The Judicialization of Politics in Pakistan

Since 2007, the Supreme Court of Pakistan has emerged as a dominant force in Pakistani politics through its hyper-active use of judicial review, or the power to overrule Parliament's laws and the Prime Minister's acts. This hyper-activism was on display during the Supreme Court's unilateral disqualification of Prime Minister Yousef Raza Gilani in 2012 under the leadership of Chief Justice Iftikhar Chaudhry. Despite the Supreme Court's practical adoption of restraint subsequent to the retirement of Chief Justice Chaudhry in 2013, the Court has once again disqualified a prime minister, Nawaz Sharif, due to allegations of corruption in 2017.

While many critics have focused on the substance of the Court's decisions in these cases, sufficient focus is not paid to the amorphous case-selection process of the Supreme Court of Pakistan. In order to compare the relatively unregulated process of case-selection in Pakistan to the more structured processes utilized by the Supreme Courts of the United States and India, this book aims to understand the historical roots of judicial review in each country, dating back to the colonial era and extending through the foundational period of each nation impacting present-day jurisprudence. As a first in its kind, this study comparatively examines these periods of history in order to contextualize a practical prescription to standardize the case-selection process in the Supreme Court of Pakistan in a way that retains the Court's overall power while limiting its involvement in purely political issues.

This publication offers a critical and comparative view of the Supreme Court of Pakistan's recent involvement in political disputes due to the lack of a discerning case-selection system that has otherwise been adopted by the Supreme Courts of India and the United States to varying degrees. It will be of interest to academics in the fields of Asian Law, South Asian Politics and Law and Comparative Law.

Waris Husain is a comparative constitutional law expert with a focus on South Asia, having written on legal developments in Pakistan, India, and Nepal. He teaches international legal advocacy and advises the international moot court program at the Howard University School of Law.

Routledge Contemporary South Asia Series

Sri Lanka's Global Factory Workers
(Un)Disciplined Desires and Sexual Struggles in a Post-Colonial Society
Sandya Hewamanne

Migration of Labour in India
The Squatter Settlements of Delhi
Himmat Singh Ratnoo

Gender, Nation and Popular Film in India
Globalizing Muscular Nationalism
Sikata Banerjee

Media as Politics in South Asia
Edited by Sahana Udupa and Stephen D. McDowell

Death and Dying in India
Ageing and End-of-Life Care of the Elderly
Suhita Chopra Chatterjee and Jaydeep Sengupta

Documentary Film in India
An Anthropological History
Giulia Battaglia

The Rule of Law in Developing Countries
The Case of Bangladesh
Chowdhury Ishrak Ahmed Siddiky

New Perspectives on India and Turkey
Connections and Debates
Edited by Smita Tewari Jassal and Halil Turan

The Judicialization of Politics in Pakistan
A Comparative Study of Judicial Restraint and Its Development in India, the US and Pakistan
Waris Husain

The Judicialization of Politics in Pakistan

A Comparative Study of Judicial Restraint and its Development in India, the US and Pakistan

Waris Husain

Routledge
Taylor & Francis Group
LONDON AND NEW YORK

First published 2018 by Routledge

2 Park Square, Milton Park, Abingdon, Oxfordshire OX14 4RN
52 Vanderbilt Avenue, New York, NY 10017

Routledge is an imprint of the Taylor & Francis Group, an informa business

First issued in paperback 2020

British Library Cataloguing-in-Publication Data
A catalogue record for this book is available from the British Library

Library of Congress Cataloging-in-Publication Data
Names: Husain, Waris, author.
Title: The judicialization of politics in Pakistan : a comparative study of judicial restraint and its development in India, the US and Pakistan / Waris Husain.
Description: New York, NY : Routledge, 2018. | Series: Routledge contemporary
South Asia series ; 123 | Includes bibliographical references and index.
Identifiers: LCCN 2017058534 | ISBN 9780815392705 (hardback) | ISBN 9781351190114 (ebook)
Subjects: LCSH: Political questions and judicial power — Pakistan. | Political questions and judicial power — India. | Political questions and judicial power — United States. | Judicial process — Pakistan. | Judicial process — India. | Judicial process — United States. | Law — Political aspects.
Classification: LCC KPL3409. H87 2018 | DDC 347.5491/05 — dc23
LC record available at https://lccn.loc.gov/2017058534

ISBN: 978-0-8153-9270-5 (hbk)
ISBN: 978-0-367-59177-9 (pbk)

Typeset in Times New Roman
by Apex CoVantage, LLC

To my family, wife, and dog Brooklyn.

Contents

List of illustrations

Figures

Table

Preface

Since 2007, the Supreme Court of Pakistan has emerged as a dominant force in the tripartite constitutional system in Pakistan. In some instances, the Court has engaged in hyper-active use of judicial review over the laws passed by Parliament or the policies of the Prime Minister. This trend was perhaps most obvious when the Supreme Court, under the leadership of Chief Justice Iftikhar Chaudhry, unilaterally disqualified Prime Minister Yousef Raza Gilani in 2012. The long-term impact of this decision led to the ouster of Prime Minister Nawaz Sharif in 2017. These decisions demonstrate one of the many dangers posed by a Supreme Court that lacks a self-restraining justiciability standard and procedure: namely, without a standard or procedure, the Court will always be open to politicization, especially under the leadership of an overly active Chief Justice. This study uses the counter-examples of India and the United States in order to present a justiciability standard and procedure for the Supreme Court of Pakistan to adopt.

Rather than attempting to apply American or Indian jurisprudence wholesale to Pakistan, the study begins by tracing the divergent development of judicial review in each country based on the impact of colonial judicial systems. The study then moves onto comparing the roles of the courts in each country as envisioned by their respective constitutional founders. Next, the structural differences in the constitutions of each country will be compared, which leads to an examination of justiciability doctrines developed by the Supreme Courts of the United States, India, and Pakistan. Lastly, the study will propose a justiciability standard and the creation of a Justiciability Council as a companion organization to the Supreme Court of Pakistan. In order to test the effectiveness of the proposed Council and test, the application section of the study will evaluate potential future petitions that request for the Court to disqualify a democratically elected Prime Minister.

The aim of this study is to take into account Pakistan's unique political and legal development and suggest a practical method to regulate and solidify the recently established power of the Supreme Court.

Acknowledgments

I would like to acknowledge my adviser and mentor, Professor Herman Schwartz, without whom this book would not be possible. I must also acknowledge Dr. Marvin Weinbaum for his mentorship and continual support over the last decade. I thank Professor Stephen Wermiel, Dr. Hassan Abbas, Yasser Latif Hamdani and Asad Jamal, for their kind guidance and unending support. A special acknowledgement goes to Chief Justice (retired) Tassaduq Hussain Jillani for being so generous in sharing his time and wisdom with me.

I am also forever indebted to my father for providing inspiration, my mother for nourishment, and my sister for providing mental support throughout this process. I thank Melvin and Celie Mobley for their endless encouragement. I would finally like to acknowledge my wife, Brittany, for believing in me when I did not and my dog, Brooklyn, for his unmatched companionship which sustained my writing and research efforts.

1 Introduction

In the summer of 2012, the Prime Minister of Pakistan, Yusuf Raza Gilani, was unilaterally and retroactively disqualified from his democratically elected post by the Supreme Court of Pakistan.[1] This disqualification was considered by critics as a unnerving and abrupt end to the dream of judicial independence promised by the Lawyers' Movement which rose to prominence in 2007, under the leadership of Chief Justice Iftikhar Chaudhry.[2] That movement deposed a military ruler and helped usher in the re-establishment of democratic rule in Pakistan.[3] Yet afterwards, the Court began escalating a confrontational relationship with the ruling regime, which was under the leadership of the Pakistan's People's Party (PPP). Critics accused the Court of judicial bias against the PPP and of applying judicial review without any structural limits, thereby interfering with the work of Parliament and the Prime Minister. These critiques were met with the defense that the Court was properly using its judicial review powers to punish rampant political corruption and apply the rule of law to the political elites of the country – actions that until now were unprecedented.[4]

While the Court has somewhat relaxed its use of power and informally adopted a policy of judicial restraint since Chaudhry's retirement in 2013,[5] it took an equally confrontational approach with the PPP's successor administration, run by Pakistan Muslim Leave (Nawaz) (PML-N). This has led to the Court repeating its decision from *Gilani* by disqualifying Prime Minister Nawaz Sharif for allegations of corruption in 2017,[6] which has reinvigorated public interest in the proper role of the judiciary in the process of executive disqualification. There is a structural issue underlying this case, as well as other manifestations of judicial overreach by Pakistan's Supreme Court over the last decade: the Supreme Court has yet to adopt a self-limiting standard of justiciability[7] or a procedure to assess the justiciability of petitions before granting oral hearings. Without a case-selection process or standard, the Court may continue to take action on petitions that wrongfully invoke judicial remedies for purely political issues.

I. Chaudhry court

Chief Justice Chaudhry led what some have described as the most interventionist Court in Pakistan's history.[8] The Supreme Court under Chaudhry's leadership was accused of abusing judicial review power[9] by invoking it without limitations and exacerbating the caseload of the already-overworked Court.[10] One can see that the Court's overuse of judicial review was evident in the matter of executive disqualification.

However, it is important to remember that while the Supreme Court under Chief Justice Chaudhry's leadership was the most active in its history, the evolution of judicial review began several decades ago and has been impacted by the historical and socio-political context of a country facing extreme poverty, illiteracy, political instability, and inability of minorities to gain access to forums of justice like the Supreme Court.

II. Global growth of judicial review

The hyper-active quality of the Chaudhry Court is an extreme example of a world-wide trend of the 'judicialization of politics' recognized by Ran Hirschl, who explains that

> over the past few years the world has witnessed an astonishingly rapid transition to what may be called juristocracy. Around the globe, in more than eighty countries . . . constitutional reform has transferred an unprecedented amount of power from representative institutions to judiciaries.[11]

This "global trend toward juristocracy" is based on the principle that "democracy must protect itself against the tyranny of majority rule through constitutionalization and judicial review."[12] Accordingly, "judicial empowerment through the constitutionalization of rights and the establishment of judicial review appear to be [the] widely accepted conventional wisdom of contemporary constitutional thought."[13] The global trend towards judicialization of politics can disturb the balance of power between branches in a tripartite system. Yet, this trend can be attributed to "multiple institutional, political, and judicial behavioral factors," including "the existence of tangible rights, an enabling constitutional framework, and an independent judiciary with an activist outlook[, which] are widely accepted as vital prerequisites for judicial involvement in the political domain."[14]

This runs counter to the argument put forth by Professor James B. Thayer in his seminal law review article from 1893 entitled *The Origin and Scope of the American Doctrine of Constitutional Law*.[15] In this work, Thayer describes that while the creation of judicial review was novel at the time of America's independence, its usage was minimized by the Supreme Court, which strictly adhered to the separation of powers enumerated in the Constitution and rejected improper or non-justiciable petitions.[16]

However, a global trend has emerged in the opposite direction of Thayer's assertion of judicial restraint in the context of the nineteenth-century United States, and the Pakistani Supreme Court, led by Chief Justice Chaudhry, became known as the "most activist court in the region's history."[17] The hyper-active tendency of the Chaudhry Court has implications for "our understanding of the phenomenon of judicialization of politics" around the world.[18] Despite the relevance of such activism by courts for the global study of judicial review, "American scholarship on constitutional law and politics still tends to ignore comparable developments in other countries."[19] This study addresses this gap by comparing the United States Supreme Court's restrained use of judicial review to the more activist court in Pakistan and, to a lesser degree, India. While justices on the Supreme Courts of India and Pakistan cite jurisprudence from the United States Supreme Court, these citations often ignore the contextual and structural differences between the nations and their respective common law. The same goes for legal scholars in the region, many of whom reject American principles of judicial restraint without contextualizing the varying degrees of judicial power guaranteed in the constitutions of the United States, Pakistan, and India.

This study uses Pakistan as the centerpiece of its analysis with India and the United States as comparative points of reference. The aim is to contextualize the use of judicial review dating back to the colonial period in each country and propose a method for the Supreme Court of Pakistan to institutionalize limitations to its use of judicial review.

III. Defining activism

The term judicial activism was introduced in 1947 to describe the split in ideologies on the United States Supreme Court at the time,[20] with one group of justices arguing in favor of "judicial activism" as a means "to achieve social justice" and another arguing in favor of judicial restraint as a means of allowing elected officials the right to pursue policies "that a majority [of voters] might wish."[21] Nearly six decades later, there is still great disagreement about what "judicial activism" actually means, and a definitive definition becomes more elusive when moving beyond the analysis of one country's Supreme Court to comparing the jurisprudence of three Supreme Courts with very different histories.

Nevertheless, scholars have attempted to define judicial activism in the following ways:[22]

- i "the Court's willingness to invalidate statutes"[23]
- ii "departing from text and or history or judicial precedent"[24]
- iii "significant court-generated change in public policy"[25]
- iv "asserting itself against an elected branch of government; it is decreeing that some issue will not be settled through the democratic process"[26]
- v "the abuse of unsupervised power that is exercised outside the bounds of judicial role"[27] which may or may not be "to promote progressive ideologies of individual rights."[28]

While there is not one definition, some of these explanations focus on the difference between activist judges who "believe that it is legitimate for them to formulate social policy," as opposed to self-restraining judges who "would confine the judiciary to the task of applying to specific cases laws and regulations made by the so-called 'political branches' of government."[29] The focus of this debate is therefore "the proper relationship between the courts, on one hand, and the legislature and administration, on the other."[30]

Another element of this issue revolves around the political ideologies which might guide the Court; as one jurist notes,

> advocates of judicial activism tend to regard it as progressive judicial conduct responding to changing economic, political, and social circumstances, while critics of judicial activism tend to characterize it as judicial impropriety usurping the power of the other branches of government.[31]

The advocates for judicial activism in Pakistan and India have used this line of argument to justify their Supreme Courts' expanded use of judicial review and as a means to push elected officials towards politically progressive policies that help the poor or disenfranchised citizens.

However, as described by Herman Schwartz, judicial activism in the United States Supreme Court has often been used to implement a politically conservative ideology that is friendlier towards corporations and the protection of private property than the needs of the 'common man.'[32] This political ideology could be one explanation for why the Court's eras of activism have coincided with proactive and progressive presidents like Roosevelt[33] and, more recently, President Barack Obama.[34]

Another scholar, Kermit Roosevelt, argues that the analysis of a Court's level of activism is not based on political ideology, but on judicial philosophy:

> A judge's views on these questions could be called political but they are "political" considerations removed to any level of generality at which they will not consistently favor any particular partisan side. They are formed not by narrow political preferences but by broader beliefs about the appropriate roles of judges and legislatures, their relative abilities to decide certain questions, and the relative dangers of too much or too little judicial supervision of majoritarian politics. They are, in short, the sorts of views that will affect how a judge acting in good faith will approach constitutional cases.[35]

Accordingly, rather than attempting to propose a singular definition for judicial activism, this study will examine the evolution of "beliefs about the appropriate roles of judges and legislatures" based on each country's varied colonial judicial history as well as constitutional and jurisprudential differences. This approach merits using all the definitions for activism provided above collectively in order identify the symptoms of judicial activism or hyper-activism as was the case in Pakistan.

IV. Method of analysis and spectrum graph comparison

As illustrated below in Figure 1.1, the method of analysis for this study will first examine the colonial underpinning of each country's judicial institutions; second, evaluate the intent of the constitutions' founders regarding the judiciary; third, compare the common law approaches to the use of judicial review in each country; and lastly, assess the proper judicial role in the executive impeachment or disqualification in each country. These four factors form the foundation for comparison of judicial review in these countries, a comparison which is used to formulate a specific proposal for the Supreme Court of Pakistan to adopt a justiciability standard and process.

On a spectrum of judicial activism today, the Supreme Court of Pakistan stands at one end, the United States at the other, and the Supreme Court of India takes a place somewhere in in between. As can be seen in Figure 1.2, the spectrum is based on how each court balances and checks the powers of the elected branches, and how difficult it makes accessing justice at the Supreme Court for potential litigants.

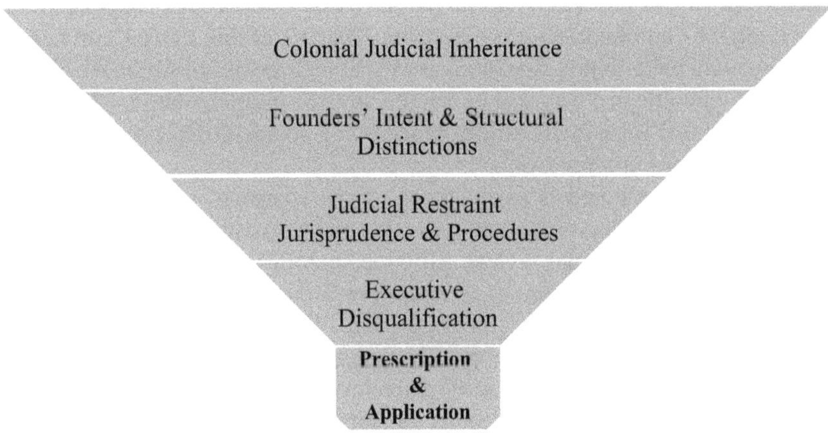

Figure 1.1 Method of analysis

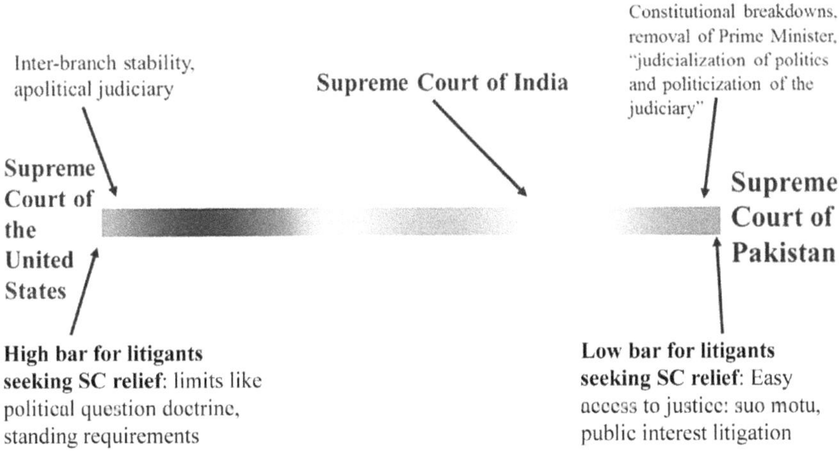

Figure 1.2 Judicial review spectrum

V. Scope and limitations of the study

Many topics found in this study have been debated for decades by highly specialized experts in the field: for example, when discussing the proper role of the judiciary as envisioned by American founders, thousands of pages have been written by legal historians and constitutional experts like Edward Surrency, A. V. Dicey, Gordon Wood, Akhil Reed Amar, and others. Similarly, in relation to common law doctrines concerning justiciability and the political question doctrine, there has been a great deal of scholarship in all three countries, which this study aims to generally summarize. Lastly, when examining the basic structure doctrine[36] as it exists in Pakistan and India, many well-recognized Indian and Pakistani jurists have dedicated a great deal of ink to analyzing the complexities of the doctrine. The aim of this study is not necessarily to contribute to this vast amount of scholarship, but to summarize these academic opinions in a way that builds towards the ultimate thesis, which concerns a proposal for a justiciability process and standard that can be adopted by the Pakistani Supreme Court.

The proposed standard is partly based on the comparative examples of the United States and India, which both provide unique insights for potential limitations on the use of judicial review. All three countries share a colonial history under British rule and operate as common law jurisdictions in the modern-day, and each has a unique interpretation of the role of the courts in government and society. As a testament to the comparative value of the United States and Indian Supreme Courts, one can see that the Supreme Court of Pakistan has relied on jurisprudence from both of these courts throughout its history.

At the same time, the comparative approach and proposed prescription in this study is meant to take into account limitations of legal, political, and historical context unique to Pakistan. This includes the Court's historical reluctance in adopting self-limiting standards concerning justiciability, which is one reason Iftikhar Chaudhry was able to engage in hyper-activism when he was Chief Justice of Pakistan. As the Court stated in *Sindh High Court Bar Association*,

> as to the maintainability of the review petitions, the Supreme Court observed that no yardstick could be fixed as to who could file review petition against a judgement of the court nor any embargo could be placed on the right of an ordinary litigant to file a review petition for the redress of his grievance, which would always be decided on the basis of the facts and circumstances of each case.[37]

This study attempts to address the Court's historical reluctance to adopt a repeatable standard by proposing a flexible justiciability test that could allow the Court to maintain its ability to provide justice to all citizens while establishing definite boundaries for its exercise of judicial review.

VI. Colonial judicial inheritance and Lord Coke's impact

Chapters 2 & 3

The modern expansion of judicial review and judicial power in general in Pakistan and India can be traced to both nations' complex relationship to British colonial judicial institutions. Colonial heritage is also relevant for the limited review exercised by the United States Supreme Court, as the American colonies lacked a positive experience with colonial judicial institutions and distrusted courts as non-elected appointed institutions. Chapter 2 examines the relative ineffectiveness and rejection of colonial courts by citizens of the American colonies, when lawyers and judges lacked public credibility.[38] The same could not be said for the Indian colonies, where judges and lawyers were often held in high regard, many of whom had been formally trained in Britain and were able to hold high posts in the colonial administration.[39]

Chapter 3 moves away from the colonial history of the British crown in general to examine the impact of one British jurist, Lord Edward Coke, whose theories impacted colonial and post-colonial courts in all three countries. Lord Coke is one of the forefathers of modern judicial review, as he controversially suggested in 1610 that the courts had the power to assess when an Act of Parliament violated natural law.[40] While he was punished by the King for this decision,[41] his ideas were adopted by some state courts in the United States,[42] and some even argue that "the American Revolution was a lawyers' revolution to enforce Lord Coke's theory of the invalidity of Acts of Parliament in derogation of the common rights and of the rights of Englishmen."[43] Lord Coke's theory also impacted the founders of the Indian and Pakistani constitutions, as they recognized the power of judicial review in their constitutional documents,[44] going one step further than their American counterparts, who did not enumerate this judicial right in 1776.

Therefore, while the Supreme Court from each country was impacted in different ways by a varied colonial heritage, each Court inherited and adopted the concepts presented by Lord Coke as they relate to the exercise of judicial review.

VII. Constitutional structure and judicial procedures

Chapters 4 & 5

How the judiciary fits into each country's constitutional structures is very relevant to the intended and actual power of the judiciary in each country. The role of the Supreme Courts in Pakistan, India and the United States is designated in two parts: i) the constitutional powers granted to the Court and ii) interpretation of those powers through common law jurisprudence.

Chapter 4 compares the constitutional structure of all three countries. There are basic differences between the American presidential system and the presidential–parliamentary system adopted by Pakistan and India, yet all three nations have rejected legislative supremacy in favor of constitutional supremacy.[45] The adoption of a written constitution that enumerates inviolable civil and political rights is also a structural aspect all three nations share. However, the jurisdictional clauses of the respective constitutions grant the Supreme Courts of Pakistan and India expansive power to address violations of fundamental rights, while the United States Supreme Court is limited to "cases and controversies."[46]

Chapter 4 also looks at the socio-political factors that distinguish Pakistan from both the United States and India. As Ran Hirschl explains, "Pakistan is a country in a near-constant political limbo,"[47] which means its judiciary has been forced to adapt to the nation's history of political instability. Unlike the comparative examples, Pakistan has suffered a civil war that split the country in half, repeated coups by the military, and the passage of three different constitutions in the country's first three decades of existence.[48] This creates the need for flexibility in any standard meant to restrain the Court, as the Supreme Court of Pakistan has to face far more difficult challenges in protecting their Constitution than their American and Indian counterparts.

These structural and socio-political differences have impacted the subsequent jurisprudence of the Supreme Courts of all three nations, which is the focus of Chapter 5. The United States Supreme Court has adopted a filtering process for petitions through the convening of a regularly scheduled writ of certiorari meeting wherein at least four justices must agree to grant a hearing to a petition in order for it to proceed.[49] Further, the Court has created relatively rigid standards to assess justiciability and standing as a means to limit the Court's exercise of judicial review to proper cases. These standards created hurdles for petitioners seeking to access remedies from the Court by requiring them to prove that they had an interest at stake in the case and that, among other things, the case did not violate the political question doctrine.[50]

While the Indian Supreme Court has not adopted such a rigid limitation on its review powers through justiciability standards, the Court does hold biweekly admissibility meetings to assess petitions.[51] Both the Indian and Pakistani Supreme Courts have refused to adopt American-style limitations to the Courts' judicial review powers to facilitate access to justice for the most disadvantaged classes in society.

However, the Pakistani Supreme Court lacks both justiciability standards as well as a filtering procedure for petitions,[52] which has left the Court overworked and subject to the demands of each Chief Justice. The negative impact of this was felt during the hyper-activism of the Supreme Court under the leadership of Chief Justice Iftiqhar Chaudhry. This hyper-activism destabilized the trichotomy of powers in many cases, but the judicial role in the disqualification of a sitting Prime Minister merits special consideration, as will be discussed in Chapter 6.

VIII. Executive disqualification

Chapter 6

After examining the historical, structural, and jurisprudential contexts for the use of judicial review by the Supreme Courts of Pakistan, India, and the United States, this study will move forward to the modern era, focusing on the narrower question of the proper role for the Supreme Court in executive branch disqualification or impeachment. The hyper-active role Pakistan's judiciary has played in this issue in the recent past illustrates the conflict-prone relationship between the executive and judiciary, and how contentiously those conflicts are resolved. This also leads into a theoretical discussion which applies to all three Supreme Courts, namely, how the Court must balance judicial independence with the democratic demands of the electorate in a republic.

The overuse of judicial review in Pakistan has been criticized by experts and the public alike.[53] While some of his political opponents have lauded the Supreme Court's ouster of Prime Minister Nawaz Sharif in 2017,[54] his disqualification reaffirms the fear of some legal scholars that the Supreme Court of Pakistan is continuing a dangerous trend started in 2012. The Supreme Courts of India and the United States offer examples of restraint in response to petitions requesting the Court to unilaterally disqualify the head of the government.[55] On the other hand, the Supreme Court of Pakistan did just that when it unilaterally disqualified Prime Ministers Gilani and Sharif, bypassing the constitutionally mandated parliamentary process for disqualification.[56]

When presented with a similar opportunity to remove Prime Minister Indira Gandhi based on a corruption conviction, the Supreme Court of India demurred and dismissed the charges, allowing the Prime Minister to remain in office.[57] While the same situation has never occurred in the United States, it is important to note that the U.S. Supreme Court did decide a narrow question of immunity in the trial of President Richard Nixon, but the Court left the actual impeachment in the hands of Congress.[58] Pakistan can learn lessons from both countries in forging a new path of standardized judicial restraint in the face of executive disqualifications or impeachments.

Further, Chapter 6 elaborates on the need for Pakistan's Supreme Court to use a filtering process for petitions and create justiciability standards. A petition-filtering or case-selection process will enhance the Court's ability to avoid taking on cases that do not warrant judicial intervention based on the separation of powers designated by Pakistan's constitution.

IX. Prescription

Chapter 7

Before prescribing a method to regulate the use of judicial review in the Supreme Court of Pakistan, it is important to set out the perimeter of this examination. The proposed standard and procedure offered in this study are intentionally flexible to accommodate the historical and socio-political factors that make Pakistan unique. Accordingly, the proposed standard allows the Court to set aside restraint in favor of activism in extraordinary instances, such as when facing off against an extra-constitutional military coup. By adopting a self-restrained approach when dealing with civilian-elected branches, the Court could expand on its public legitimacy and political credibility among Parliamentarians, both of which would be necessary for the Court to effectively confront a potential extra-constitutional coup.

Even without the possibility of a coup, the proposed standard would foster the Supreme Court's pursuit of its goal to grant immediate justice to impoverished or disenfranchised communities. In the past two decades, the Court has involved itself in political questions and attempted to manage elected branches and executive agencies, which has limited its ability to deliver justice to disenfranchised or poor communities. Chief Justice Jillani alluded to this in his seminal judgment on the protection of minorities: an unrestrained overuse of judicial review by the Court in non-justiciable matters will limit the Court's ability to deliver justice to the least-advantaged groups of Pakistan.[59]

The evaluation of each petition according to this standard could overburden the Court if it were to perform this function on its own like Supreme Court Justices in the United States and India. Instead, this study suggests that the proposed standard be implemented by a Justiciability Council, composed of former justices. This Justiciability Council would become a companion organization to the Supreme Court, acting as a filter for petitions before submission to the Supreme Court for initial oral hearings. Not only would this minimize the Court's caseload and improve time-management, it would solidify the implementation and development of the proposed standard.

In the final part of Chapter 7, the proposed standard and Justiciability Council will be put to the test to interpret the justiciability of petitions calling for the unilateral disqualification of the Prime Minister. This will bring the study full circle by applying the proposed method to recommend proper judicial responses to hypothetical cases that are based on currently relevant facts.

Notes

1 *Muhammad Azhar Siddiqui and Others v. Federation of Pakistan and Others* (2012) — PLD (SC) 774 (Pak.)

2 Qaiser Zulfiqar, *PM Contempt: Asma Jahangir Terms August 8 as Black Day in Judicial History*, Express Tribune, Aug. 10, 2012. Available at http://tribune.com.pk/story/419356/pm-contempt-asma-jahangir-terms-august-8-as-black-day-in-judicial-history/ (last accessed on Aug. 11, 2016). ("Former president Supreme Court Bar Association (SCBA) Asma Jahangir termed Wednesday as yet another 'black day' in the judicial history of the country after the Supreme Court issued show-cause notices to Prime Minister Raja Pervaiz Ashraf in the National Reconciliation Ordinance (NRO) implementation case.")

3 Khan Faqir, Fakhrul Islam & Shahid Hassan Rizvi, *The Lawyers' Movement for Judicial Independence in Pakistan: A Study of the Musharraf Regime*, 2 Asian J. Soc. Sci. and Human. 345 at 355 (2013). ("But in 2007 a proper struggle started in the shape of lawyers' movement for independence of judiciary. In short term objectives they succeeded in the restoration of Chief Justice and other deposed judges and in the long term, in overthrowing a military rule.")

4 Faisal Siddiqi, *Judicial Accountability*, Dawn, Aug. 1, 2016. Available at www.dawn.com/news/1274492/judicial-accountability (last accessed on Aug. 1, 2016). ("The messiah, when it comes to the issue of corruption, is an exercise in accountability overseen by the higher judiciary i.e. the High Courts and the Supreme Court. But this confidence in the higher judiciary is based on the premise that the higher judiciary itself is not corrupt, that it is beyond influence and acting in a transparent manner. Secondly, the Supreme Judicial Council is composed of specified judges of the Supreme Court and specified chief justices of the High Court. In other words, it is a system of internal accountability as opposed to external accountability by the legislature or the executive.")

5 Hasnaat Malik, *2014: From Judicial Activism to Judicial Restraint*, Express Tribune, Dec. 31, 2014. Available at http://tribune.com.pk/story/814921/2014-from-judicial-activism-to-judicial-restraint/ (last accessed on July 24, 2016.)
6 *Imran Ahmed Khan v. Mian Muhammad Nawaz Sharif*, C.M.A. No. 4978/2017 in Constitutional Petition No. 29/2016 and C.M.A. No. 2939/2017 in Constitutional Petition No. 29/2016. (SC) (Pak.) (July 28, 2017.) Available at www.supremecourt.gov.pk/web/user_files/File/Const.P._29_2016_28072016.pdf
7 Justiciability, *Black's Law Dictionary* (10th ed., 2014) ("The quality, state, or condition of being appropriate or suitable for adjudication by a court.")
8 Mark Tushnet & Madhav Khosla, *Unstable Constitutionalism* (2015). Osama Siddique, Chapter 6: *The Judicialization of Politics in Pakistan: The Supreme Court After the Lawyer's Movement.*
9 Judicial Review, *Black's Law Dictionary* (10th ed., 2014) "1. A court's power to review the actions of other branches or levels of government; esp., the courts' power to invalidate legislative and executive actions as being unconstitutional. 2. The constitutional doctrine providing for this power." Charles Grove Haines, Judicial Review of Legislation in the United States and the Doctrines of Vested Rights and of Implied Limitations on Legislatures, 2 Tex. L. Rev. 257, 270 (1924). "The original idea of judicial review seems to have been conceived primarily to preserve the integrity and uphold the independence of the courts as against the other departments, and to preserve and protect certain personal and private rights, such as the right of trial by jury, which were thought to be natural and inalienable."
10 See id. See also Maryam S. Khan, *Genesis and Evolution of Public Interest Litigation in the Supreme Court of Pakistan, Toward a Dynamic Theory of Judicialization*, 28 Temp. J. Intl. & Comp. l. 284 (2015).
11 Ran Hirschl, *Towards Juristocracy: The Origins and Consequences of the New Constitutionalism* (2007) at 1.
12 Id at 2.
13 Id.
14 Mark Tushnet & Madhav Khosla, *Unstable Constitutionalism* (2015) at 160.
15 James B. Thayer, *The Origin and Scope of the American Doctrine of Constitutional Law*, 7 Harv. L. Rev. 3 (1893).
16 Id.
17 Tushnet & Khosla, *supra* note 14.
18 Id.
19 Hirschl, *supra* note 11, at 6.
20 Arthur M. Schlesinger, Jr., *The Supreme Court: 1947*, Fortune, Jan 1947.
21 John Q. Barrett, *Arthur M. Schlesinger, Jr. – in Action, in Archives, in History*. Citing Arthur M. Schlesinger, Jr. *A Life in the 20th Century: Innocent Beginnings 1917–1950*, at 352 (2000).
22 John O. Haley & Toshiko Takenaka, *Legal Innovations in Asia: Judicial Lawmaking and the Influence of Comparative Law* (2014), at 165. Vai Io Lo, *Judicial Activism in China, Chapter 3.4* (the following summaries of definitions explained in Lo's chapter).
23 Frank B. Ross & Stefani Lindquist, *The Decisional Significance of the Chief Justice*, 154 U. Pa. L. Rev. 1665, 1701 (2006).
24 Earnest A. Young, *Judicial Activism and Conservative Politics*, 73 U. Colo. L. Rev. 1139, 1144 (2002).
25 Bradley C. Canon, *Defining the Dimensions of Judicial Activism*, 66 Judicature 236, 238 (1082–3).
26 Kermit Roosevelt, *The Myth of Judicial Activism: Making Sense of Supreme Court Decisions* (2008) at 39.
27 Craig Green, *An Intellectual History of Judicial Activism*, 58 Emory L. J. 1195, 1222 (2009).
28 Haley & Takenaka, *supra* note 22, at 165.

29 Kenneth M. Holland, ed. in his Preface to *Judicial Activism in Comparative Perspective* (1991), at vii.
30 Id.
31 Haley & Takenaka, *supra* note 22, at 165.
32 Herman Schwartz, *Right Wing Justice* (2004), at 10. ("federal courts have been a bastion of conservative rather than a leader in protecting human rights and promoting social justice . . . Except for relatively brief periods, the courts have been primarily concerned with protecting the haves against the have-nots – the poor, workers, farmers, blacks, and women.")
33 See Anna Sale, *Obama v. SCOTUS: Learning from FDR's Court Comeback*, WNYC, Mar. 28, 2012. Available at www.wnyc.org/story/194795-last-incumbent-courtwatcher/ (Citing Jeff Shesol, Supreme Power, Franklin Roosevelt vs. the Supreme Court (2011). "Between 1933 and 1936, the Court overturned acts of Congress at ten times the traditional rate.")
34 See Ilya Shapiro, *Obama's Abysmal Record Before the Supreme Court*, Cato Institute, Feb. 11, 2016. Available at www.cato.org/blog/obamas-abysmal-record-supreme-court (last accessed on Oct. 22, 2016).
35 Roosevelt, *supra* note 26, at 89.
36 The basic structure doctrine has been used by the Supreme Courts of Pakistan and India to strike down constitutional amendments passed by Parliament when the amendments has been deemed to violate the "basic structure" or salient features of the Constitution.
37 *Sindh High Court Bar Association v. Federation of Pakistan* (2009) — PLD (SC) 879 (Pak.) Available at https://pakistanconstitutionlaw.com/p-l-d-2009-sc-879-2/
38 Edwin C. Surrency, *The Courts in the American Colonies*, 111 Amer. J. Leg. Hist. 253 at 255–6 (1967). ("Throughout the colonial period, the courts, with few exceptions, were poorly staffed; the effects of this were felt in the organization of American courts well into the Nineteenth Century.")
39 Mitra Sharafi, *A New History of Colonial Lawyering: Likhovski and Legal Identities in the British Empire*, 32 L. & Soc. Inquiry, 1059 (2007), at 1070 ("South Asians began to have a major presence in the upper echelons of the legal system from the late nineteenth century on.") See also Abhinav Chandrachud, *An Independent, Colonial Judiciary: A History of the Bombay High Court During the British Raj, 1862–1947* (2015).
40 *Dr. Bonham v. College of Physicians* (1610), 77 Eng. Rep. 638, 8 Co. Rep. 107 ("it appears in our books, that in many cases, the common law will control Acts of Parliament, and sometimes adjudge them to be utterly void; for when an act of Parliament is against common right and reason, or repugnant, or impossible to be performed, the common law will control it, and adjudge such an Act to be void.")
41 Theodore F. T. Plucknett, *Bonham's Case and Judicial Review*, 40 Harv. L. Rev. 30, 50 (1926)
42 See generally William W. *Crosskey, Politics and the Constitution in the History of the United States* at 944 (I 953). (Listing nine cases in which state Supreme Courts debated the use of judicial review.)
43 *New York State Bar Association, Yearbook- 1915* at 238.
44 Mauro Cappelletti, *Judicial Review in Comparative Perspective*, 58 Cal. L. Rev. 1017, 1031 (1970). ("other ex-colonies, including Canada, Australia, and India, which likewise adopted judicial review upon attaining independence.")
45 Umama Moin, *Parliament and the Supreme: The Indian Experience* (2011) (Aligarh Muslim University). Available at http://shodhganga.inflibnet.ac.in/handle/10603/11379 (last accessed on Oct. 31, 2016), at 59. (India "adopted some modified form of the American pattern to suit Indian needs.")
46 Compare U.S. Constitution Article III Section 2 to Constitution of India Article 32 and Constitution of Pakistan Article 184(3).
47 Ran Hirschl, *The New Constitution and Judicialization of Pure Politics Worldwide*, 75 Ford. L. Rev. 721, 733 (2000).

48 See Hamid Khan, *Constitutional and Political History of Pakistan* (Oxford Pakistan, 2nd ed., 2009); Tayyab Mahmud, *Praetorianism and Common Law in Post-Colonial Settings: Judicial Responses to Constitutional Breakdowns in Pakistan*, 1993 Utah L. Rev. 1225

49 H. W. Perry Jr, *Deciding to Decide: Agenda Setting in the United States Supreme Court* (1994).

50 See generally Lea Brilmayer, *The Jurisprudence of Article III: Perspectives on the "Case or Controversy" Requirement*, 93 Harv. L. Rev. 297 (1979).

51 Manoj S. Mate, *The Variable Power of Courts: The Expansion of the Power of the Supreme Court of India in Fundamental Rights and Governance Decisions* (2010) (University of California, Berkley) Available at http://escholarship.org/uc/item/3f1640wm (last accessed on Oct. 31, 2016), at 14.

52 Moeen Cheema & Ijaz Shafi Gilani, *The Politics and Jurisprudence of the Chaudhry Court 2005–2013* (2015), at 293–4. Asher A. Qazi, *Suo Motu: Choosing Not to Legislate Chief Justice Chaudhry's Strategic Agenda* ("The Supreme Court "conventionally . . . grants an oral hearing to most, if not all, appeals and petitions fixed before it. It should thus come as no surprise that even as a court of 17 justices hears various cases in smaller benches of three judges or at times only two judges, it may take years before a particular action is heard.")

53 For expert critiques see Khan, *supra* note 3 and Tushnet, *supra* note 8. For public reaction to Supreme Court Under Chief Justice Chaudhry see Babar Sattar, *Judicial Restraint or Complacency?* Dawn, July 14, 2014. Available at www.dawn.com/news/1118993 (last accessed on July 25, 2016). ("average Joe mocking the lawyers' movement and its wages.")

54 *Panamagate Decision: Musharraf Congratulates Nation on SC's Verdict*, Geo News, July 28, 2017. Available at www.geo.tv/latest/151432-panama-verdict-musharraf-congratulates-nation-on-scs-decision (last accessed on Oct. 14, 2017).

55 See *Indira Nehru Gandhi v. Shri Raj Narain* (1976) AIR 1975 SC 2299, 1975 (Supp) SCC1, 2

SCR 347 (India); and *Richard M. Nixon v. United States*, 418 U.S. 683 (1974).

56 '*Pakistan's Supreme Court and the National Reconciliation Ordinance: What now for Pakistan?*' ISAS Brief no. 147, Dec. 22, 2009, at 6. Citing Jamaluddin Jamali, '*PPP Lawyers, Asma Jahangir Rant Against SC Verdict*', Pakistan Today, 27 Apr. 2012. Available at www.pakistantoday.com.pk/2012/04/27/news/national/ppp-lawyers-asma-jahangir-rant-against-sc-verdict/?printType=article 9 (last accessed 20 June 2016.) (noted jurist Asma Jahangir argued that the decision did not set "a good tradition to disqualify the prime minister under Article 63, and that no Prime Minister would survive in future if that same tradition continued.")

57 See *Indira Nehru Gandhi v. Shri Raj Narain* (1976) AIR 1975 SC 2299, 1975 (Supp) SCC1, 2 SCR 347 (India).

58 See *Richard M. Nixon v. United States*, 418 U.S. 683 (1974).

59 Interview with retired Chief Justice Tassaduq Hussain Jillani, Supreme Court of Pakistan, in Lahore (Mar. 9, 2015).

2 Colonial justice

I. Introduction

While Pakistan, India, and the United States all share a colonial history of British rule, the legal systems of colonial administration differed greatly between the American and Indian colonies. This difference is key to understanding how the founding fathers of each nation envisioned the roles for the judiciary in their post-colonial state based on their experience with colonial justice.

There are several colonial legal developments that must be examined concerning this analysis: the varied treatment of native justice systems, the establishment and administration of colonial courts, and the legal education available for advocates in those courts. Each of these developments differed between the Indian and American colonies. While the administration of justice was criticized in the American colonies for being improvised and haphazard,[1] the British Crown approached the establishment of legal institutions in a more systematic way with the assistance of local collaborators in the Indian subcontinent.[2]

There are several reasons for this distinction that bear mentioning before beginning a discussion of these legal institutions. First, the British Crown operated for a far greater period of time in the Indian subcontinent compared to the American colonies.[3] This created an imbalance of effective judicial institutions between the two colonies. Second, and relatedly, the British Crown was able to reform and redevelop legal institutions in the Indian subcontinent over time with more extensive experience in colonial administration than they had in their experience in America.[4] The Crown lacked this experience with the American colonies, which were one of the Crown's first colonial projects.[5]

The disparate development of justice in the American and Indian colonies was reflected in the judicial ethos of all three of the post-colonial states. The result was that constitutional founders in Pakistan and India envisioned a more wide-ranging role for the judiciary than their American counterparts, who were wary of granting powers to unelected justices in the wake of ineffective colonial legal institutions.

II. The American experience with colonial justice

A. Native justice

For the United States, experience with colonial jurisprudence began with the setting aside of native customs concerning justice developed by the Native Americans. As a general policy, European settlers in the American colonies intended "to replace meaningful or threatening Native ideas and ways of life with European versions."[6]

These customs once included tribal courts and councils established to administer justice in pre-colonial America.[7] Some of these tribal courts continue to operate today on Native American reservations, administering justice based on Native American customs and treaties.[8] However, rather than attempt to incorporate these systems into the newly created colonial justice system established through the British Crown, "native justice" was limited to application within the native population and not on European-born settlers.[9]

This could partially be related to the perception of European settlers that the Native American culture was in some way crude or underdeveloped.[10] Further, the colonies experienced rapid population changes with an increase of European settlers and the steady demise of the Native American population, leading to burgeoning common law courts and increasingly limited use of Native American judicial customs.

Regardless of the reason, two separate and distinct systems began to operate in the North American colonies: the newly expanding colonial courts and the indigenous peoples' justice systems. The former would eventually supplant the latter almost completely, but prior to independence, the British allowed the Native American tribes to govern themselves as foreign nations with their own legal customs.[11]

On the one hand, this allowed the Native Americans to continue their traditional judicial practices. On the other hand, this agreement treated the Native Americans and their justice systems as alien and incompatible with the common law British system. The result was that the British common law dominated and marginalized Native American law and customs.[12]

The same could not be said for the traditional native justice systems in the Indian subcontinent colonies, which were adapted and used by the British Crown; native customs were mixed with its own methods for the rule of law.[13] The marked difference in treatment of native justice systems demonstrates that the post-colonial Indian subcontinent was more willing to adopt the British common law system due to the Crown's adaptations for Indian society. However, because the United States did not develop such a hybrid system based on tradition, there was relatively less deference to the British judicial system after independence was won – although some state courts did adopt many British common law principles after independence.

A hybrid system such as that used in the Indian subcontinent would be difficult to establish in the United States, whose native populations were purposefully marginalized by European settlers. While the American colonies were "settler colonies" created to attract European settlement and displace native populations, the Indian colony was an "extractive colony" meant to produce natural resources for the Crown, rather than to serve as a new home to European settlers.[14] The extractive colonies fostered the hybridization of British and native legal customs, leading to the persistence of those hybrid customs for a longer period of time than in the settler colonies in which there was no hybridization.

The settler colonies in America had European customs for justice transported by the settlers themselves, so it is logical that the post-colonial United States retained some of its colonial British common law concepts. However, many British concepts, including scope of judicial power, parliamentary supremacy, and unwritten constitutional principles, were outright rejected by the Americans as "foreign" to the newly independent United States. The same did not occur in extractive colonies like India, where British common law retained its influence after independence because the Crown adapted colonial legal institutions to meet the social and political demands of the native population.

B. Development of colonial courts and the blurring line between branches

One of the issues raised by the settlers in the American colonies was the lack of separation of powers between the courts and the executive, or the Governor General. While the doctrine of separation of powers can by its nature be ambiguous when it comes to the specific distribution of power and duties between branches, the overall value of this doctrine is that it allows each branch to specialize in its own sphere: it allows the legislator to legislate, the executive to enforce the laws, and the courts to interpret the laws.

This was not the case for the American colonies, in which each colony was assigned a Governor General with the power to both implement and interpret the law. The Governor General had a wide scope of judicial power in the colonies and "would act as judge and jury" in cases involving criminal allegations or civil complaints.[15] Therefore, there was "no separation between the functions of the executive, legislative and judicial branches . . . and the distinctions between different bodies or courts were blurred."[16]

Eventually, a council was formed in some colonies to advise the Governor General on cases, general jurisdiction courts were created, and eventually there were Supreme Courts and justices of the peace.[17],[18] However, despite the creation of these judicial institutions, the Governor General and his council served either in the Court of Appeals or a general court. Further, there were accusations that some Governor Generals were using the lack of separation of powers as a means to further their own interests, denying real access to justice in the colonial judicial institutions. For example, in 1704 a Governor General was accused of "abus[ing] counsel" and "hector[ing] judges if they disagreed with him," which amounted to a "gross and visible partiality in most cases of his friends."[19]

The second major issue regarding colonial judicial institutions in the American colonies relates to the lack of uniformity between each colony.[20] Despite staking an exclusive claim for creating courts in the American colonies, the British Crown "never tried to make the judicial system in the colonies uniform."[21] Surrency states that

> initial courts generally were established by executive action, but later the judicial system was formalized by legislation. However some courts were created by virtue of rights arising from a grant; the grant of a large estate carried with it the authority to hold a court baron.[22] . . .
>
> the courts in the colonies often had their origins through some other source, [but] were later regularized by a statute. Under English law, certain grants of power from the King to his subjects carried with them the privilege to create courts, and these principles were applied in America.[23]

Further, although each colony was created through similar colonial charters, most charters "made no attempt to govern the rules of decision or procedures in the courts unless, of course, a colonial statute was involved [with the exception of Pennsylvania]."[24] This sowed the seeds for distrust in colonial judicial institutions by the American colonists as there was a lack of uniformity in the creation and administration of colonial courts.

Along with deficiencies in each charter and disparities among them, another reason for the lack of inter-colony uniformity in America's judicial development was "the [varied] conditions of settlement and of development within each colony." This uneven development "meant that each [colony] evolved its own individual legal system,"[25] which led to critiques of the colonial justice system near the time of the American Revolution.

Although the colonial courts in the Americas lacked uniformity, they all shared the common critique that the courts failed to provide effective justice to the colonists. Surrency states that even when trained judges arrived in the colonies to deal with the inadequacies of the court system,

> they had to accommodate their aims to the reality of colonial courts. Throughout the colonial period, the courts, with few exceptions, were poorly-staffed; the effects of this were felt in the organization of American courts well into the Nineteenth Century.[26]

C. Public perception of colonial courts

While there is a paucity of data on public opinions regarding colonial courts, it seems likely that the British were interested in having an impact on the low public opinion of the colonial courts in the American colonies. Many scholars have attempted to trace the opinion of the legal community and public at large to understand how colonial courts were perceived. As with most communities, "the colonists expected their courts to render justice and to handle the problems arising in a competent manner, the same objectives modern society sets for its courts."[27] However, when legal institutions failed to deliver these simple requirements, the perception of courts, lawyers, and judges was tarnished.

This dissatisfaction with colonial courts was so widespread across the American colonies that the "government in London became concerned with the problems of the courts at the close of the seventeenth century as a result of constant complaints against the administration of justice."[28] This led to an order calling for an investigation into the administration of justice in the colonies. Further, the Council on Trade and Plantations stated that "there had been constant complaint of great delays in the proceedings of the courts in the colonies," and the Council instructed the governors to see that justice was impartially administered.[29] Therefore, it seems evident that the colonial subjects were not satisfied with the lack of impartiality or the efficiency of court proceedings.

The suspicion of the colonial courts also bred animosity towards practitioners of the law. Gordon S. Wood explains that "Colonial America considered judges dangerous because they regarded judges essentially as appendages or extensions of royal authority embodied in the governors, or chief magistrates."[30] Despite the large number of colonial lawyers, the lawyer remained an "unpopular figure" through most of the colonial period.[31] Lawyers were prohibited from collecting fees in some jurisdictions[32] and were excluded from becoming legislators in Rhode Island.[33] Further, while there were many lawyers leading the Revolution who gained popularity among the colonists, "this was offset by the popular feeling against the many who were loyalists, a feeling that persisted even after the Revolution."[34]

As a result, lawyers and judges were seen at times to be instruments of colonial exploitation that threatened justice and liberty, values upon which the founding fathers of the United States focused so greatly. This created a special suspicion among the founding fathers regarding the over-empowerment of the judiciary, which experienced an unplanned and non-uniform evolution throughout the colonial period.

D. Legal education

One of the major early problems with the colonial courts was the dearth of trained lawyers. For example, in Pennsylvania throughout the seventeenth century, "legal matters seem to have been cared for by a class of part-time practitioners who were informally, and most likely often indifferently, trained."[35] Reisch states that

> a technical system can of course be administered only with the aid of trained lawyers. And these were generally not found in the colonies during the 17th and even far down into the 18th, we shall find that the legal administration was in the hands of laymen in many of the provinces.[36]

In fact, many of the general, Appeals, and even Supreme Courts for the colonies were administered partially by non-legal laymen or freemen.[37] This led both to an uneven development of the earlier colonial laws but also fed into public perception of colonial courts as lacking efficiency and effectiveness.

However, for the small numbers that did pursue a career in law, the training of members for each colony's bar was as inconsistent as the colonial courts themselves. While some attained their license to practice through apprenticeships or law school degrees in the colonies,[38] others traveled to Britain to be part of a renowned legal Inn. Prior to the eighteenth century, there were only seven American-born legal students admitted to the Inns of Court.[39] Therefore, "the clear inference is that English-trained lawyers were so few and so scattered in the colonies in the seventeenth century as to have, by themselves, a negligible effect upon the practice of law."[40]

Many would acknowledge the legal training at British Inns as more substantive than any programs offered in the colonies considering the historical prominence of these Inns. By 1815, "236 American-born students had traveled to London to study law at all four Inns."[41] Eventually, each colony's bar varied in population between self-trained lawyers and a limited number of British Inn-trained lawyers. Charles Warren's treatise on the American Bar "lists no Rhode Island lawyer trained in England, and he says there were only a few with American legal training."[42] Throughout the seventeenth century, it has further been shown that "in Maine, there were only six 'educated lawyers' in 1770, none of whom was English-trained."[43] Further, while Pennsylvania's bar was moderately advanced in comparison to its peers, the bar was still "comparatively late in getting a body of trained lawyers."[44]

This lack of lawyers formally trained in the common law mixed with a substantial number of self-trained or part-time lawyers limited the ultimate evolution of colonial courts. However, there were some successful attempts made at teaching law through apprenticeship. Stoebuck explains that "the great George Wythe, who himself apparently received his legal education in Virginia, provided in his single office the legal educations of Jefferson, Marshall, Madison, and Monroe."[45] These were some of the legal minds that helped develop the role of courts in the United States, and without great debate, have been recognized as both unique and adept legal thinkers despite their lack of training in a British Inn.

However, outside of these notable exceptions, the lack of formally trained lawyers affected the capability of colonial courts to deliver justice. Unlike their counterparts in the Indian subcontinent, thousands of whom trained in British Inns,[46] the lawyers of the American colonies did not share as strong a link with the tradition of British common law. The absence of this link, while challenging the evolution of colonial courts, allowed for American legal theorists to create an original perspective on the role of courts that has impacted post-colonial constitutionalism ever since.[47]

E. Impact on founders

The distrustfulness of the judiciary among the founders can be evidenced by the fact that the courts were constitutionally designated as the least powerful branch. The founders' hostility towards the judiciary was shaped, in part, by their experiences with the inadequate and sometimes unjust colonial judicial system. As described above, the founders needed to address the lack of uniformity in courts and the blurred lines between branches, and to decide whether or not to accept the common law tradition.

The first revolutionary concept that addresses the first two issues was the written constitution, which was crucial to the development of judicial review. By contrast, the unwritten British Constitution "referred to the traditions, practices, understandings, principles, and institutions that collectively structure the basic British system of government and way of life."[48]

The concepts that constitute the unwritten British Constitution did not protect colonial judicial institutions from becoming impacted by bias, ineffectualness, and nepotism. Further, a written constitution was needed to address the fact that colonial judges exercised "an enormous amount of discretionary authority"; therefore, "by having the new state legislatures write down the laws in black and white, many of the revolutionaries aimed to turn the judge into what Jefferson hoped would be 'a mere machine'."[49] This is why the founders of the United States focused on the format of their rules as contained in a central document called the Constitution.[50] The federal and state constitutions set out the roles for the judiciary,[51] while supplementary statutes like the Judiciary Act of 1789 created uniformly organized courts.

The third issue was determining the scope of the newly formed judiciary's acceptance of British common law. While the U.S. Constitution formally created a national Supreme Court with both original and appellate jurisdiction, the documents fail to mention what legal theory this court would apply. As stated by Professor Charles Lofgren, "the members of the Philadelphia Convention were silent about how they expected the Constitution to be interpreted."[52]

The relationship of post-colonial courts and British common law was described as follows by the Supreme Court in 1829:

> The common law of England is not to be taken in all respects to be that of America. Our ancestors brought with them its general principles, and claimed it as their birthright; but they brought with them and adopted only that portion which was applicable to their situation.[53]

While there was adoption of some British common law principles, Reinsch explains that "we find from the very first originality in legal conceptions departing widely from the most settled theories of common law and even a total denial of the subsidiary character of English jurisprudence."[54]

Therefore, unlike their Indian counterparts, the founders of the American system favored creating "a newly wholly American judicial philosophy as well as accepting the common law as a basic feature of the American system linking us to British common law."[55] While adopting some of the legal reasoning from the British, the arrival of America's written constitution made it "rather clear that Americans could no longer look back to England's original contract . . . as the source of their constitutional rights."[56] The partial rejection of British common law in America introduced "a period of rude, untechnical popular law" in the administration of justice in some of the American colonies.[57]

Throughout the debates leading up to the constitution's adoption, one sees a reluctance in empowering judges. Brutus states in Anti-Federalist Paper #11 that "judges will be interested to extend the powers of the courts" and that this power "will enable them to mold the government into almost any shape they please."[58] Brutus agrees that legislators who pass laws that violate the Constitution deserve to be removed from power through elections, but

> when this power is lodged in the hands of men independent of the people, and of their representatives, and who are not, constitutionally, accountable for their opinions, no way is left to control them but *with a high hand and an outstretched arm*.[59]
>
> (emphasis added)

The fear of unelected judges exercising their will over the people and displacing the legislature was founded partly on the experience with colonial courts as described above. Brutus feared that empowering the courts with such powers would make judges "independent of the people, of the legislature, and of every power under the heaven."[60] This could help explain why James Madison, writing as Publius in Federalist Paper #78, argued in favor of creating a federal judiciary but stated that "the judiciary is beyond comparison the weakest of the three departments of power; that it can never attack with success either of the other two."[61] Madison even argues that the Courts should have a role in checking the actions of the elected branches but that

> *the judiciary, from the nature of its functions, will always be the least dangerous to the political rights of the Constitutio . . . The judiciary, on the contrary, has no influence over either the sword or the purse . . .* [courts] must ultimately depend upon the aid of the executive arm even for the efficacy of its judgments.[62]
>
> (emphasis added)

Despite these debates, it is important to note that the founders of the United States were attempting the first experiment with constitutional democracy in the world. Therefore, one can assume that the founders did not know exactly what kind of system they were creating at the time. In fact, when it came to the ability of the judiciary to invalidate laws passed by the legislature, "many of the delegates to the Philadelphia Convention in 1787 still regarded judicial nullification of legislation with a sense of awe and wonder, impressed."[63] Therefore, in the end, the Constitution that was ratified created a Supreme Court without explicitly enumerating its right to judicial review. This right was developed over time through common law jurisprudence, as will be described in the Chapter 3.

III. Indian subcontinent's expansive experience with colonial justice

There are two especially notable differences that must bet set out in regards to comparing the American and Indian subcontinent colonies. First, while the American colonies were largely established and inhabited by European settlers, the Indian colony remained dominated by native groups that historically lived on the land. Second, the colonial period of rule in the American colonies was far shorter in time than British rule of India, which began in the late seventeenth century and extended up until 1947.[64]

A. Native justice

Unlike the indigenous peoples of North America, whose population and culture were largely wiped out, India retained both its population and its heterogeneous culture.[65] Cheryl McEwan explains that

> colonialism took different forms in different places . . . British colonization of the Americas was largely through the complete destruction and subjugation of indigenous communities . . . the British colonization of India was achieved less through military force, although this was always a threat, and more through creating a hierarchical administrative structure that incorporated and co-opted Indian elites.[66]

The coopting of the elites came with the British also deferring the resolution of some matters to local religious courts. There were various religious groups living in India at the time, including Muslims, Parsis and Hindus, all of whom possessed codes of law and dispute resolution institutions for their communities. These religious institutions were allowed to dispense justice under the monarchial rule of the Mughal Empire and later by the British Empire as well.[67]

While the British set aside native laws as foreign in the Americas, they sought to temper British rule with the adoption of local customs in the Indian colony. One reason for this difference could be that while the American natives lacked a single ruling tribe, the British witnessed the last vestiges of the vast Mughal Empire upon entering the territory. As John F. Richards explains,

> the Mughal Empire was one of the largest centralized states known in in pre-modern world history . . . [wherein] the Mughal emperor held supreme political authority over a population numbering 100 and 150 millions . . . The uniform practices and ubiquitous presence of the Mughals left an imprint upon society in every locality, and region of the subcontinent over several decades, when they first entered the territory.[68]

These Mughal practices were generally adopted and reformed by the British in an effort to create a native–colonial hybrid system of laws in the Indian Colonies.

This approach is remarkably different from the British rule in the American colonies. For example, while the British unilaterally introduced the Stamp Act in the face of opposition from the colonists in America, the British East India Company "secured the right to revenues in Bengal *in the name of* the Mughal emperor, rather than through an act of Parliament."[69] The East India Company created many treaties and engagements with various "Native Princes and States" in India to allow the leaders of these regions to continue their rule while granting land and trading rights to the Company for export of goods back to Britain.[70]

Based on these agreements, the British demarcated areas wherein the colonial courts would not have jurisdiction, granting autonomous rule to certain "princely states." Therefore, "while most of India was ruled directly through colonial officials in so-called British India, nearly one-fifth of the population resided in one of over five hundred 'princely states' whose internal governance was largely outside the jurisdiction of British authorities."[71] By granting autonomous rule for natives in some areas while exercising direct control in others, "India was thus administered as a direct/indirect rule hybrid, with varying degrees of involvement by colonial officials."[72]

Part of the hybridization can be linked to the British Empire's attempt at capitalizing on the institutions and credibility of the Mughal Empire as a means to establish its rule in India. Dr. Osama Siddique discusses the work of Christopher Bayly, who argues that there were "collaborators, beneficiaries, allies and even converts" that took part in the transformation of the Mughal-administered territory to a British Colony.[73] Bayly argues that there was a transition between a "crumbling Mughal empire" and the British judicial system that encouraged the British to coopt some of the judicial concepts and institutions designed for Mughal rule.[74] Therefore, some have argued that

> colonial policy essentially pushed forward/promoted trends that had already existed in the pre-colonial evolutionary stage of Indian society. In other words, British policy choices were not very different from those of their predecessors, the Mughals. As to the modus of change, while violence and coercion may have at times played a role in pursuit of certain policy objectives, so did compromise, cooperation, and acceptance.[75]

While it would be a mistake to assert that the entire native population was freely accepting of colonial domination, it is clear that the British were attempting to learn and coopt native traditions to make colonialism more acceptable to the native population. Washbrook goes further in saying, "early colonial India operated under a 'state mercantilist' form of economy in which the institutions of the ancient regime were made more efficient, brutalized and bastardized but, significantly, not dissolved."[76]

There was a substantial pre-colonial tradition for the administration of justice, which continued in force throughout the colonial period:

> while colonial officials were slow to engage the native populations in the lawmaking process in British India, their cautious approach to the transplantation of the legal system and rules reflected their acknowledgement of the preexisting Hindu and Muslim codes of conduct.[77]

Historians of India have crafted a theory called "change–continuity" which makes the argument that colonial laws were never meant to "drastically change the basic structure and purposes" of native traditions but were aimed at adapting those traditions to British rules of law.[78,79]

This amalgamation of British common law with native traditions of justice produced a long-standing colonial rule that influenced the subsequent developments of law in both Pakistan and India after independence.[80] In the United States, where native justice was viewed as "foreign," there was less influence by the British model on the jurisprudence that would come from the United States Supreme Court. While the imprint left by the British on both colonies was significant, one could expect that the Americans were more likely to diverge from commonly accepted principles in British justice than their Indian or Pakistani counterparts.

B. Development of colonial courts

While the development of colonial courts in America was unplanned, the British attempted a more organized effort for the Indian colonies. However, in the beginning there was a period where laws transmitted by British colonial entities "lacked systematic organization and were poorly publicized."[81] This was amended with the annual publication of laws in English, Bengali, and Persian by Lord Cornwalis.[82]

Informing and involving natives in decisions made by the Crown became necessary in order to ensure long-term stability in the Indian colony. Lord Bartle Frere during Parliamentary debates argued that failing to include natives in the legislative process would be a "perilous experiment of continuing to legislate for millions of people, with few means of knowing, except by a rebellion whether the laws suit them or not."[83]

Therefore, one can see a marked difference between the British approach to ruling its American and Indian colonies. This difference could be attributed to the lessons learned by the British in dealing with the rebellious American colonists, which led to a concerns relating to creating a more cooperative rule in India. Therefore, rather than granting ad hoc and innumerable powers to the Governor General, the British relied upon three sources of law to govern the Indian colonies

> (1) wisdom literature – left to Hindu theologians, Brahmins and European philologists, (2) positive colonial law – a mix of English common law, dharmashastra, Sharia, and compiled customary law – with the latter three subject to uniform English court procedures and thereby distorted the process; and (3) what he calls "local ways."[84]

Eventually, through a purposefully gradual codification process, the British began "implanting values such as consistency and formality" into "modified indigenous courts before being replaced by British institutions."[85] This gradual approach

> provided the British with the opportunity to test their policies, while also ensuring that the native population had time to adjust to the new laws . . . By

> slowly adapting the legal system they were able to create a court hierarchy and a body of law that was both effective and accepted by the native population – two points vital to the success of the rule of law.[86]

The process of codifying India's laws for interpretation by the courts started with the 1833 Charter Act. The Charter Act of 1833 "mandated the codification of Indian law, calling for its amalgamation of legal sources" in a way that married acts of Parliament to Islamic, Hindu, and regional traditions of justice.[87] The Charter also "strengthen[ed] this movement towards legal standardization, centralizing the legislative process in the Governor-General and his Council."[88] The aim of this endeavor was to create "one great and entire work symmetrical in all its parts and pervaded by one spirit."[89]

This legal movement gained momentum "in the second half of the nineteen century with the introduction of several Indian legal codes."[90] These codes demonstrated how "the principles of the English common and statute law took root gradually in India . . . [becoming] firmly embedded in the structure of the great Indian Codes."[91]

Codification with Acts spurred development and increased power for the Indian colonial courts. Despite the persistence of native alternative dispute mechanisms, "with codification, the colonial regime, it is argued, appropriated the right of interpretation and rewriting. Now courts were to decide disputes, judges reinterpreted them."[92]

C. Public perception of colonial courts

Despite the overall success of the codification process infusing British common law with traditional Indian sources of law, there was "native discontent at the various displacements brought on" by codification.[93] This discontent was displayed in many ways, including "violations of rules, a public flouting of norms, a silent persistence with alternative practices."[94] These protests would continue to gather steam in the lead up to independence and partition in 1947.

Further, by supplanting the native forms of justice with Anglo-Saxon legal principles,

> the British clearly intended to bring justice, [but] their legal system often produced results that were experienced and understood as injustice, not because the British desired or intended such a result, but because most Indians did not appreciate the system's morality and logic.[95]

However, as Siddique concludes, "one could reasonably argue that a century-and-a-half of British rule would have been untenable if there had been no concomitant change in the Indian people's reception of British laws."[96] The begrudging acquiescence to British laws by Indian subjects "may have evolved into something acceptable and beneficial to the people."[97] With the involvement of colonial subjects in the legislative process, the codification of codes, and the incorporation of traditional native customs in the codes, the British were able to gain a stronger foothold among their Indian colonial subjects, as compared to the more contentious relationship the Crown had with its American colonies.

While the legal community had a tarnished public image in the American colonies due to its supposed loyalist leanings, lawyers in India were regarded with greater honor. While some have described colonial era lawyers as either protagonists or antagonists, there is a new historical approach that treats them "as intellectual middlemen molding colonial forms of ethnographic knowledge and collective self-image."[98]

Most significantly, the favorable image of colonial courts and lawyers in India informed the founders' decisions on creating powerful and independent judicial bodies in post-colonial Pakistan and India, as did the native Indian public's acceptance of these colonial courts, which will be discussed in Chapter 3. In the United States, some founding fathers were suspicious of the courts due to their experience with ineffective or biased colonial courts. This attitude may have partially inspired the American post-colonial focus on empowering the elected branches of government rather than enabling an active appointed judicial branch.

D. Legal education and native lawyers

As mentioned earlier, the legal education received by Indian and American colonial subjects varied greatly. While both nations allowed for a system of apprenticeship as a means of learning to practice law, Indian elites preferred British-based education. Unlike their American counterparts, thousands of Indians went to London in order to seek training at the local universities and be called to the bar at the many famous Inns of Court.[99] Their arrival in Britain was "an unexpected phenomenon given the cultural stereotype of the period that characterized Muslims as 'backward' and resistant to Anglicized forms of education."[100]

While pursuing their studies in London, "South Asian bar students tended to lodge together in neighborhoods, like Paddington and Bloomsbury, and to study at the University of London and Inns concurrently."[101] Many successfully completed their training, and returned home to earn greater respect and prestige in the colonial courts. Many graduates from these British institutions went on to create the nations of Pakistan and India, including Mohammad Ali Jinnah (Lincoln's Inn),[102] Mohandas K. Gandhi (Inner Temple), and Jawaharlal Nehru (Inner Temple).[103]

While there was a glass ceiling for most colonial subjects taking part in their master's legal systems, the British allowed some Indians to hold posts of great power.[104] For example, "lawyers like Mohammad Ali Jinnah and judges like Syed Ameer Ali and Dinshaw Mulla played critical roles in creating 'legal India' through the Judicial Committee of the Privy Council, the final court of appeal for the British Empire."[105] As a result,

> South Asians began to have a major presence in the upper echelons of the legal system from the late nineteenth century on. By the early twentieth, a number had risen to the ranks of the presidency [of] High Courts, and in 1909

> Syed Ameer Ali became the first South Asian judge to be appointed to the Judicial Committee of the Privy Council.[106]

Not only did these jurists elevate themselves in the colonial legal order, they were able to address long-standing issues within their own communities. At one point there were "two South Asian judges in the Bombay High Court in the same period, using law as a way of settling debates over reform within their own communities."[107] These judges, as part of the native legal elite that was given power to interpret colonial laws, made the effort to reformulate "Parsi and Hindu law in the image of their ideal communal visions."[108]

Therefore, lawyers in colonial India trained through the British Inn system were given positions of authority as well as the responsibility to settle issues and modernize dispute resolution institutions in their own native communities. This training and role gave credibility to lawyers, judges, and the justice system overall in the Indian colony and explains the greater persistence of the British legal traditions in post-independence Pakistan and India than in America, where lawyers lacked training in and reverence for British legal traditions.

E. Impact on founders

British-trained lawyers from India were involved in the independence movement and helped shape the nation's justice system. Therefore, "by admitting overseas students in the previous century, the Inns of Court had played a significant part in preparing the British colonies for independence."[109] This combination of British-trained lawyers with power to settle issues in their communities created a long-lasting colonial control for the Crown.

This control influenced the decisions of independent India and Pakistan. For example, the colonial legal system established by the British "was followed by [India's] 1950 Constitution, which although drafted by an Indian Constituent Assembly, still in many ways looked like a very Western document (perhaps not surprisingly given that many players at the Assembly were Western educated)."[110]

British training allowed common law legal traditions to impact India well beyond the constitution-writing process: "for over a hundred years . . . [Indian jurists] have been basing themselves upon the theories of English common law and statutes."[111] These jurists have, however, "evolved doctrines of their own, suited to the peculiar need and environment of India."[112]

Therefore, while one must understand the "foreign roots" of British legal traditions in India and their long-standing impact, modern Indian law is "unmistakably Indian in its outlook and operation."[113] The British colonial policy of mixing native customs and laws with British common law allowed the post-colonial legal regime to be rooted in the British legal tradition while allowing indigenous legal concepts to evolve over time.

The same can be said for Pakistan, where a gap continues to exist between the Pakistani people and "inherited laws from its colonial legacy," which were "in some cases [left] intact in their original forms."[114] Not only were some of the laws carried over from the colonial era, but also other legislation "promulgated after independence" was crafted in the mold and ethos of the colonial era.[115] Therefore, much like India, Pakistan's legal evolution was partially based on British traditions. However, there was also a space for the creation of unique concepts of justice, which are embodied in both the Constitution of Pakistan and its common law jurisprudence, which will be discussed in Chapter 3.

IV. Conclusion

The actions of the post-colonial founders of the United States, the Federation of Pakistan, and the Republic of India must be understood in the context of their colonial history of justice. Perhaps having learned lessons from the shortcomings of colonial rule in the American colonies, the British aimed at creating a flexible, rule-based, and long-standing colonial experiment in India. In many ways their method was effective – by gradually mixing native traditions of justice with British common law, the British were able to affect even the post-colonial development of courts in India and Pakistan.

Accordingly, Indian and Pakistani lawyers were more committed to the concepts of traditional British legal traditions than their American counterparts. Many reasons have been laid out for this distinction, including: i) the difference in legal education, ii) the way in which the Indian colony's judicial institutions were mixed with native systems, unlike in America where the natives were set aside, iii) the way in which the colonial courts were also widely accepted as being effective and properly established, unlike in America, and iv) the way in which natives in India were given British legal training and were thus better able to ingrain themselves in the colonial ruling system. All of this collectively allowed for the persistence of that system into the modern era in Pakistan and India, unlike in the United States.

Undoubtedly, Pakistanis and Indians responded to continuing colonial control after gaining independence like their American counterparts. Unlike their colonial master, the Pakistanis and Indians followed the American example of creating a written constitution and allowing the courts to interpret that supreme law. However, the power to interpret creates far greater powers for the Indian and Pakistani judiciaries, in part due their historical lineage dating back to effective British colonial courts. By contrast, in the United States, which lacked effective and customized colonial courts, uniquely American concepts of judicial power and restraint evolved over time in relation to the court's right to interpret the Constitution.

Notes

1 Edwin C. Surrency, *The Courts in the American Colonies*, 111 Amer. J. Leg. Hist. 253 (1967) ("The British government claimed the sole power to create courts, and the early courts, except those in the charter and proprietary colonies, were created by executive action. However, after the initial settlement the judiciary received little attention from the King, and colonial courts were left to evolve without much thought or consideration. England never tried to make the judicial system in the colonies uniform.")

2 See Dr Osama Siddique, *Pakistan's Experience with Formal Law: An Alien Justice* (2013), at 46. ("Others have similarly asserted 'continuity' at several levels of Indian polity and society in order to maintain that colonial knowledge of the colonized and the resulting colonial rule, was not a unique colonial invention. It was in fact the product of collaboration between European rules and their 'chosen and trusted indigenous informers'.")

3 See generally James Olson, *Historical Dictionary of the British Empire* (1996). (The British Crown took direct control over India first through the East India Trading Company in 1612 and then with the establishment of the British Raj in 1824, which lasted until 1947. The United States was only under colonial rule from the early 1600s to the late 1700s.) See also Ronald J. Daniels et al., *The Legacy of Empire: The Common Law Inheritance and Commitments to Legality in Former British Colonies*, 59 Am. J. Comp. L. 111, 134 (2011) ("Perhaps attributable to its unique importance to the Empire as well as the lengthy duration of British engagement in the Subcontinent.")

4 For example, during Parliamentary debates in 1860 Lord Bartle Frere commented that applying the confrontational colonialism strategy they had used in America to India or other colonies would be a "perilous experiment of continuing to legislate for millions of people, with few means of knowing, except by rebellion whether the law suits them or not." Sir Bartle Frere, minutes to the Parliamentary debates of the Act, reprinted in Cecil Meme Putnam Cross, the Development of Self Government in India, 1858–1914 at 42.

5 See generally Nicholas Canny, *The Oxford History of the British Empire: Volume I: The Origins of Empire : British Overseas Enterprise to the Close of the Seventeenth Century: British Overseas Enterprise to the Close of the Seventeenth Century* (1998).

6 Nonso Okafo, *Reconstructing Law and Justice in a Postcolony* (2012).

7 Robert O. Saunooke, *Tribal Justice the Case for Strengthening Inherent Sovereignty*, 47 Judges' J. 15, 17 ("Although there is evidence of judicial and dispute resolution systems in place throughout Indian Country prior even to Columbus, the development of tribal courts as they are now known can be traced to a case in the 1880s.") See also Mitra Sharafi, *A New History of Colonial Lawyering: Likhovski and Legal Identities in the British Empire*, 32 L. & Soc. Inquiry1059–1094 (2007) ("given the unusual phenomenon of the independent Cherokee courts that operated during the nineteenth century") citing Rennard Strickland, *Fire and the Spirits: Cherokee Law from Clan to Court* (1975).

8 Vine Deloria Jr & Clifford M. Lytle, *American Indians, American Justice* (2010).

9 Okafo, *supra* note 6. (There was an "ambivalent separation of the Native American reservations justice systems from the official US system.")

10 Joan-Pau Rubies, *Texts, Images, and the Perception of 'Savages' in Earlier Modern Europe: What We Can Learn from White and Harriot*, British Museum Organization, Available at www.britishmuseum.org/pdf/4-Rubies-Text%20Images%20and%20the%20Perception%20of%20Savages.pdf (last accessed on Oct. 17, 2016).

11 Laurence French, *Native American Justice* (2003) at 3. ("during the colonial era of America, the British Crown . . . made treaties and other alliances with American Indians.")

12 Okafo, *supra* note 6, "English common law or its derivative dominates the Native American law and justice systems."

13 Daniels, *supra* note 3, at 173–4 (2011) (Though it may be assumed that the British completely transformed pre-existing legal institutions in all of their colonies, "this was never true" outside of the settler colonies like the United States, Canada, or Australia. Daniels states that "indeed, in almost every case, the British imperial authorities attempted to grapple with the challenge of integrating elements of the common law system with preexisting or traditional systems or modes of maintaining social order.")

14 Id at 119–20 (2011) ("In regions in which European settlement was unattractive or infeasible, the colonists tended to create extractive colonies lacking strong property protections and safeguards against government expropriation, while in areas with more hospitable climates, Europeans were more inclined to establish settler colonies characterized by more representative governance structures and trade-friendly policies.")
15 Surrency, *supra* note 1, at 258.
16 Id at 253.
17 Surrency, *supra* note 1, at 258.
18 Id.
19 Id at 255.
20 William B. Stoebuck, *Reception of English Common Law in the American Colonies*, 10 Will. & Mary L. Rev. 393 (1968).
21 Surrency, *supra* note 1, at 253.
22 Id at 254
23 Id at 257.
24 Stoebuck, *supra* note 20, at 393.
25 Id.
26 Surrency, *supra* note 1, at 255–6.
27 Surrency, *supra* note 1, at 255.
28 Surrency, *supra* note 1, at 256 citing Order of the Lords Justices in Council, 1700 Calendar of State Papers American West Indies 423, Order 651.
29 Surrency, *supra* note 1, at 257 citing Circular Letter to the Governors of all H.M. Plantations in America relating to Courts of Justice, 1702–1703 Calendar of State Papers American West Indies 356, Order 578i.
30 Gordon S. Wood, *The Origins of Judicial Review Revisited, or How the Marshall Court Made More Out of Less*, 56 Wash. & Lee L. Rev. 787 (1999).
31 Stoebuck, *supra* note 20, at 393.
32 Paul S. Reinsch, *The English Common Law in the Early American Colonies* (1899) at 395 and 406.
33 See Thomas Durfee, *Gleanings from the Judicial History of Rhode Island* (1883) at 37–8.
34 Francis R. Auman, *The Changing American Legal System* (1940) at 80–1.
35 For example Stoebuck, *supra* note 20, at 404 citing Charles Joseph Hilkey, *Legal Development in Colonial Massachusetts, 1630–1686*, 37 Columbia University Studies in History, Economics, and Public Law, 216–21 (1910).
36 Reinsch, *supra* note 32, at 367.
37 Stoebuck, *supra* note 20, at 411 ("Not only were there practically no English-trained judges on the colonial bench during the seventeenth century, but it seems to have been made up in large part of men who were not lawyers at all.")
38 The first law school in the United States was at the College of William and Mary in 1780. https://law.wm.edu/about/ourhistory/index.php (last accessed on Oct. 17, 2016).
39 Randy J. Holland, *Anglo-American Templars: Common Law Crusaders*, 8 Del. L. Rev. 137, 144 (2006)
40 Stoebuck, *supra* note 20, at 405.
41 Holland, *supra* note 39.
42 Stoebuck, *supra* note 20, at 414. Citing Charles Warren, *A History of the American Bar* (1913).
43 Id at 414.
44 Id at 402. Citing Charles Warren, *A History of the American Bar* (1913).
45 Stoebuck, *supra* note 20, at 414.
46 See generally Mitra Sharafi, *South Asians at Inns, South Asian Legal History Resources*. Available at http://hosted.law.wisc.edu/wordpress/sharafi/south-asian-law-students-at-the-inns-of-court/ (last accessed on Oct. 17, 2016).

47 Carl J. Friedrich, *The Impact of American Constitutionalism Abroad* (1967).
48 Akhil Reed Amar, *America's Unwritten Constitution: The Precedents and Principles We Live By* (Reprint ed., 2015).
49 Wood, *supra* note 30. Citing Letter from Thomas Jefferson to Edmund Pendleton (Aug. 26, 1776), in *The Papers of Thomas Jefferson* 503, 505 (Julian P. Boyd ed., 1950).
50 Thomas MacAffee, *Inalienable Rights, Legal Enforceability and American Constitutions: The Fourteenth Amendment and the Concept of Unenumerated Rights*, 36 Wake Forest L. Rev. 758. Citing Thomas Macafee, *Inherent Rights, the Written Constitution, and Popular Sovereignty: The Founder's Understanding* (2000) at 10–12. ("Indeed, by 1787 many thoughtful Americans had come to see Great Britain's unwritten constitution as lacking an essential element of constitutionalism in failing to provide explicit and binding limits on the government power.")
51 See generally Akhil Reed Amar, *America's Constitution: A Biography* (1st ed., 2010).
52 Charles A. Lofgren, *The Original Understanding of Original Intent?*, 5 Constitutional Commentary 77, 79 (1988).
53 *Van Ness v. Pacard*, 27 U.S. (2 Pet.) 137, 143–44 (1829).
54 Reinsch, *supra* note 32, at 7.
55 Id.
56 MacAffee, *supra* note 50, at 758.
57 Reinsch, *supra* note 31, at 8.
58 Brutus, "Anti- Federalist #11," in Ralph Ketcham, ed., *The Anti Federalist Papers and the Constitutional Convention Debates* (2003).
59 Brutus, "Anti- Federalist #15," in The Ralph Ketcham, ed., *Anti Federalist Papers and the Constitutional Convention Debates* (2003).
60 Id.
61 Alexander Hamilton, "Federalist #78," in Clinton Rossiter, ed., *The Federalist Papers* (1961).
62 Id.
63 Wood, *supra* note 30, at 796.
64 Daniels, *supra* note 3, at 135 (2011). ("Ultimately, the English took full advantage of the opportunity to create a functional legal system during their lengthy stay in India.")
65 See generally C. A. Baylyl, *Rulers Townsmen and Bazaars: North Indian Society in the Age of British Expansion 1770–1870* (1983).
66 Cheryl McEwan, *Post-Colonialism and Development* (2008), at 82.
67 See generally BBC, Mughal Empire (1500s, 1600s), Available at www.bbc.co.uk/religion/religions/islam/history/mughalempire_1.shtml (last accessed on Oct. 17, 2016).
68 John F. Richards, *The New Cambridge History of India: The Mughal Empire* (1995), at 2.
69 Kavita Saraswathi Datla, *The Origins of Indirect Rule in India: Hyderabad and the British Imperial Order*, 33 Law & Hist. Rev. 321, 325–6 (2015)
70 See generally a Collection of Treaties and Engagements with the Native Princes and States of Asia Concluded on Behalf of the East India Company by the British Governments in India, Viz. by the Government of Bengal Etc. Also Copies of Sunnuds or Grants of Certain Privileges and Imunities to the East India Company by the Mogul and Other Native, United East India Company (1812).
71 Daniels, *supra* note 3, at 134–5.
72 Id.
73 Siddique, *supra* note 2, at 46 citing C.A. Bayly, *supra* note 65.
74 See generally C.A. Bayly, *supra* note 65.
75 Siddique, *supra* note 2, at 57.
76 Siddique, *supra* note 2, at 83 citing D.A. Washbrook, "Law, State and Agrarian Society in Colonial India," in C. Baker, G. Johnson, & A. Seal, eds., *Power Profit and Politics: Essays in Imperialism, Nationalism and Changes in the Twentieth Century India*

(Cambridge University Press, 2009). Vol. 15, Pt. 3 (originally published as a collection of essays in a special issue of Modern Asian Studies, July 1981), at pp 661.

77 Daniels, *supra* note 3, at 134–5 (2011).

78 Siddique, *supra* note 2, at 46 citing C.A. Bayly, *supra* note 65.

79 Siddique, *supra* note 2, at 36–7 (There are three other models of analysis for Indian historians according to Siddique: 1. Radical Displacement theory which argues that colonial legal systems displaced local, intelligible and accessible systems, 2. Inevitable Modernization or the Change–Continuity Argument wherein colonial laws were part of an unavoidable modernization of already existing local customs and 3. Desirable Modernization argument which describes colonial legal system as necessary and desirable to modernize India.)

80 Daniels, *supra* note 3, at 135.

81 Daniels, *supra* note 3, at 134–5. Citing Abdul Hamid, *A Chronicle of British Indian Legal History* (1991), at 102–4.

82 Id.

83 Sir Bartle Frere, *Minutes to the Parliamentary Debates of the Act*, reprinted in Cecil Meme Putnam Cross, *The Development of Self-Government in India, 1858–1914*, at 42.

84 Siddique, *supra* note 2, at 88 describing D.H.A. Kolff, *The Indian and the British Law Machines: Some Remarks on Law and Society in British India*, in European Expansion and Law (1992).

85 Daniels, *supra* note 3, at 135.

86 Id.

87 Id at 147–8 (2011).

88 Id at 147–8 citing Minutes dated Jan. 2, 1837, in C.D. Dharker, *Lord Macaulay's Legislative Minutes* (1946).

89 Id.

90 Siddique, *supra* note 2, at 52.

91 M. C. Setalvad, Padma Vibhufan, Attorney-General of India, *The Common Law in India* (1960) at 224.

92 Neeladri Bhattacharya, "Remaking Custom: The Discourse and Practice of Colonial Codification," in *Tradition, Dissent and Ideology: Essays in Honour of Romila Thapar* (2001).

93 Siddique, *supra* note 2, at 90.

94 Bhattacharya, *supra* note 92, at 51.

95 Lloyd I. Rudolph & Susanne Hoeber Rudolph, *The Modernity of Tradition: Political Development in India* (1984), at 245.

96 Siddique, *supra* note 2, at 45.

97 Siddique, *supra* note 2, at 49.

98 Sharafi *supra* note 7, at 1084.

99 See generally Sharafi, *supra* note 46.

100 Sharafi, *supra* note 7, at 1083 citing (see Hunter 1872, 151–216; Hardy 1872, 92–115; Strangman 1931, 201; Nehru 1946, 390).

101 Sharafi, *supra* note 7, at 1083.

102 Lincoln's Inn, *Mohammad Ali Jinnah Factsheet*, Available at www.lincolnsinn.org.uk/images/word/Library/jinnah.pdf (last accessed on Oct. 17, 2016).

103 Inner Temple, *The Admission of Overseas Students to the Inner Temple in the 19th Century*. Available at www.innertemple.org.uk/history/historical-articles/35-admission-of-overseas?showall=&start=2 (last accessed on Oct. 17, 2016).

104 See Abhinav Chandrachud, *An Independent, Colonial Judiciary: A History of the Bombay High Court During the British Raj, 1862–1947* (1st ed., Oxford University Press, 2015).

105 Sharafi, *supra* note 7, at 1082.

106 Sharafi, *supra* note 7, at 1070 citing (see Abbasi 1989; Muhammad 1991).
107 Id.
108 Id.
109 Inner Temple, *supra* note 103.
110 Jayath K. Krishnan, *Professor Kingsfield Goes to Delhi: American Academics, the Ford Foundation, and the Development of Legal Education in India*, 46 Am. J. Legal Hist. 447 (2004).
111 Setalvad, *supra* note 91, at 225.
112 Id.
113 Id.
114 Siddique, *supra* note 2, at 45.
115 Siddique, *supra* note 2, at 45.

3 The origins of judicial review

Having reviewed the judicial institutions established by the British in the American and Indian colonies, one must understand the historical origins of the Court's exercise of judicial review over the executive or legislative branch in the American and Indian colonies. The use of legal history to explore the genesis of judicial review will foster a contextualized understanding of the development of judicial review in Pakistan, India, and the United States.

This chapter will first examine the emergence of parliamentary supremacy as a legal doctrine that empowered the legislative branch and limited the development of judicial review in early English jurisprudence. Subsequently, the concept of ultra vires will be discussed as an antecedent legal principle to judicial review, which was employed by English courts in some cases during the seventeenth century. Next, Lord Coke's seminal decisions setting out judicial review will be examined, along with the responses both from his colleagues in Britain and in the Indian and American colonies. This will lead to a discussion of the varied early uses of judicial review in Pakistan, India and America that impacted its subsequent development in each nation.

I. Parliamentary supremacy

A counterpoint to the emergence of judicial review in British jurisprudence was the gradual but widespread acceptance of parliamentary supremacy. During the time of monarchical rule, Parliament was seen as a secondary source of law, while the King possessed expansive legislative powers through orders and decrees.[1] Through laws like the Statute of Proclamations Act of 1539, the King was granted formal powers to legislate through unilateral Proclamations.[2]

These Proclamations were not reviewed by judges or the courts, as

> prior to the American Revolution, so far were the English courts from sustaining the later doctrine of parliamentary absolutism that in the reign of James II, ten of the twelve judges of England held that the King was an absolute sovereign.[3]

Therefore, in the power battle that emerged between Parliament and the monarchy in the eighteenth century, the judiciary was seen as an ally of the King. Critics challenged the absolutism of the King's rule by arguing in favor of transferring this same power to Parliament due to many factors, including "Parliament's claim to represent the wisdom of the entire community; distrust of the ability of the king's judges to withstand improper royal influence . . . [and] the presumed equal right of every generation to change its laws."[4]

Eventually, parliamentary supremacy came to be defined as "the right to make or unmake any law whatever," meaning that "no person or body is recognized by the law of England as having a right to override or set aside the legislation of Parliament."[5] This doctrine of parliamentary supremacy signified a challenge to the once-absolute powers of kings, although this supremacy was not based on democratic principles initially. Very few British citizens were given the right to vote and between 1430 and 1836; only forty-shilling freeholders, or men who owned land worth at least 40 shillings, were allowed to vote in elections for the House of Commons.[6] However, the fight between the King and his Parliament was an attempt to devolve power from a monarchy to an oligarchy or aristocracy, which would eventually evolve into a democratic order.

While the judiciary had been known to legitimize rather than challenge the King's law, one judge emphasized the role of parliamentary supremacy as a check on the King's powers. In *Case of Proclamations*,[7] Lord Justice Edward Coke championed parliamentary supremacy as a means of weakening the king's power, while ultimately carving out a niche that would eventually allow judicial review of parliamentary acts.

He wrote that "of the power and jurisdiction of the parliament, for making of laws in proceeding by bill, it is so transcendent and absolute, as it cannot be confined either for causes or persons within any bounds."[8] This can help explain the quotation from William Blackstone concerning the supremacy of parliament. Blackstone argued that even where Parliament enacted an unreasonable law,

> no power can control i . . . . where the main object of a statute is unreasonable, the judges are [not] at liberty to reject it; *for that were to set the judicial power above that of the legislature, which would be subversive of all government.*[9]
>
> (emphasis added)

Though many have debated the meaning of Lord Coke's assertions and the extent to which parliamentary supremacy should be recognized,[10] A. V. Dicey explained that

> in England we are accustomed to the existence of a supreme legislative body, i.e. a body which can make or unmake every law; and which, therefore, *cannot be bound by any law*. This is, from a legal point of view, the true conception of a sovereign, and the case with which the theory of absolute sovereignty has been accepted by English jurists.[11]
>
> (emphasis added)

Some English jurists believed any review of Parliament's acts by the judiciary was a violation of Parliament's rights and duties as the institution that inherited much of the King's power. Judges like Lord Justice Coke were the first to challenge this seemingly impenetrable wall of parliamentary supremacy. Additionally, the doctrine of ultra vires played a role in developing judicial review as a means to challenge legislative supremacy.

II. Ultra vires: forbearer of judicial review

Ultra vires is an ancient doctrine[12] that allow courts to assess whether an organization has acted beyond the scope of its delegated powers. Many have argued that the doctrine was a source for judicial review.[13] It has been described as "the central principle of administrative law," and its impact extended to the birth of judicial review as a means for the courts to assess the legality of executive or legislative action.[14] This doctrine confers on the judiciary the right to "declare a particular action or decision . . . as being beyond the scope of powers that had been delegated by the Parliament to the officer or body."[15] It was cited by British courts in the late nineteenth century in cases like *Coleman v. Eastern Counties Railway Company* (1840), *East Anglican Railway Company v. Eastern Counties Railway Company* (1851) and *Ashbury Railway Carriage and Iron Company v. Riche*.[16]

Stated differently, through ultra vires, judges have the power to declare acts illegal because they go beyond a legitimate scope. As one American scholar has observed:

> [British] judges have this power because Parliament intends them to and . . . it should be exercised only to ensure that the executive branch of government does not act ultra vires – beyond the authority granted to it by Parliament through legislation . . . These twin notions, the doctrines of parliamentary intent and ultra vires, formed the backbone of British theories of judicial review for almost one hundred years.[17]

More specific to the United States, British jurist and Ambassador to the United States Lord Bryce[18] concluded that "Judicial Review in the United States in derived directly from Judicial Review in Britain."[19] Lord Bryce explained how ultra vires became a foundation for judicial review in the American colonies, because most of the colonies were established by charters:

> Many of the American colonies received charters from the British Crown . . . and endowed [their assemblies] with certain powers of making laws for the colony. Such powers were of course limited, partly by the charter, partly by usage . . . questions sometimes arose in colonial days whether . . . statutes . . . were in excess of the powers conferred by the charter; and if the statutes were found to be in excess, they were held invalid by the courts . . . by the colonial courts, or, if the matter was carried to England, by the Privy Council.[20]

Christopher Forsyth and Dawn Oliver have more recently updated and confirmed Lord Bryce's insights.[21]

For the Indian colonies, "judicial review based on the doctrine of ultra vires dates back to the inception of British rule."[22] An early example of the colonial courts using ultra vires dates back to 1878, in the case of *The Empress v. Burah*, in which the Calcutta High Court assessed the legality of the Lieutenant Governor's order to prohibit the exercise of the Court's jurisdiction in a certain geographical area.[23] Justice William Ainslie established the court's review power in holding that "if [the Lieutenant Governor's act] was ultra vires, this Court is bound to take notice of the fact."[24]

It must be noted, however, that there is a major distinction to be drawn between the ultra vires principles and judicial review. While both speak to the ability of the court to strike down executive action that exceeds Parliament's intent, ultra vires generally does not allow the "judiciary [to] substitute its judgement for that of the executive or Parliament – it is the will of Parliament, not the will of the judiciary, that determines when and if an executive action is to be declared invalid."[25] The focus is on legislative intent with the presumption that Parliament could pass any law. However, the modern use of judicial review sets aside that presumption in favor of assessing the constitutionality of legislative action, which can implicitly allow the "judiciary to substitute its judgement" for that of the legislature.[26]

Nevertheless, one cannot ignore the influence of ultra vires on the emergence of judicial review in the colonies. Even before Lord Coke declared the right of the judiciary to assess whether a law ran afoul of "common right and reason," the long-term usage of ultra vires was the intellectual foundation for the creation of judicial review in the United States, Pakistan, and India.

III. Lord Coke's introduction of judicial review

The first direct reference to judicial review dates back to the seventeenth century and came from Lord Chief Justice Coke. In 1608, Coke went beyond ultra vires and directly challenged parliamentary supremacy. In *Calvin's Case*, Lord Coke recognized "a law eternal, the Moral law, called also the Law of Nature," that Parliament had no right to limit through its actions.[27] This implicitly allowed the courts to assess when Parliament violated "the Moral law" or the "law of nature," opening the door for judicial review.

It wasn't long before Coke explicitly mentioned the right of the courts to annul parliamentary actions in *Dr. Bonham v. College of Physicians*, in 1610, where he decided that:

> it appears in our books, that in many cases, the common law will control Acts of Parliament, and sometimes adjudge them to be utterly void; for when an act of Parliament is against common right and reason, or repugnant, or impossible to be performed, the common law will control it, and adjudge such an Act to be void.[28]

It is important to note that since there was no written constitution or bill of rights yet in England, the judges compared legislative acts against "moral law,"

"law of nature," or "common right and reason."[29] The lack of enumerated rights led to critiques that Lord Coke's reliance on principles like common right would dangerously allow the courts to spread their power and eventually become the masters of elected Parliament.

IV. Vindication of Lord Coke in the United States

When judicial review was first introduced, there was an immediate clash between the judiciary on one hand and the legislature and the monarch on the other.[30] This can be partly attributed to the radicalism of Coke's claim. His concept was so radical that his peers in the legal community generally rejected his suggestions. Further, King James requested Lord Coke to withdraw his ruling on behalf of Dr. Bonham[31] In response to the King's request, Coke

> refused to acknowledge any substantial error in his writings, and boldly met his accusers by repeating the offending passages word by word as he first wrote them. He had been suspended from office some months earlier and commanded to correct his *Reports*, but the only defects he would acknowledge were a few trifling slips which he protested were extremely few, considering the magnitude of his work.[32]

This led to King James eventually removing him from the bench on the Court of Common Pleas in 1613.[33]

Though there were a few jurists who began exploring judicial review at the time, Coke's concept was mostly rejected by British judges.[34] Some judges expressed their acceptance of judicial review, but only through non-binding obiter dicta in some cases.[35] For example, in *City of London v. Wood*, Justice Holt wrote that

> what my Lord Coke says in Dr. Bonham's case . . . is far from any extravagancy, for it is a very reasonable and true saying, that if an Act of Parliament should ordain that the same person should be . . . [a] Judge in his own cause, it would be a void Act of Parliament.[36]

Yet, despite adopting Coke's reasoning from the *Bonham* case, Justice Holt later "acknowledged that the judiciary could not employ judicial review to void acts of parliament."[37]

While some English jurists accepted the basic principles of Coke's argument in theory, this did not lead to the kind of expansion of judicial review powers in England as it eventually did in the United States.[38] In some ways, American jurists adopted Coke's theory as a basis for revolting against the British Crown when "just as Bonham's Case was becoming a historical curiosity in the UK, in the British North American colonies it was being invoked in legal arguments that were instrumental in the events leading up the American Revolution."[39] In fact, the New York State Bar Association asserted in 1915 that "the American Revolution was a lawyers' revolution to enforce Lord Coke's theory of the invalidity of

Acts of Parliament in derogation of the common rights and of the rights of Englishmen."[40] As one scholar explains,

> This dictum of Coke, announced in *Dr. Bonham*'s case was soon repudiated in England, but the doctrine announced in Coke's dictum found fertile soil in the United States and sprouted into such a vigorous growth that it was applied by the United States Supreme Court in the decision of cases coming before it; and it has been said that the doctrine of the supremacy of the Supreme Court is the logical conclusion of Coke's doctrine of control of the courts over legislation.[41]

Therefore, Coke's ideas were studied and, in some ways, adopted by American jurists even in the first decade of the country's independence, predating the *Marbury* decision.[42] Accordingly, the history of judicial review dates earlier to its use by colonial courts in the Indian and American colonies and its use by courts in Britain.

V. Early review cases in the United States

While Lord Coke's ideas were less commonly accepted by British jurists, "judicial invalidation of legislation, in America, had been a feature of the pre-Revolution era, and even prior to the 1787 Constitution State Supreme Courts had exercised this power against statutes enacted by the new State legislatures."[43]

Specifically, Coke inspired the "judicial invalidation of legislation" when the Massachusetts Assembly declared that the Stamp Act of 1765 was void because its provisions violated the Magna Carta.[44] The Royal Chief Justice of Massachusetts stated that the Stamp Act violated the "Magna Charta and the natural rights of Englishmen, and [was] therefore, according to the Lord Coke, null and void."[45]

Judicial review powers were also raised in a colonial court case concerning the state seizure of private property and tax-payment coercion. Judge Symonds explained:

> Let us not (here in New England) despise the rules of the learned in the lawes of England, who have great helps and long experience . . . First rule is, that where a law is . . . repugnant to fundamental law, it's voyd; as if it gives power to take away an estate from one man and give it to another.[46]

A major distinction between Lord Coke's concepts of judicial review and the American adaptations of this theory is that Coke determined the legality of legislative action based on "natural law" or "common right," while American jurists were able to rely on enumerated rights from their state and later national constitutions. As mentioned earlier, a major early distinction between the United States and its former colonial master was the creation of written constitutions.[47] Though many founders like Thomas Jefferson did not believe the judiciary possessed the right to exercise judicial review, the founders set the foundation for it simply by enumerating certain rights in a supreme legal document. Unlike Lord Coke, who compared parliamentary action to theoretical principles of "natural law," judges in the United States could rely on their state or national constitutions to evaluate the legality of actions by the executive or legislative branches.

A. Common right

There are a few notable American cases that did not rely upon constitutions, but on the "natural law" language of Coke, as explained by Douglas Edlin.[48] Edlin cites the *Ham v. M'Claw's* (1789) case, in which judges in a South Carolina court held that it was "the duty of the court, in such case, to square its decisions with the rules of common right and justice . . . if laws are made against those principles, they are null and void."[49] Also, in *Bowman v. Middleton (1792)*, a South Carolina court declared that a law violating the "common right" "was therefore ipso facto void [and] . . . that no length of time could give it validity, being originally founded on erroneous principles."[50] In Virginia, Judge Carrington wrote that the use of judicial review could be based either on the constitution or on issues related to "common right."[51]

Some judges also asserted that the rights embedded in documents like the Magna Carta, state constitutions or the national Constitution were not "declaratory of a new law but confirmed all the ancient rights and principles which had been in use in the state."[52] Some state judges also concluded that the rights included in documents like the Magna Carta or the Constitution had always existed as part of natural law or common right before the documents were written.

Going beyond the state courts, the U.S. Supreme Court discussed the scope of judicial review in *Calder v. Bull*, which predates *Marbury v. Madison*. In *Calder*, the justices asserted their de jure right to assess the legality of a law while emphasizing their de facto reluctance to use this power.[53] Justice Chase held that

> there are certain vital principles in our free Republican governments, which will determine and over-rule an apparent and flagrant abuse of legislative power . . . . [but] if I ever exercise the jurisdiction I will not decide any law to be void, but in a very clear case.[54]

This seems to grant deference to the democratic institutions while restraining the court's use of review powers. Justice James Iredell agreed with this in part:

> If any act of Congress or of the Legislature of a state, violates those constitution provisions, it is unquestionably void; though, I admit, that the authority to declare it void is of a delicate and awful nature, the court will never resort to that authority but in a clear and urgent case.[55]

B. Early constitutional cases

Returning to American state courts, Coke's *Bonham* case-report was crucial for the establishment of judicial review. One of the first examples of a major civil liberties case involving the sanctity of the home was *Paxton's Case on the Writ of Assistance (1761)*.[56] In this case, James Otis argued that

> an act against the Constitution is void: an Act against natural equity is void: and if an Act of Parliament should be made, in the very words of this Petition, it would be void. The Executive Courts must pass such Acts into disuse.[57]

Though this argument was rejected by the Court at the time, it had a long-term impact:

> Otis's reliance on *Bonham* in *Paxton* would have an important and discernable influence on the development of judicial review by state courts in the period following the Revolution.
>
> The next three decades of American legal history saw the increasing influence of Bonham on state courts that based their power of judicial review on the common law. In the thirty years following Otis's argument in *Paxton*, state courts would assert, in several cases, a common law authority to invalidate statutory enactments.[58]

There were many state cases that continued the trend inspired by *Bonham* and echoed by Otis's argument in *Paxton*, though many judgments may not have referred directly to *Bonham*. Some of these cases did not relate to the constitution, but to "natural right and justice," in the case of in *Robin v. Hardaway (1772)*,[59] and a treaty with Britain[60] in the case of *Rutgers v. Waddington (1784)*.[6162]

Aside from these cases, many other state courts evaluated laws based on state constitution. In *Trevett v. Weeden (1786)*,[63] judges held that the Rhode Island Paper Money Act violated the state constitution's guarantee of jury trial for the criminally accused, though the attorney for the case raised natural law as well.[64] In *Bayard v. Singleton (1787)*,[65] the Supreme Court of North Carolina determined that a statute prohibiting trial by jury for citizens attempting to recover confiscated land from the state was invalid because it violated the North Carolina Constitution.[66] In *Vanhorne Lessee v. Dorance (1795)*, Justice Patterson distinguished between American and British uses of judicial review, concluding that "whatever may be the case in other countries, yet in this there can be no doubt, that every act of the legislature, repugnant to the constitution, is absolutely void.[67]

Perhaps the most important of all these state cases was the *Case of the Prisoners* in 1782, which demonstrated the active role that some state courts like Virginia adopted in employing judicial review very early in the nation's history. In that case, "two of the eight judges on the court of appeals took the position that the court had the power to declare statutes unconstitutional . . . and these may have been the first American judges to take this position."[68] William Treanor points to this case as proof that there were activist jurists in the founding generation who grounded their judicial activism on a "broad reading of a constitution," moving beyond the concepts of natural law that once dominated the judicial review debates.[69] Further, the court in *Marbury* was following the example set by some of the judges in the *Case of the Prisoners*, such as George Wythe, who trained Chief

Justice John Marshall in the practice of law.[70] As a result, when *Marbury* came before Marshall and the Supreme Court,

> the Chief Justice was applying the lesson that he had learned over twenty years before when he heard his former law professor's judicial opinion in the *Case of the Prisoners*, and he was ensuring that the national judiciary had a power that his state's judiciary had long exercised without challenge.[71]

Evaluating these various legal precedents for judicial review by the U.S. Supreme Court, four categories appear: state court decisions, Supreme Court decisions, decisions based on common rights or natural law, and decisions based on constitutional rights. Altogether, these formed the collection of legal concepts that led to Chief Justice Marshall's decision in *Marbury v. Madison*, which will be discussed in Chapter 5. These cases are especially important for the United States, where judicial review was a judge-created concept that was not directly enumerated in the Constitution.

VI. Origins of judicial review in Indian colonies

Although the constitutions of Pakistan and India enumerate the right to judicial review, unlike the United States, the history of judicial review in India and Pakistan dates back to colonial courts similar to the United States. There are some instances where the courts of colonial India invalidated laws referring to the right to judicial review. Dr. More Atul Lalasaheb explains that:

> it is pertinent to note that during the pre-independence period, Indian courts were exercising judicial review power and in fact struck down acts of legislature or executive as being ultra vires. *But, such occasions used to be rare and the scope for judicial review was restricted, until the Government of India Act, 1935 was enacted.*[72]
>
> (emphasis added)

Much like the colonies in America, the Indian courts retained the power to declare certain legislative acts or executive policies as ultra vires but were reluctant to use that right. As the pre-constitution laws in the Indian colonies did not contain "any declaration of fundamental rights, the only ground on which a legislative or executive act could be struck down was lack of power," or ultra vires.[73] Without a written declaration of rights, the Courts could only assess when the Parliament or executive acted beyond the scope of its proper power through ultra vires review; yet, "in India, judicial review based on the doctrine of ultra vires dates back to the inception of British rule . . . therefore, the legitimacy of judicial review has never been an issue."[74]

The use of ultra vires review linked to judicial review in the colonial courts dates back to the case of *The Empress v. Burah* and *Book Singh* (1878), where "the Calcutta High Court as well as Privy Council adopted the view that the Indian courts had [the] power of Judicial Review under certain limitations."[75] In that judgment, Justice William Markby wrote:

> Where an Act has once been passed by a Legislature which is supreme, I consider it to be absolutely binding upon Courts of law. Where it is passed by a legislature the powers of which are limited, it is not the less binding, provided it be not in excess of the powers conferred upon the limited Legislature . . . *it is our duty to say whether the authority given to the Lieutenant-Governor to take away the jurisdiction of this Court was validly conferred.*[76]
>
> (emphasis added)

Unlike Lord Coke and jurists from state courts in the United States, Justice Markby denied the ability of the judiciary to "question the validity of Acts of the legislature upon . . . natural justice" in a different case, *Queen v. Ameer Khan* (1878).[77] However, by taking the position that the courts could assess when Parliament exceeded its mandate of power, Markby nevertheless set the foundation for judicial review in India and Pakistan. Thus, in a case decided by the Judicial Committee of the Privy Council in 1913, Lord Haldane dismissed a statute as being ultra vires because it denied "fundamental principles" of Indians that were enumerated in the Parliament Act of 1858.[78] In *Annie Besant v. Government of Madras* (1918), "the Chief Justice of the Madras High Court concluded that the Indian legislature was inferior to the Imperial Parliament, and any law created by the Indian legislature in excess of the powers delegated from the Imperial parliament was illegitimate."[79]

As Professor S. P. Sathe, explains while judicial review existed in the Indian colony, its use was greatly limited by courts:

> The courts struck down very few statutes during the colonial period. Professor Allen Gledhill observed that instances of invalidation of laws by courts were so rare that "even the Indian lawyer generally regarded the legislature as sovereign and it was not until the Government of India Act of 1935 came into force that avoidance of laws by judicial pronouncement was commonly contemplated." However, the courts continued to both construe the legislative acts strictly and to apply the English common law methods for safeguarding individual liberties.[80]

The strict interpretation of legislative acts was denounced by the Joint Committee on Indian Constitutional Reforms when it considered adding a declaration of rights to the Government of India Act of 1935. However, rights were not enumerated by the Committee in the Government of India Act in order to prohibit the expansion of judicial review:

> Either the declaration of rights is of so abstract a nature that it has no legal effect of any kind or its legal effect will be to impose an embarrassing restriction on the power of the Legislature and to create a grave risk that a large

> number of laws may be declared invalid by the courts because of the inconsistency with one or other of the rights so declared.[81]

This fear of a "large scale invalidation of the laws by the courts" was at the heart of the British decision not to include a bill of rights in the Government of India Act of 1935.[82] Nevertheless, debate concerning judicial review continued until 1950 and 1956, when India and Pakistan adopted their own constitutions, respectively. The Act was in effect for Pakistan and India after they won independence in 1947, when the Constituent Assemblies of each country drafted their own Constitution.[83]

The Act of 1935 did create a Federal Court, which was meant "to scrutinize the violation of the constitutional directions regarding the distribution of the powers on the introduction of federalism in India."[84] However, much like the American Constitution, the Act did not explicitly grant powers to the judiciary to assess the legality of legislation. In fact, several issues were excluded from judicial review, including:

- i No High Court shall have any original jurisdiction in any matter concerning the revenue.[85]
- ii The Court would have no jurisdiction to assess the validity of legislative proceedings or the acts of legislators either at the federal or provincial level.[86]
- iii Neither the federal nor any court has jurisdiction to hear a case challenging the Governor General's control of water for the colony.[87]
- iv The Governor General's acts are final and cannot be challenged in court so long they are not ultra vires.[88]

Despite these limitations on judicial review, the Act of 1935 inspired a debate within the Indian colony concerning the proper role for the judiciary. Though the courts were not expressly granted the power of judicial review, some argued that the courts were "implicitly empowered to pronounce judicially upon the validity of the statutes."[89] In his inaugural address in 1939 to the newly created Federal Court, Sir Brojendra Lal Mitter, Advocate General of India, stated that

> Your function as the Federal Court will be to expound and define the provisions of the Constitution Act, and as guardians of the Constitution it will be for you to declare the validity or invalidity of statues passed by the legislatures in India, on the one hand, and on the other, to define true limits of the powers of the executive. The manner in which you will interpret the Constitution will largely determine the constitutional development of the country.[90]

While the Federal Court did evaluate several laws and statutes, they exercised "judicial self-restraint,"[91]which fostered calls for empowering the judiciary through the new constitution that would succeed the Government of India Act. Some argued that "in post-independence India, the inclusion of explicit provisions for judicial review was necessary in order to give effect to the individual and group rights guaranteed in the Constitution."[92]

VII. Early post-colonial judicial review in India

Through the 1950 Constitution, India expanded judicial review, making the courts "the most powerful organ for scrutinizing the legislative lapses." Dr. B. R. Ambedkar, Chairman of the Constitution Drafting Committee in India, argued that judicial review was the heart of the Constitution, which meant that "the Supreme Court of India and various High Courts were given the power to rule on the constitutionality of legislative as well as administrative actions."[9394] Despite this expanded right of judicial review, the Supreme Court of India was influenced by the restraint exercised by its predecessor Federal and High Courts during the colonial period. As M. V. Pylee argues,

> during the span of a decade of their career as constitutional interpreters the Federal Court and the High Court of India reviewed the constitutionality of a large number of legislative Acts with fully judicial self-restraint insight and ability. The Supreme Court of India as the successor of the Federal Court intended the great traditions built by the Federal Court.[95]

Two early cases discuss the debate concerning the scope of judicial review under India's new constitution. In *Gopalan v. State of Madras* (1950), the Court began by utilizing the language of natural justice to assess the legality of Parliamentary or executive action much as did Lord Justice Coke and his successors in the United States. Chief Justice Harilal Jekisundas Kania, writing the majority opinion of the court, concluded that

> in spite of the fact that in England the Parliament is supreme I am unable to accept the view that the Parliament in making laws, legislates against the well-recognised principles of natural justice accepted as such in all civilized countries.[96]

The Court then compared the English concepts of parliamentary supremacy to the rights guaranteed in the U.S. that are supreme over legislative or executive acts:

> The Constitution of India is a written constitution and though it has adopted many of the principles of the English Parliamentary system, it has not accepted the English doctrine of the absolute supremacy of Parliament in matters of legislation. In this respect it has followed the American Constitution and other systems modelled on it.[97]

The Court went on to say that it had the power of judicial review under the Indian Constitution, Article 13(2), which requires that "the State shall not make any law which takes away or abridges the rights conferred by this Part and any law made in contravention of this clause shall, to the extent of the contravention, be void."[98] Much like the United States, the Constitution and its enumerated list of fundamental rights were held to be supreme over subsequent acts of the legislature.

The Supreme Court of India issued a similar ruling in *State of Madras v. V. G. Row* (1952), in which the justices addressed critique by some that under the new constitution, the courts would "seek clashes with the legislatures in the country."[99] The Court accepted that a certain degree of deference must be given to the legislature as it forms and debates policy, but held that the judiciary "cannot desert its own duty to determine finally the constitutionality of an impugned statute."[100] *State of Madras v. V. G. Row* and *Gopalan* are especially pertinent to explore the early development of judicial review in the 1950s after India's constitution was passed, which will be discussed in Chapter 5.

In sum, the Supreme Court of India recognized that it had "been assigned the role of a sentinel on the qui vive" for the fundamental rights listed in the Constitution, and concluded that the aim of judicial review was not to "tilt at legislative authority in a crusader's spirit, but in discharge of a duty plainly laid upon them by the Constitution."[101]

VIII. Early post-colonial judicial review in Pakistan

Pakistan's post-colonial history can be distinguished from both the United States and India because there have been several military coups and declarations of martial law since 1947, which will be described in Chapter 4. This instability has also been reflected in the constitution-writing process, as Pakistan has adopted three different constitutions – in 1956, 1962, and 1973. It is accordingly more difficult to mark the beginning of judicial review in Pakistan after its independence, since three different constitutional documents controlled the judiciary at various times, granting varying scopes of review power for the judiciary.

Regardless, certain cases from the 1950s illustrate the early debate concerning the role of judicial review in post-colonial Pakistan. Though the Supreme Court of India limited its judicial review power, it exerted the right to exercise this power in defense of fundamental rights enumerated in the Constitution. The judiciary in Pakistan initially went further in limiting its review powers, especially when those review powers needed to be exercised against a powerful executive branch represented either through the Governor General or military generals.

Since Pakistan did not adopt its first constitution until 1956, the Government of India Act of 1935 was the controlling legal document for nine years after independence was declared in 1947. During this period, the predecessor to the Supreme Court of Pakistan was the Federal Court, created during the end of British rule. This Federal Court "created a black hole" during the decade of its existence in post-colonial Pakistan by issuing decisions that "made bad precedents of judicial review," and limited the development of the democratic institutions.[102]

Three major cases arose in 1955 relating to judicial review during the growing conflict between the Governor General and the Constituent Assembly. Leading up to *Federation of Pakistan v. Maulvi Tamizuddin*, the Constituent Assembly had amended the Government of India Act of 1935 in order to allow High Courts to issue writs of mandamus and of quo warranto.[103] However, the Governor General did not consent to the inclusion of these judicial powers in the Act and quickly dissolved the Constituent Assembly altogether. The Court then held that the Constituent Assembly had erred and could only create laws if it had the "necessary assent" from the Governor General, or in other words the Governor General could unilaterally invalidate laws passed by the Constituent Assembly.

Syeda Shabbir, a former researcher for the Supreme Court of Pakistan, points out that this case "marked the beginning of constitutional crises in Pakistan."[104] Not only was this a dangerous precedent that would be used later to legally legitimize military coups and martial law, but the Court in *Tamizuddin* concluded that "the only issue that the Court is required to determine in such cases is whether the legal power existed or not, and not whether it was properly and rightly exercised, which is a purely political issue."[105] This holding restricted the evolution of judicial review to its historical predecessor, ultra vires.

In *Usif Patel v. The Crown*, the Court changed course by using judicial review to nullify the Governor General's Emergency Powers Ordinance (IV of 1955).[106] This was the first real confrontation of the Federal Court with an increasingly autocratic Governor General, who was determined to quash the growth of both the judicial and legislative branches in post-colonial Pakistan. The Court sided with the legislature, overturning its prior decision recognizing sweeping powers for the Governor General. It concluded that "any legislative provision that relates to a constitutional matter is solely within the powers of the Constituent Assembly and the Governor-General is, under the Constitution Acts, precluded from exercising those powers."[107] Without directly addressing the Court's right to prohibit the suspension of rights through executive orders and martial law, the Court staked its claim in the post-colonial struggle for power between the executive and all other branches.

However, with one step forward, the Federal Court took two steps back. In *Reference By Governor General*, the Court was asked to assess whether the Governor General was permitted to retroactively legitimize laws or dissolve the Constituent Assembly.[108] Shabbir explains, "the Federal Court advised the Governor General that he could continue with his extra-constitutional power of validating laws retroactively" until a new constitution could be adopted.[109] In the decision, Chief Justice Muhammad Munir recognized that "necessity knows no law" and "necessity makes lawful which otherwise is not lawful." Justice Alvin R. Cornelius concluded that the prerogative power of the Governor General was "not a justiciable matter" because "whether it is rightly or wrongly exercised *is not a matter of law*, and therefore not a suitable subject for expression of opinion by this Court."[110] By asserting that exercise of this power was non-justiciable, the Court created a constitutional crisis that stunted the development of judicial review at its outset.

By recognizing the doctrine of necessity, which will be examined in Chapter 4 of this study, the Court opened the door for the judicial legitimization of extra-constitutional actions by the executive and military. Judicial capitulation to the Governor General's over-exertion of power was the beginning of the judiciary's legitimization of anti-democratic and autocratic tendencies in the executive branch.[111]

IX. Conclusion

The emergence of judicial review in the United States predates *Marbury v. Madison*, as it was first alluded to by Lord Justice Coke in the seventeenth century. In fact, the origins could even predate Coke if one considers the ultra vires doctrine to be a predecessor of judicial review, for that had been used centuries earlier by colonial courts in America and India. Coke's analysis developed ultra vires beyond merely assessing whether Parliament had the power to enact certain laws. He went one step further in asserting that the Court could nullify a law passed by Parliament if that law violated the "natural law" and "common rights" of citizens, regardless of the scope of its designated power. Despite being criticized in Britain, Coke's views were increasingly accepted by early American state courts.

American jurists were able to carry forward Coke's ideas through the creation and interpretation of a written constitution, which set the United States apart from its constitution-less former colonial ruler. Judges in the state courts or the Supreme Court of the United States could rely on either the enumerated rights in the constitution and sometimes on "natural law" to assess the legality of Congress's actions.

For Pakistan and India, the Government of India Act of 1935 controlled the legal regime of both countries until independence, limiting the expansion of judicial review powers even after both nations drafted their own constitutions. While there was very limited judicial review by the colonial courts in India, the Indian constitution directly enumerated fundamental rights and granted the judiciary expansive jurisdiction to hear cases relating to a violation of those rights. While the Supreme Court of India agreed that it had judicial review power over government officials, violating citizens' fundamental rights, early cases demonstrated a limited use of this power and the Court granted deference to the legislative branch.

The Pakistani Federal Court went one step further in abdicating judicial review authority when it held that the Constitution and Government of India Act could be set aside completely in the face of necessity, and that the Court would do nothing to stop an autocratic executive branch from curtailing or eliminating fundamental rights for citizens. This limited the growth of judicial review in Pakistan at the outset while also assisting the anti-democratic military dictatorships that would come later in the nation's turbulent history.

Notes

1 A. Bradley, K. Ewing & Christopher Knight, *Constitutional and Administrative Law, Chapter 4: Parliamentary Supremacy*, at 49. ("Despite the existence of Parliament and the common law courts, the King, through his Council, exercised not only full executive powers but also a residue of legislative and judicial power. Acts of Parliament which sought to take away any of the 'inseparable' prerogatives of the Crown were considered invalid.")

2 E.g. Statute of Proclamations, Proclamations of the Crown Act, 31. Henry VIII, 1539, which stated that the Crown's Proclamations should be treated as "though they were made by act of parliament." See also Bradley, Ewing and Knight, *supra* note 1. ("The Statute of Proclamations 1539 gave Henry VIII wide powers of legislating by proclamation without reference to Parliament.")

3 New York State Bar Association, 63d Congress, 3d Session, Document No. 941, *Duty of Courts to Refuse to Execute Statutes in Contravention of the Fundamental Law* (1915), at 11.

4 Jeffrey Goldsworth, *Parliamentary Sovereignty: Contemporary Debates* (2010), at 275.

5 A.V. Dicey, *The Law of the Constitution* (2013), at 27.

6 Ashley Cooper & Stephen Cooper, *The Forty-Shilling Freeholder*, Chivalry and War. Available at www.chivalryandwar.co.uk/Resource/THE%20FORTY%20SHILLING%20FREEHOLDER.pdf (last accessed on Oct. 17, 2016). See also United Kingdom Parliament, "Birth of English Parliament: The Knights of the Shire." Available at www.parliament.uk/about/living-heritage/evolutionofparliament/originsofparliament/birthofparliament/overview/knights/ (last accessed on Mar. 1, 2017).

7 Case of Proclamations, King's Bench, EWHC KB J22, 1610. This case posited the concept that while the King could enforce laws, he was far more limited in the creation of new laws, which was to be left to Parliament.

8 Lord Coke, Institutes of The Laws of England: The Fourth Part 36 (1797).

9 Sir William Blackstone et al., *Commentaries on the Laws of England: In Four Books; with an Analysis of the Work*, at Section V, Subsection 10, at 91 (1829).

10 E.g. Roy Stone de Montpensier, *The British Doctrine of Parliamentary Sovereignty: A Critical Inquiry*, 26 La. L. Rev. (1966) 753–87, at 754. Available at: http://digitalcommons.law.lsu.edu/lalrev/vol26/iss4/4 (last accessed on Oct 17, 2016). (Arguing that "we should not be led, as were Blackstone, Austin, Dicey and a whole host of writers on constitutional law, political theory, or history and jurisprudence, to assert in seeking a concept of sovereignty that Parliament can do anything except bind its successors . . . [as such] Kings nor Parliament are superior to the law, are supreme, are sovereign, though they may make the laws as part of the whole law.")

11 Dicey, *supra* note 5, at 42.

12 S.P. Sathe, *Judicial Review in India: Policy and Limits*, 35 Ohio St. L. J. 870 (1974), at 870. ("Marbury was not unknown to legal theory because its ultimate source lay in the ancient doctrine of ultra vires.")

13 Christopher Forsyth, *Of Fig Leaves and Fairy Tales: The Ultra Vires Doctrine, the Sovereignty of Parliament and Judicial Review*, 55 Cambridge L.J. 122 (1996).

14 Sir William Wade & Christopher Forsyth, *Administrative Law* (7th ed., Oxford University Press, 1994), at 41.

15 David Bateman, *Judicial Review in Kingdom and Dominions: The Historical Foundations of Judicial Review in the U.K., Canada, and New Zealand* (University of Pennsylvania), at 13. Available at www.polisci.upenn.edu/ppec/PPEC%20People/bateman/LSA%20Paper%20Final1.pdf (last accessed on Oct. 17, 2016).

16 Shirani A. Bandaranayake, *The Developments in the Role of the Doctrine of Ultra Vires in Central-Local Relations*, 8 Sri Lanka Journal S.S. 25, at 29 (1985). Available at http://dl.nsf.ac.lk/bitstream/handle/1/5075/JSS8_25.pdf?sequence=1 (last accessed on Oct. 17, 2016). (Citing *Ashbury Railway Carriage and Iron Company v. Riche* (1875) 14 Eng. Rep. 42, 7 L.R.C.P. (H.L.) 653. *Colman v. Eastern Counties Railway Company* (1847) 48 Eng. Rep. 488, 10 Beav. 1. *East Anglican Railway Company v. Eastern Counties Railway Company* (1868) 11 C.B. 775, 21, L.J.C.P. 23.)

17 Lori Ringhand, *Fig Leaves, Fairy Tales, and Constitutional Foundations: Debating Judicial Review in Britain*, 43 Colum. J. Transnat'l L. 865, 871 (2005)

18 Viscount James Bryce, *The American Commonwealth*, Volume 1 (1897) at 246. ("a statute passed by Congress beyond the scope of its powers is of no more effect than a bye-law made ultra vires by an English municipality.")

19 Justice (r) Fazal Karim, *Paper on Judicial Review of Administrative Actions*, Supreme Court of Pakistan Available at www.supremecourt.gov.pk/ijc/articles/16/2.pdf (last accessed on Oct. 17, 2016.), at 2. (explaining Lord Bryce's theory.)

20 Viscount James Bryce, *The American Commonwealth* (1995), at 181–2.

21 Forsythe, *supra* note 13. See also C. F. Forsyth, *Judicial Review and the Constitution* (2000), Chapter 1: Dawn Oliver, Is the Ultra Vires Rule the Basis for Judicial Review? (explaining that the ultra vires doctrine provides the essential foundation for judicial review).
22 Sathe, *supra* note 12, at 870.
23 *The Empress v. Burah and Book Singh*, Mar. 26, 1877(1878) ILR 3 Cal 64. Available at http://indiankanoon.org/doc/600234/ (last accessed on Oct. 17, 2016) (The Court was examining the Governor-General's ordinance "Section 4 of Act XXII of 1869 (which is called the "Garo Hills Act")" in which "the Garo Hills are removed 'from the jurisdiction of the Courts of civil and criminal judicature'.")
24 Id.
25 Ringhand, *supra* note 17, at 874.
26 Id.
27 *Calvin's Case* (1608) 77 Eng. Rep. 377, 7 Co. Rep. ia, I3a, (C.P.)
28 *Dr. Bonham's Case* (1610) 77 Eng. Rep. 638, 8 Co. Rep. 107a.
29 A Statutory Bill of Rights was eventually created in 1689, nearly eighty years after the *Bonham* case. Bill of Rights, Bill of Rights of 1698, 1 William & Mary Sess 2 c 2. However, unlike Coke's explanation of a consistent moral law that binds parliament, the bill of rights could be repealed or limited.
30 T. R. S. Allan, *Constitutional Dialogue and the Justification of Judicial Review*, 23 Oxford J. L. Studies 563–84 (2003), at 565.
31 Theodore F. T. Plucknett, *Bonham's Case and Judicial Review*, 40 Harv. L. Rev. 30, 50 (1926) ("Coke's removal to the King's Bench in 1613 was the prelude to still sterner measures, in view of the fact that he was soon to give still more offense; in June, 1616, he was suspended from his office and ordered to 'correct' his Reports. In the following October there was a schedule of five questions which were put to the Chief Justice by the King, apparently on the suggestion of Bacon and the Solicitor-General, Yelverton, the fourth of which demanded an explanation of the dictum in Bonham's Case that the common law will control acts of Parliament.")
32 Id at 51 citing 8 Co. 114a (C. P. 1610).
33 Id at 50.
34 Bateman, *supra* note 15, at 13. Citing Mark D. Walters, *The Common Law Constitution in Canada: Return of Lex Non Scripta As Fundamental Law*, 51 U. Toronto L.J. 91, 141 (2001).
35 Mark D. Walters, *The Common Law Constitution in Canada: Return of Lex Non Scripta as Fundamental Law*, 51 U. Toronto L.J. 91, 141 (2001) citing *Day v. Savadge* (1615), Hob. 85 (K.B.), per Hobart C.J, at 87. *Lord Sheffield v. Ratcliffe* (1615), Hob. 334a (K.B.), *per* Hobart C.J, at 346. *R. v. Love* (1653), 5 St. Tr. 43, *per* Keble J, at 172. *Thomas v. Sorrell* (1677), Vaugh, 330, at 337. *Case of Ship-Money* (1637), 3 St. Tr. 825, per Finch C.J, at 1224, 1235.
36 *City of London v. Wood* (1702) 88 Eng. Rep. 1592, 12 Mod. 669, per Holt C.J, at 68.
37 Phillip A. Hamburger, *Revolution and Judicial Review: Chief Justice Holt's Opinion in City of London v. Wood*, 97 Colum. L. Rev. 2091 at 2093 (1994). ("Under England's parliamentary system of government, Holt's version of judicial review could not void acts of legislation, but it at least required the government to exercise its power by means of such acts and so by means of law.")
38 Randy J. Holland, *Anglo-American Templars: Common Law Crusaders*, 8 Del. L. Rev. 137, 145 (2006) citing James M. Beck, *The Constitution of the United States*, James Truslow Adams, ed. (1941). See also *The Genesis of the United States: A Series of Historical Manuscripts*, Alexander Brown, ed. at 106 (1890) (letter dated June 22, 1607, from Virginia Council to council in England). ("although this holding [from Dr. Bonham's Case] was never widely embraced in subsequent English decisions, it resonated immediately with the colonial law students and was a harbinger of judicial review in America.".)
39 Walters, *supra* note 35, at 141.

40 New York State Bar Association, *Yearbook* (1915), at 238.
41 Hugh Evander Willis, *Constitutional Law of America* (1936.)
42 See generally William W. Crosskey, *Politics and the Constitution in the History of the United States* (University of Chicago Press, 1953), at 944. (Listing nine cases of instances where state Supreme Courts debated the use of judicial review.)
43 Bateman, *supra* note 15.
44 Joyce Lee Malcolm, *Whatever the Judges Say It Is? The Founders and Judicial Review*, 26 J.L. & Pol. 1, 19 (2010) citing Charles Grove Haines, *The American Doctrine of Judicial Supremacy* (1914) at 52. ("In 1765 Governor Hutchinson of Massachusetts explained that the 'prevailing reason' for opposition to the Stamp Act 'is that the act of Parliament is against Magna Carta, and the natural rights of Englishmen, and therefore, according to Lord Coke, null and void'.")
45 Quincy, *Mass Reports*, 527. Hutchinson, the Royal Chief Justice of Massachusetts. See also Catherine Drinker Bowen, *The Lion and the Throne: The Life and Times of Sir Edward Coke (1552–1634)* at 172 (1957).
46 Sathe, *supra* note 12 citing Giddings v. Browne, 2 Hutchinson Papers I. See also, McGovney, Cases on Constitutional Law, (First ed., 1930) 8–11.
47 Thomas Jefferson, Letter to William C. Nicholas, Monticello, (Sept. 7, 1803). ("Our peculiar security is in the possession of a written constitution. Let us not make it a blank paper by construction . . . If it has bounds, they can be no others than the definitions of the powers which that instrument gives. It specifies and delineates the operations permitted to the federal government, and gives all the powers necessary to carry these into execution. Whatever of these enumerated objects is proper for a law, Congress may make the law.")
48 Douglas Edlin, *Judges and Unjust Laws: Common Law Constitutionalism and the Foundations of Judicial Review* (Reprint ed., 2010), at 84.
49 *Ham v. M'Claws*, 1 S.C. (Bay) 38 (1789). (South Carolina), at 96.
50 *Bowman v. Middleton*, 1 S.C. (Bay) 252 (1792). (South Carolina), at 102.
51 *Jones v. Commonwealth*, 5 Va. (1 Call.) 208 (1799). (Virginia), at 209. ("Therefore, whether I consider the case upon . . . the doctrines of the common law or the spirit of the Bill of Rights and the act of Assembly, I am equally clear in my opinion.")
52 *Williams Lindsay v. East Bay Street Com'rs*, 2 S.C.L. (Bay) 38 (1796). (South Carolina), at 57.
53 *Calder v. Bull*, 3 U.S. (3 Dall.) 386, 1 L.Ed. 648 (1798).
54 Id at 395.
55 Id.
56 Bateman, *supra* note 15.
57 Walters, *supra* note 35, at 115. Citing *Paxton's Case of the Writ of Assistance* (1761), reported in J. Quincy, Jr., Reports of Cases Argued and Adjudged in the Superior Court of Judicature of the Province of Massachusetts Bay Between 1761 and 1772 (1865; reissue, Russell & Russell, 1969 at 51–7.
58 Edlin, *supra* note 48, at 83–4.
59 *Robin v. Hardaway* (1772), 1 Jefferson 109, 114, 1 Va. Reports Ann. 58. (Virginia).
60 Saikrishna B. Prakash & John C. Yoo, *The Origins of Judicial Review*, 70 U. Chi. L. Rev. 887, 936 (2003).
61 *Rutgers v. Waddington* (N.Y. City Mayor's Ct. 1784), Reprinted in Julius Goebel, Jr., *The Practice of Alexander Hamilton: Documents and Commentary Volume I*, 393–419 (1964).
62 *Legal History of New York*, New York Courts. Available at www.nycourts.gov/history/legal-history-new-york/legal-history-eras-02/history-new-york-legal-eras-rutgers-waddington.html (last accessed on Oct. 17, 2016). ("The *Rutgers* case was the first to establish the principle that State legislation in conflict with the provision of a United States Treaty was void. It also set State precedent for the doctrine of judicial review that would be established in the Supreme Court of the United States in 1803 (*Madison v Marbury*, 5 U.S.137)).")

63 (R.I. 1786), described in James M. Varnum, The Case *Trevett v. Weeden:* On Information and Complaint, for Refusing Paper Bills in Payment for Butcher's Meat, In Market, at Par With Specie (1787).
64 William Michael Treanor, *The Case of the Prisoners and the Origins of Judicial Review*, 143 U. Pa. L. Rev. 491–570, 545 (1994). ("Attorney James Varnum's argument in *Trevett v. Weeden* was principally based on natural law.")
65 *Bayard v. Singleton*, 1 N.C. (Mart.) 48 (1787). (North Carolina)
66 Id at 49. ("the court asserted that the challenged statute and state constitution were in conflict because "by the constitution every citizen had undoubtedly a right to a decision of his property by a trial by jury.")
67 *Vanhorne Lessee v. Dorance*, 2 U.S. (2 Dall.) 304 (1795).
68 Treanor, *supra* note 64, at 497.
69 Id at 498.
70 Id at 497 ("one of the judges being Marshall's former law professor, George Wythe.")
71 Id at 500.
72 Dr. More Atul Lalasaheb, *An Appraisal of the Judicial System in India: A Critical Study on Judicial Independence Vis-à-vis Judicial Accountability* (2015), at Section 3.7.2 "Judicial creativity and judicial discretion- judicial activism in decision making."
73 Id.
74 Sathe, *supra* note 12.
75 Umama Moin, Parliament and the Supreme Court: The Indian Experience (2011) (Aligarh Muslim University). Available at http://shodhganga.inflibnet.ac.in/handle/10603/11379 (last accessed on Oct. 31, 2016), at 99.
76 *The Empress v. Burah and Book Singh*, [1878] 3 Indian L.R. 63, 87–8 (Calcutta).
77 Id citing *Queen v. Ameer Khan*, 6 B.L.K. 482.
78 *Secretary of State v J Moment*, ILR 40 Cal 391 (1913) (1913) 15 BOMLR 27.
79 Umama, *supra* note 75, at 102. (Citing *Annie Besant v. Government of Madras*, AIR 1918 Mad. 1210 at 1232–3).
80 S. P. Sathe, *Judicial Activism: The Indian Experience*, 6 Wash. U. J.L. & Pol'y 29, 36–7 (2001) citing Alan Gledhill, *Unconstitutional Legislation*, in 9 Indian Y.B. Intl. Affairs 40 (Madras ed., 1952).
81 Id citing Report of the Joint Committee on Indian Constitutional Reform, part I, para. 366 (1934) (H. M. Stationary Office).
82 Id at 40 (2001).
83 See G. J. Calder, *Constitutional Debates in Pakistan I*. 48 *The Muslim World* 40–60, at Page 40 (1956). ("When in August 1947, Pakistan and India became sovereign independent states, Dominions within the British Commonwealth of Nations, with the right later to secede, the Government of India Act of 1935 became, with certain adaptations, the basis of Pakistan's interim government. British rule passed to the Constituent Assembly, elected by the Provincial Assemblies in July 1947. This body was given two separate functions: to prepare a Constitution and to act as a Federal Legislative Assembly or Parliament until that Constitution came into effect.")
84 Umama, *supra* note 75, at 103.
85 Government of India Act, 1935, [26 Geo. 5. Ch 2.] Part IX, Chapter II, Article 226 (1). Available at www.legislation.gov.uk/ukpga/1935/2/pdfs/ukpga_19350002_en.pdf (last accessed Jan 2, 2017).
86 Id at Article 41 and Article 87.
87 Id at Article 133.
88 Id at Section 13(2).
89 Umama, *supra* note 75, at 99.
90 Sir Brojendra Lal Mitter, *Advocate General of India at the Inaugural Address of the Federal Court of India*, Federal Court Reports, 1939, at 4.
91 Umama, *supra* note 75 citing M. V. Pylee, *The Federal Court of India* (P.C. Manaklal and Sons Pvt. Ltd., Bombay, 1966), at 327.

92 Virendra Singh, *Indian Polity with Indian Constitution & Parliamentary Affairs* (Neelkanth Prakashan, 2016), at 264.
93 Id at 265.
94 Id at 264.
95 Umama, *supra* note 75 citing M.V. Pylee, *The Federal Court of India* (1966) at 327.
96 *A. K. Gopalan v. State of Madras*, [1950] 3- All India Rptr. 2, 34 (Sup. Ct.). (India)
97 Id.
98 India Const., art. 13(2).
99 *State of Madras v. V.G. Row Union of India & State*, 1952 AIR 196, 1952 SCR 597. (India)
100 Id.
101 Id.
102 Syeda Saima Shabbir, *Judicial Activism Shaping the Future of Pakistan*, International Islamic University Islamabad, Jan. 30, 2013. Available at http://papers.ssrn.com/sol3/papers.cfm?abstract_id=2209067 (last accessed on Oct. 17, 2016).
103 *Federation of Pakistan v. Maulvi Tamizuddin* (1955) PLD (FC) 240 (Pak.)
104 Shabbir, *supra* note 102.
105 Tamizuddin, *supra* note 103.
106 *Usif Patel v. The Crown*, PLD 1955 Federal Court 387. (India)
107 Id.
108 Reference By Governor General (1955) PLD FC 435. (India)
109 Shabbir, *supra* note 102.
110 Reference By Governor General, *supra* note 108.
111 See generally Victor V. Ramraj & Arun K. Thiruvengada, *Emergency Powers in Asia: Exploring the Limits of Legality* (2010). ("the executive seeks judicial validation of the takeover under the 'doctrine of state necessity' which recognizes extraconstitutional authority or the executive to take extraordinary actions as necessary against existential threats to the state.")

4 Structural and constitutional differences

In order to properly contextualize modern case law from each country, the constitutional structural differences for the judiciary in each country must first be examined. Both Pakistan and India employ a parliamentary system of representative democracy, while the United States has a presidential system. This difference affects the role of judicial review in relation to the doctrine of legislative supremacy.[1] Also, while the American Constitution limits the jurisdiction of the Supreme Court in several ways, the constitutions of Pakistan and India expand the Supreme Court's power.

The final section of this chapter will move away from the text of the constitutions in order to explore the additional socio-political factors that demonstrate Pakistan's uniqueness in comparison to India or the United States. Unlike the comparative cases, Pakistan's political structure is impacted by the substantial role of the military in civilian affairs, the non-continuity of constitutional documents, and the dissolution of the country in 1971.

All of these constitutional and socio-political differences are structural in nature and set the context for the evolution of judicial review in each country.

I. United States

In order to understand the structural differences between each country, one must first grapple with the motivations of the founding fathers of each nation and the debates held in the Constituent Assemblies.

A. Presidential system and parliamentary supremacy

In reviewing the adoption of the presidential system in the United States, it is important to remember that "the Framers had no relevant model of republican government to give them guidance. Most of all, they lacked any suitable model for the executive branch."[2] The framers had studied the British parliamentary model and its practices as indicated by Jefferson,[3] but as Robert Dahl goes onto explain, while the British parliamentary system inspired the framers in some ways, "as a solution to the problem of the executive, it utterly failed them," because there was little support for establishing an American monarchy.[4] The framers did consider adopting a democratic parliamentary form of government where "the choice of the chief executive [was] in the hands of the legislature," under the Virginia Plan, but this too was eventually rejected,[5] in part because the framers "feared that the president might be too beholden to Congress."[6] The framers understood that

> a republic would need an independent judiciary, a bicameral legislature consisting of a popular house and some kind of second chamber to check the popular house and an independent executive. But how was the independent executive to be chosen?[7]

The solution was to create an office for the president that would be independent from the legislature and elected by the people for a specified term. While presidents are elected by the Electoral College in the United States, the Prime Minister in a parliamentary system is elected by Parliament. For the presidential system, the "separate election of legislators and the chief executive officer" fosters "a greater degree of separation of powers and less concentration of lawmaking power than parliamentary systems."[8] Further, while the president is allowed to serve a fixed term of four years, a Prime Minister is beholden to the legislature as he or she can be removed with a parliamentary vote of no-confidence at any time. Therefore, in a parliamentary system, "the legislative and executive branches are in a sense fused . . . [and] the parliamentary system confer[s] a lawmaking monopoly on the winners of the parliamentary elections for their term of election."[9]

The framers of the United States Constitution wished to diffuse the powers of the legislature. As Madison stated, "the federal legislature will possess a part only of that supreme legislative authority which is vested completely in the British parliament."[10] James Leonard and Joanne Brant explain, "the Framers saw a need to emphasize the limited grant of authority to Congress,"[11] because the "Framers' overriding fear was the expansion of the legislative power to the point of tyranny and . . . they especially feared the union of legislative and executive powers."[12] Without a diffusion of the legislature's power through the creation of the presidency, Madison argued that "the legislative department is everywhere extending the sphere of its activity and drawing all power into its impetuous vortex."[1314]

This was a clear rejection of the doctrine of parliamentary supremacy by the Founders. By creating a presidential system, the American framers provided the president with a form of review power over the legislature.[15] As the president was independently tasked with executing the laws created by the legislature, he or she could determining the priority and manner of execution according to their own view of the Constitution.[16] The president was also granted a veto power over the legislature in order ensure that congressmen "engaged in unjustifiable pursuits" will be stopped by the threat of a presidential veto.[17]

The separation of powers in the presidential system undermined legislative supremacy, which implicitly paved the way for judges to develop judicial review in order to reject the decisions of the legislature.[18] As Gordon Wood explained, "the concept of the constitution as fundamental law was not by itself a sufficient check on the legislative will, unless it possess some other sanction than the people's right of resistance."[19] This implicitly meant that the Supreme Court would need to issue "some other sanction" that would prohibit any legislature from passing a law inconsistent with the Constitution.

James Madison, who "did not have full confidence in the representation at the national level," proposed an alternative check on the legislature in the form of the Council of Revision, which would have the authority to "veto acts of the legislature."[20] This Council was not adopted by the framers of the Constitution "chiefly because it would give the Supreme Court a double negative over laws passed by Congress."[21]

Nevertheless, some have argued that without setting aside the doctrine of parliamentary supremacy, the expansion of judicial review in American jurisprudence would have never taken place:

> it is also regularly contended that American-style judicial review, under which the courts are empowered to invalidate statutes, is not compatible with parliamentary sovereignty . . . Parliamentary sovereignty has traditionally been understood to require . . . that no judicial review power over primary legislation is granted to the courts.[22]

Therefore, while the British adopted the principle that parliamentary supremacy should limit the review powers of the courts, the Americans set aside parliamentary sovereignty by adopting a Presidential system that would directly foster an independent executive and indirectly lead to the judiciary gradually developing its powers of judicial review.

While Pakistan and India differed from the United States in adopting a parliamentary system with a presidential head of state, all three nations rejected parliamentary supremacy because there is an independent judiciary that can assess the legality of legislative actions based on the Constitution.[23]

B. Establishment of the Supreme Court and federal judiciary

While the Pakistani and Indian constitutions contained specific provisions that created a Supreme Court and federal judicial systems, the American constitution fell silent on some of these major issues. Article III of the United States Constitution creates the Supreme Court, but many issues relating to the structure and scope of the judiciary were left unanswered.

i. Judiciary Act of 1789

Due to the silence of the United States Constitution on many issues, statutes became an immediate necessity during the post-colonial era. This was partly by design, as the framers intentionally deferred some issues to be addressed through laws passed by the first Congress. The most significant of these statutes was the Judiciary Act of 1789 passed by the first Congress,[24] which became the subject of the Supreme Court's seminal judicial review holding in *Marbury*.

ii. Form of the judiciary

Article III of the U.S. Constitution "vests the whole judicial power of the United States in one supreme court, and such inferior courts as Congress shall, from time to time, ordain and establish."[25] Rather than set out the form and scope of the federal judiciary, the American constitutional founders delegated this duty to the first Congress, which subsequently passed the Judiciary Act of 1789. This Act created the federal court system by establishing thirteen federal district courts with jurisdiction over national and interstate issues.[26] This greatly differs from the Pakistani and Indian systems, which mandate the form of the federal judiciary in the national constitution itself. For the United States, it is important to note that there were major issues regarding judicial power left unaddressed by the Constitution, and the legislature needed to step in subsequently to create statutes to fill in the gaps.

iii. Scope of the judiciary's jurisdiction

The Judiciary Act also filled in the constitutional silence on the scope of judicial power and the jurisdiction of the district courts and Supreme Court. The Act "put in place all the crucial elements of judicial review, including an explicit authorization to declare federal and state laws constitutional."[27] Some have argued that "had Congress not passed the Judiciary Act of 1789 or some similar measure, federal judicial review would have existed only in constitutional theory," and that "the Judiciary Act of 1789 did far more than *Marbury* to establish judicial review."[28]

The question at the center of *Marbury* was whether the legislature could expand the scope of the Court's power through the Judiciary Act when the Constitution did not grant such authority. The decision of Marbury came at an especially divisive time in American history, with a showdown erupting between the Jeffersonians and Federalists. In *Marbury*, the Court was evaluating Section 13 of the Judiciary Act, which granted the Supreme Court the exclusive jurisdiction to issue writs of mandamus, orders to a government official or lower court to do or refrain from doing an action.[29] Chief Justice Marshall rejected the mandamus powers created by the legislature through statute as they "appear[ed] not to be warranted by the constitution."[30] The Court limited its jurisdiction in relation to writs of mandamus, only to establish a far more expansive scope for its jurisdiction through its judicial review and nullification of legislative acts.

Though the Court asserted its right to assess the legality of legislative acts in *Marbury*, it pulled back from this position one week later when it delivered the judgment for *Stuart v. Laird*.[31] In this case, the Court upheld the validity of a provision in the Judiciary Act of 1801 which removed several federal judges and their circuit court seats. This was part of the "Jeffersonian purge" of Federalist judges who had been appointed by Jefferson's predecessor, President John Adams.[32] The Supreme Court justices considered launching a judicial strike to protest "the purge of their colleagues from the circuit courts,"[33] but they eventually settled on "the proposition that the Supreme Court should give way to the central claims made by a victorious president and his party in the name of the People."[34]

An important commonality between the two cases was a silence in the Constitution on the scope and limits of the Supreme Court's judicial review power. This silence was partially filled by various Judiciary Acts passed throughout the nation's history that, for example, created a federal court structure and allowed the Court to regulate which cases would be granted writ of certiorari. However, as evidenced by *Marbury* and *Stuart*, there were times when legislative acts were compared against the Constitution itself, which opened the door to judicial review in the United States Supreme Court.

The same could not be said for Pakistan and India, whose constitutions set out expansive judicial review powers within the constitution itself, doing away with the requirement of Judiciary Acts. While there was a still a great deal of common law interpretation and analysis of the constitution in Pakistan and India, just like the United States, there were fewer supplementary legislative acts that needed to be passed in Pakistan or India, as the constitutions of both countries directly molded the form of the judiciary.

C. Federalism

The differing models of federalism in the United States, India, and Pakistan also affect the judicial power of the nations' Supreme Courts. All three nations are federal republics, meaning power is shared between the federal government and provincial (or state) governments, as opposed to unitary systems that vest power exclusively in the national government.[35] However, the Constitution of the United States grants much more autonomy to states than India or Pakistan.[36] The U.S. Constitution limits the national legislature or Congress to a list of powers enumerated in Article I Section 8. However, over time, Congress has increased its powers under three clauses from Section 8, including the Spending Clause, the Necessary and Proper Clause, and the Commerce Clause. In its early history, the Supreme Court did not challenge the expansion of the national government's power and invalidated only three federal laws in the first hundred years of its existence.[37]

Even taking into account the national government's expansion of power and the Supreme Court's tacit approval thereof, the United States still grants greater autonomy to its states than Pakistan and India. Two major differences have influenced the autonomy of states and indirectly affected the differing uses of judicial review by the Supreme Court of the United States as compared to Pakistan or India.

First, unlike the provinces in Pakistan and India, the states in the United States each have their own constitutions to complement the U.S. Constitution.[38] Second, each state in the United States has a Supreme Court that has the right to exercise judicial review for questions of state law.[39] While the federal judiciary in the United States determines only questions of federal law except in limited cases of diversity jurisdiction, and a separate system of state courts handles questions of state law, the High Courts in Pakistan and India operate as both a provincial appeals court and a lower court subject to review by the Supreme Court.

This distinction means that in the United States, questions of state constitutional and statutory law usually lie outside the jurisdiction of the Supreme Court and exclusively within the jurisdiction of state courts: "the classic example of a non-reviewable state court decision arises when the state court relied exclusively upon specific state constitutional provisions to strike down a state statute."[40] Outside of very limited examples like *Cooper v. Telfair* (1800), the Supreme Court asks state courts for guidance on purely state constitutional issues.[41] There is no such analog in Pakistan or India, which both have a singular federal constitution that is interpreted by the Supreme Court.

However, when it comes to actions by the state legislatures that affect federal rights established under the national constitution, the Supremacy Clause has allowed for the United States Supreme Court to retain its judicial review powers. While the Supremacy Clause establishes the federal constitution as a supreme source of law, above all other law including state constitutions,[42] the Supreme Court has set out its dominant role in evaluating the constitutionality of state legislative acts or even state constitutional provisions that might violate the national Constitution.

The Supremacy Clause was meant to stymie renegade state courts or legislatures that attempted to "defy the union by striking down federal measures."[43] To deal with the threat of renegade state or provincial courts, the Constitution was "relatively clear concerning federal review of state acts . . . the founders relied . . . on compulsion by law – that is, national supremacy imposed by what is now called judicial review."[44] This clause provided the legal authority to the Supreme Court to exercise judicial review over state legislatures when they passed acts that violated the federal rights enumerated in the national Constitution, because that Constitution was recognized as being supreme over any state law. Therefore, "the Supremacy Clause establishes a rule of decision for courts adjudicating the rights and duties of parties under both state and federal law."[45] This right was further supplemented by Article 25 of the Judiciary Act of 1789, which "explicitly authorized Supreme Court review of state court decisions upholding state measures, or invalidating federal measures, challenged on federal constitutional grounds."[46]

Yet, the general rule remains that the state Supreme Courts retain the exclusive right to take action on cases that focus solely on the state constitution. This is dissimilar to Pakistan and India, where there are no provincial constitutions. The relatively more unitary nature of federalism in Pakistan and India has expanded the scope of judicial review by the Supreme Courts of those countries at a more extreme rate than in the United States. However, despite the higher level of autonomy granted to the states in the United States than Pakistan and India, the United States Supreme Court has used the Supremacy Clause, among other clauses, as the legal basis for the extensive use of judicial review.

D. Jurisdictional limitations on U.S. Supreme Court

Article III of the Constitution of the United States contains limiting language on the jurisdiction of the court, which is starkly different from the constitutions of Pakistan and India with their expansive jurisdiction clause language. For the U.S. constitution, "judicial power shall extend to all cases in law and equity arising under this constitution,"[47] including controversies between citizens of different states or controversies between two or more states. Article III goes onto to describe the limited instances of original jurisdiction for the court in matters concerning public ministers or ambassadors. As will be described in later in this chapter, this jurisdiction clause is far more limited than the clauses in the Indian and Pakistani constitutions, which vest expansive power in the Supreme Courts.

Many of the doctrines developed concerning Article III have limited the use of judicial review by the Supreme Court, but cannot be found in the text of the Constitution itself.[48] These ideas were developed through common law or judge-made rules, which will be the focus of Chapter 5. However, this chapter has a narrower focus on the language of the Constitution itself, with the "case or controversy" and its underlying injury-in-fact requirement. These standing requirements have been set aside in many cases by the Pakistani and Indian Supreme Courts, but are important limitations to the United States Supreme Court's judicial review powers.

i. Case or controversy

The "case or controversy" language included in Article III of the U.S. Constitution is meant to prohibit the Supreme Court from solving "abstract, intellectual problems" and instead focus on "concrete living contest[s] between adversaries."[49] Justice Felix Frankfurter explained that the framers of the Constitution "explicitly indicated the limited area within which judicial action was to move" and that the Courts would only have authority "over issues which are appropriate for disposition by judges."[50] This limitation precluded the Court from acting on "matters that require no subtlety to be identified as political issues,"[51] which will be later explained as the political question doctrine in Chapter 5.

The limitation on the Supreme Court's power to hear only "cases or controversies" was partially based on "eighteenth century forms of adjudication . . . and most notably, a belief that the courts should not interfere in proper democratic processes."[52] In order to understand what the framers intended through the inclusion of "case or controversy" language, legal historians have debated what forms of adjudication were imagined at the time of the Constitution's framing.[53] While conceding that the Constitutional Convention never provided enough explanation for the "case or controversy" language, Leonard and Brant conclude that

> a fair reading of the proceedings of the Constitutional Convention and the contemporary legal environment makes it more likely than not that the Framers envisioned that the federal courts would be limited, as a constitutional matter, to cases where individual plaintiffs brought their own grievances for resolution and relief.[54]

This limitation on judicial power to cases where individual plaintiffs brought their own grievances is known as the injury-in-fact requirement and is related to the case or controversy issue.

ii. Injury-in-fact

The injury-in-fact requirement was developed subsequent to the 1930s, but it is directly connected to the question of whether there is an actual case or controversy presented before the Court. The injury-in-fact rule requires plaintiffs to prove that they suffered an individual and actual harm that can be remedied by judicial decision.

One must keep in mind that the judicial system envisioned by the framers was based on the premise that the Courts can only decide traditional lawsuits where one individual's rights has been violated.[55] The framers did not envisage a protection of "group rights," and by choosing to exclusively protect individual rights in the Bill of Rights, the framers limited the scope of the Court's review powers.

Without a direct harm to the plaintiff in the case, the Court was limited in its actions, partly to protect the political branches from encroachment by the judiciary. Where there was a lack of demonstrable harm to the plaintiff caused by the defendant and capable of judicial remedy, the political branches had the right to create a policy and the courts could not preempt the political branches. This requirement limited the growth of judicial review and kept "the courts out of policy making functions of the legislative and executive branches except when individual claims made judicial participation unavoidable."[56]

Accordingly, the Court would only involve itself "when necessary to protect the rights of the individuals,"[57] which meant that plaintiffs would need to prove that their rights had actually been violated and could be remedied by the judiciary in some way. This is strikingly different from Pakistan and India, which have a far broader view of the justiciability of cases involving both individual and group rights. The distinction in the U.S. precludes claimants from bringing two types of claims, which would otherwise be considered justiciable in Pakistan and India:

i Claims brought by a group that has not directly suffered a concrete and judicially remediable injury itself, but is raising claims on behalf of a community at large.
ii Unripe claims concerning non-imminent future harm from proposed legislation or executive order.

While the "case or controversy"' rules have developed over time, raising the bar for the plaintiff to seek remedy at the United States Supreme Court, the Pakistani and Indian Supreme Courts take a less stringent approach by lowering the bar for standing through public interest litigation, which will be described in the next section.

II. India and Pakistan

A. Parliamentary system

Both India and Pakistan have adopted similar versions of the parliamentary system, although Pakistan experimented with a presidential system for a short period of time. Both nations had some experience with the parliamentary system through their colonial history under the Government of India Acts of 1919 and 1935. These Acts created parliamentary houses for the entire colony or Federation, and these houses were populated by a mix of Indian and British officials.[58] Based on this history, India's constitutional framers "preferred the parliamentary system of Government to the presidential system . . . [as] [t]he people of India were already familiar with the working of the parliamentary system."[59] The same applied for the people of Pakistan who shared in the colonial experience with India. Imtiaz Omar explains that

> it is therefore not surprising to find that the Colonial Act in many aspects determined the general pattern of constitutions of both countries . . . both Constitutions were based on the Westminster model of parliamentary democracy, each with a president who was to assume many of the functions of the British monarch.[60]

i. India's parliamentary–presidential system

The continuation of the parliamentary system in India was also meant to ensure "harmony between the executive and the legislature."[61] This is based on a major difference in the parliamentary versus presidential system; namely, that the parliamentary system's executive or Prime Minister must answer to the legislature, while the presidential system allows for a more independent Executive with the power to frustrate the policies of the legislature. The parliamentary form of democracy was adopted in India partly as a means to avoid the political breakdowns that can take place in a presidential system when the President and Congress disagree.

The Indian President can be compared to the monarchy in Britain in many ways. First, much like the British king, the Indian President is duty-bound to abide by the advice and aid of his or her Council or Cabinet of Ministers.[62] Further, the Council of Ministers are

> responsible for every executive act and accountable for their actions to the parliament. Their responsibility is collective. Wherever the constitution requires the satisfaction of the President for the exercise of any power or function, that satisfaction is not his personal satisfaction but in the constitution sense that of the Council of Ministers.[63]

Second, as ceremonial head of state, the President of India can declare an emergency and dissolve Parliament's leadership under Article 355–360 of India's Constitution. One of the constitution's founders, Dr. B. R. Ambedkar, argued that despite the danger posed by granting such a right, "he was hopeful of proper role played by the president."[64] But, even if one considers the limited instances where emergency proclamation powers could be used by the President, he or she is left with very few powers because real political power is vested mostly in the Prime Minister and the Council of Ministers.

ii. Pakistan's parliamentary–presidential system

Though Pakistan's development of parliamentary democracy has been more complicated than India's, both nations share a starting point in British colonial rule. As discussed earlier, the Government of India Acts 1919 and 1935 established the parliamentary institutions that trained many of the future leaders in the territory that would become Pakistan. Once Pakistan declared its independence in 1947, it took nine years for the nation's first Constituent Assembly to draft a constitution. During this nine-year interim period, the Government of India Act 1935 "remained the Constitution of Pakistan until the framing and enforcement of the first Constitution in 1956."[65]

The long shadow of the Government of India Act fostered the continuation of some parliamentary institutions inherited from the British and eventually led to the 1956 Constitution, which was "was founded on the concept of parliamentary democracy."[66] This included a loose separation of powers between the Prime Minister working with the President, Parliament, and the judiciary.

However, this constitution was set aside through the imposition of martial law, and a new constitution was created in 1962 that created a purely Presidential model with the National Assembly being stripped of most of its powers.[67] This temporary presidential model was unlike the United States in that it granted expansive powers to the executive while leaving the legislature with almost no real political power. This constitution was utilized by authoritarian military leaders to single-handedly rule the nation while suspending or silencing Parliament.[68] Justice Muhammad Munir stated that the 1962 Constitution was "a parody of a presidential form of government . . . which had actually set up a disguised dictatorship."[69]

Eventually, this led to the framing and adoption of a new constitution in 1973, which reinstated the parliamentary system but allowed the continued existence of the President's office. In this final formulation in 1973, the President's powers were greatly narrowed and, much like in India, the President is meant to serve as a ceremonial head of state. Article 48 of Pakistan's Constitution requires the President to accept the advice of the Prime Minister and his or her cabinet.[70] Further, "the Prime Minister is neither answerable to the President nor in any way subordinate to him . . . [but] only to the National Assembly."[71]

However, as in India, the President of Pakistan has the right to issue a proclamation of emergency. Unlike in India, the Pakistani President has used this right several times to suspend provisions of the constitution in times of supposed emergency.[72] As Paula Newberg concludes, "the conflict between head of state and head of government is inscribed in an internally contradictory constitutional instrument that will continue to thwart political progress."[73] Further, due to the praetorian nature of Pakistan's state, Pakistan's President has continually exceeded his proper role by legitimizing and assisting military coups and the imposition of martial law.[74]

iii. Parliamentary sovereignty in India and Pakistan

While both Pakistan and India adopted parts of the parliamentary model from the British, the concept of parliamentary sovereignty certainly did not carry over from British colonial rule. From the outset, by creating substantial power for the judiciary and the executive, it was clear that neither the Indian and Pakistani Parliaments were considered infallible nor institutions deserving complete deference from the other branches of government.

By creating vast judicial review powers for the Supreme Court, the framers of Pakistan and India's Constitutions pitted judicial power that had emerged from the United States in the wake of *Marbury* against the parliamentary sovereignty native to Britain. The framers of the Indian and Pakistani Constitutions "preferred a proper synthesis" between the British and American models.[75] In other words, India rejected "legislative absolutism" much like the United States and "adopted some modified form of the American pattern to suit Indian needs."[76] This modified form attempted to balance the rights of the legislature and the duties of the judiciary. Though the U.S. Supreme Court invalidated very few federal laws in its early days,[77] setting out the general power of the Court to challenge legislative supremacy was an inspiration to the framers of India and Pakistan's constitutions.

Shah Nawaz points out that, "the contradiction between the principles of parliamentary sovereignty and judicial review that is embedded in India's constitution has been a source of major controversy over the years."[78] This controversy has been resolved through decisions by the Supreme Court of India in a way that empowers the Court far more than its American counterpart. The same can be said for Pakistan, as its Constitution mirrors the language of India's Constitution regarding the conflict between the judiciary and legislature, and the Court has interpreted the Constitution to greatly empower the judiciary. This jurisprudential phenomenon will be discussed further in Chapter 5.

B. Establishment of courts

Not only did the Government of India Acts of 1919 and 1935 establish a parliamentary system in the Indian Colony, the Acts also established a Federal Court of India that eventually became the Supreme Courts of India and Pakistan after independence. This court was meant to "to adjudicate upon in the conflicting claims of those units [provinces] in the matter of legislation and to interpret the Constitution."[79] While there was no formal constitution during the colonial period, the Federal Court of India relied upon legal principles commonly accepted at the time to assess the legality of state action or legislation.

This Court was essentially adopted by both Pakistan and India through the creation of Supreme Courts in their respective Constitutions. Therefore, the Supreme Courts of India and Pakistan date their lineage to the colonial era under British Rule. This was certainly not the case in the United States, where the Supreme Court was a new institution at the time of the drafting of the Constitution.

Another distinction from the United States Constitution is that both Pakistan and India's constitutions mandate and control the creation of lower courts in the federal judiciary.[80] While the U.S. Constitution creates a Supreme Court like Pakistan and India, it leaves the establishment of a federal court structure to a future legislative body, unlike its counterparts.

Chapter V of India's constitution lays out the jurisdiction of the High Courts along with the composition and qualification for judges. In Chapter VI, the Constitution calls for the creation of subordinate provincial courts that will be controlled and can be overruled by the provincial High Courts. The same goes for Pakistan's Constitution in Part VI, Chapter 3, which established the High Courts. High Courts were originally created for Lahore, Peshawar, Sindh, and Balochistan through the Government of India Act, but all of them were carried over after independence and enumerated in the Constitution that was passed in 1953.

The U.S. Constitution grants limited jurisdiction to the federal courts, leaving the rest for the state courts to decide. For Pakistan and India, which have more centralized models of federalism than the United States, the scope of federal or central courts is very different.

C. Federalism

All three nations use federalist models of republican government, yet the level of autonomy enjoyed by provinces in each country greatly varies. Pakistan and India's Constitutions go further in consolidating power in the national government than the United States. While each state in the United States has its own constitution and Supreme Court, India and Pakistan have a unitary national constitution that is adjudicated by either the Supreme Court or its subordinate federal High Courts. Despite this structural difference, the Supreme Courts of all three nations have exercised their review powers in cases concerning federalism and conflict of laws.

i. Residual powers

The Constitutions for each country establish varying levels of control for the national government through residual powers clauses. In the United States Constitution, there are a few issues enumerated that are under the exclusive control of the national government, including the clauses for interstate commerce, necessary and proper, and spending. All three of these areas of control by the national government have expanded over time with more federal legislation, but all residual issues not mentioned in the U.S. Constitution or related to the clauses described above are reserved for the states.[81] Despite the expansion of federal legislation, the rule for residual powers in the United States is opposite that of India.

India's Constitution contains a provision that all residual powers not enumerated in the Constitution are vested in the national legislature.[82] India's Constitution is also more detailed, with its Federal Legislative List, Provincial Legislative List, and Concurrent Lists delegating control of certain subjects to either the national government, provincial governments, or both. There are 99, 66, and 47 subjects respectively for each list, which demonstrates the power of the national government in India. Hamid Khan concludes that "India's constitution has strengthened the Union more than any other federal country."[83] This is augmented by the absence in the Indian Constitution for recognition of "states' rights," "dual government," or "divided sovereignty." The result is an empowerment of the federal government at the cost of provincial autonomy.[84]

The 1973 Constitution of Pakistan mirrors the empowerment of the national government in India by creating a Federal Legislative List and a Concurrent List. However, Article 143 of the Constitution "reveals [that] the true locus of power" is in the national government, because it mandates that federal laws prevail over provincial laws when the two conflict and appear on the Concurrent List.[85]

Pakistan has attempted to devolve federal powers to the provinces over time. One major difference between Pakistan and India's Constitutions regarding the question of federalism is that Pakistan's Constitution "did not provide for a separate provincial legislative list and Provincial Assemblies were extended the power to make laws on the residuary subjects, that is, matters not enumerated in either the federal or in the concurrent list."[86] This meant that while the national government was limited to the subjects listed in either the Federal or Concurrent Lists, the Provinces could legislate on any issue not mentioned in the Constitution. In 2010, the passage of the Eighteenth Amendment made major changes to the constitution to devolve federal legislative duties to the provinces even further.[87] The Concurrent List was abolished through this Amendment,[88] which pulled Pakistan's Constitution towards the provincial-empowerment model of the United States over the more unitary model of India.

ii. Impact on judicial review

Questions concerning federalism have expanded the exercise of judicial review by the Supreme Courts of Pakistan and India. This is similar to the United States, where the Supremacy Clause, Interstate Commerce Clause, Spending Clause, Necessary and Proper Clause and various Judiciary Acts have allowed the Supreme Court to decide myriad questions concerning federalism. Accordingly, the Supreme Courts in all three countries "act as the policemen of federalism."[89] Hamid Khan explains:

> Of course, in the case of disputes between the Union and the States, the nature of the jurisdiction of the Indian Supreme Court may differ considerably from that of the Supreme Court of the United States, owing to the difference in the very nature of the federation in the two countries . . . . [T]he very elaborateness of the legislative lists and the attempt at exhaustiveness tends to the growth of justiciable doubts and disputes as to the legislative powers, at least so long as the principles of interpretation applied by the Supreme Court are not well settled.[90]

Even though the Indian and Pakistani constitutions attempted to address the question of federalism directly by delegating many duties through exhaustive legislative lists, questions remain concerning the interpretation of those lists. Much as the United States, questions concerning the interpretation of federal or provincial rights have fostered the growth of judicial review by the Supreme Courts of India and Pakistan.

D. Jurisdictional limits

The most significant difference concerning the judicial review powers between the United States on the one hand and Pakistan and India on the other is the way in which each constitution lays out the jurisdiction of the Supreme Court. As discussed above, the United States Constitution limits the jurisdiction of the Supreme Court to a few areas, and Article III requires the existence of a "case or controversy" in order to trigger review by the Supreme Court. This case or controversy requirement has been developed to require proof that the plaintiff has suffered a tangible injury before coming to the Supreme Court in order to prohibit the judiciary from getting involved in litigating group rights that are not generally enumerated in the U.S. Constitution or purely political matters. However, this requirement has often been set aside in Pakistan and India, partially because the Constitutions of each country allow for an expansion of the Supreme Court's power more than the United States' Constitution.

i. Protection of fundamental rights

The Indian and Pakistani Constitutions adopt a far more expansive approach than America to the jurisdiction of the Supreme Courts as a means to protect the fundamental rights of citizens against State infringement. In India's Constitution, Part III enumerates a list of fundamental rights that the State is prohibited from "taking away or abridging." Article 32 designates the Supreme Court as the proper institution to adjudicate whether the state has "taken away or abridged" fundamental rights and guarantees for citizens "the right to move" the Supreme Court.

Unlike India's Constitution, Pakistan's Constitution does not guarantee the right to seek a remedy before the Supreme Court for violations of fundamental rights. However, Article 8 requires that any law or ordinance that violates fundamental rights is void, and the Supreme Court has the power to declare such laws void in part according to Article 184(3), which states that

> the Supreme Court shall, if it considers that a question of public importance with reference to the enforcement of any of the Fundamental Rights conferred by Chapter I of Part II is involved have the power to make an order of the nature mentioned in the said Article.

This Article was the impetus for the expansion of the Supreme Court's powers in the 2000s under Chief Justice Chaudhry.[91]

The Supreme Courts of both countries have relied on these constitutional provisions as the basis for judicial review.

ii. Other powers/High Court powers

There are residual appeals powers that are also vested in the Supreme Court of India through Article 136, which states that "the Supreme Court may, in its discretion, grant special leave to appeal from any judgment, decree, determination, sentence or order *in any cause or matter passed or made by any court or tribunal in the territory of India*" (emphasis added). Further, the Supreme Court has exclusive jurisdiction over any conflict of laws between the provinces and federal government through Article 131. Finally, Article 226 lays out the jurisdiction of the Supreme Court's subordinate High Courts, which enjoy the power to issue "directions, orders or writs, including writs in the nature of habeas corpus, mandamus, prohibition, quo warranto, and certiorari, or any of them, for the enforcement of any of the rights conferred by Part III and for any other purpose."

For Pakistan, Article 184 (1) grants the Supreme Court original and exclusive jurisdiction over any dispute between the federal and provincial governments with language that directly mirrors Article 131 of the Constitution of India. The Pakistani Supreme Court relies on Article 143 to adjudicate disputes between the provincial and federal governments because this Article mandates that any provincial law that is repugnant to federal law is void. The Supreme Court has the exclusive power to declare those provincial laws void.

There is also one last similarity that demonstrates the expansive reach of the Supreme Court in the Pakistani and Indian constitutions. Under Article 143 of India's Constitution and Article 186 of Pakistan's Constitution, the President can seek the "opinion of the Supreme Court on any question of law which he considers of public importance."

All of this is in striking contrast to the limitations on the power of the Supreme Court in the United States. First, the United States Supreme Court would not provide an advisory opinion on the constitutionality of a law nor would a president request one because of the "case or controversy" limitation in the Constitution, which requires proof of actual injury to the plaintiff. American presidents seeking the prospective analysis of a law before its passage or even after its adoption but before a valid lawsuit is filed could not go to the U.S. Supreme Court, but Pakistani and Indian presidents could obtain such opinions from their Supreme Courts.

Prospective or hypothetical rights violations are far outside the scope of the U.S. Supreme Court, but often arise before the Supreme Courts of India and Pakistan because of the Constitution. While all three Constitutions enumerate civil rights or fundamental rights, the Indian and Pakistani Constitutions directly allow the Supreme Court to protect these rights.

III. Pakistan

Pakistan and India share many constitutional similarities that can be distinguished from the United States. However, there are socio-political issues that are unique to Pakistan and affect the evolution of judicial review in the nation's Supreme Court. These issues include the power of the military, the dissolution of the nation in 1971, and the constitutional breaks that have caused Pakistan to adopt four different constitutions in its short post-colonial history. Knowing these issues is necessary for one to understand the history of the Pakistani Supreme Court, which has included the judicial legitimization of military coups.

A. Fourth branch

It has been said that while some nations possess armies, Pakistan is a place where the army possesses the nation. The military has remained Pakistan's most powerful and domineering institution since the country's independence and has influenced the democratic evolution of the country.[92] It follows that Pakistan has been described as a praetorian state,

> one in which the military tends to intervene and potentially could dominate the political system . . . The political processes of this state favor the development of the military as the core group and the growth of its expectations as a ruling class.[93]

Unlike either the United States or India, Pakistan has experienced intermittent periods of democratic leadership broken by four military dictatorships in 1958, 1969, 1977 and 1999.[94] This means that Pakistan has "been under some form of martial law for one third of its 53 years as an independent state,"[95] and the Army has ruled "directly or indirectly for more than half the life of the country.[96]

The Army has taken direct action through the imposition of martial law and the suspension of various constitutions through the passage of various Provisional Constitutional Orders (PCO) or Legal Framework Orders (LFO). However, even more significant than these PCOs or LFOs is how the Army has manipulated the political process:

> The army's wide political influence distorts the democratic process . . . . Earlier periods of military intervention created new political divisions. Groups that found themselves benefited by authoritarian rule were opposed by others, often linked to the mainstream political parties, that were sidelined or repressed. During these times, the army itself became an increasingly powerful vested interest in society.[97]

The judiciary was one of the groups that has been accused of acting on behalf of the military's interests. In the past, the Supreme Court has been used as a vehicle of legitimization by the Army for military coups and the suspension of the constitution. These extra-constitutional acts were justified through the development of the doctrine of necessity, which was based on Kelsen's theory that efficacy of a regime is the source of its validity or legality.[98] While a great deal of scholarship has been dedicated to a critical analysis of Kelsen's theory, the objective of this section is merely to point out that this theory was adopted and applied by the Supreme Court of Pakistan to legitimize coups. Chief Justice Muhammad Munir in *State v. Dosso* (1952) "purported to rely on Kelsen's authority to argue that the essential condition to determine whether a constitution has been annulled is the efficacy of the change."[99] The majority opinion concluded that "a victorious revolution or a successful coup d'état is an internationally recognized legal method of changing a constitution."[100]

The necessity, as formerly interpreted by the Pakistani judiciary, could be political, economic or territorial, but it essentially meant that if a military coup was successful, it was legal, and the successful military leader would have the legal right to suspend the constitution in order to preserve 'national order and security.' The current status of the doctrine of necessity is that it has been overruled by the Supreme Court of Pakistan;, however, as Figure 4.1 illustrates, the history of the Court's use of the doctrine is complex.

The paradox of judges legitimizing the suspension of the very Constitution they are sworn to defend has not been lost on many observers of the Court's jurisprudence. Newberg concludes,

> judges have supported the government of the day and accepted limits on their jurisdiction, and extensions of executive rule inconsistent with the conceptual foundations of their rulings in order to judge at all . . . [which has] endowed judicial actions with a political consequentialism that itself has restricted judicial autonomy.[101]

The Army has used the Supreme Court to act against the Court's own self-interest of preserving the rule of law.

The Army has not only suspended the Constitution, but it also was able to influence the drafting of the various constitutions that Pakistan has adopted since declaring independence in 1947. The cumulative effect of this has made constitutions into "vehicles [that] legalize the exercise of power [more] than they have to legitimize its sources."[102] This means that unlike India and the United States, the Constitution of Pakistan is

> as much about the uses of power as about the way that constitutional documents articulate rules. The judiciary's relationship to written constitutions, civil law and military regulations has been part of a process of give and take among those holding power rather than strictly a process of enforcing rules.[103]

This lack of rule enforcement has historically left civilian institutions like the Supreme Court and Parliament without real power, and their "search for stable and democratic constitutional frameworks is repeatedly derailed by the military's extra-constitutional usurpations of power."[104]

The lack of a rule-based regime has presented challenges and opportunities for the Supreme Court in its judicial review power. Though the judiciary has legitimated military coups, there have also been instances where judges fought back against the usurpation of political and legal power by the Army.[105]

Nevertheless, the continual three-way struggle between the Supreme Court, elected parliamentary members, and the Army leadership in Pakistan has exacerbated intra-branch conflicts, unlike in India or the United States. As Newberg explains, "unlike the Indian dialogue between legislative and judicial powers, the Pakistani experience has combined overwhelming executive power, uncertain constitutional resilience and a cautious but consistent judicial quest for jurisdiction and justiciability."[106]

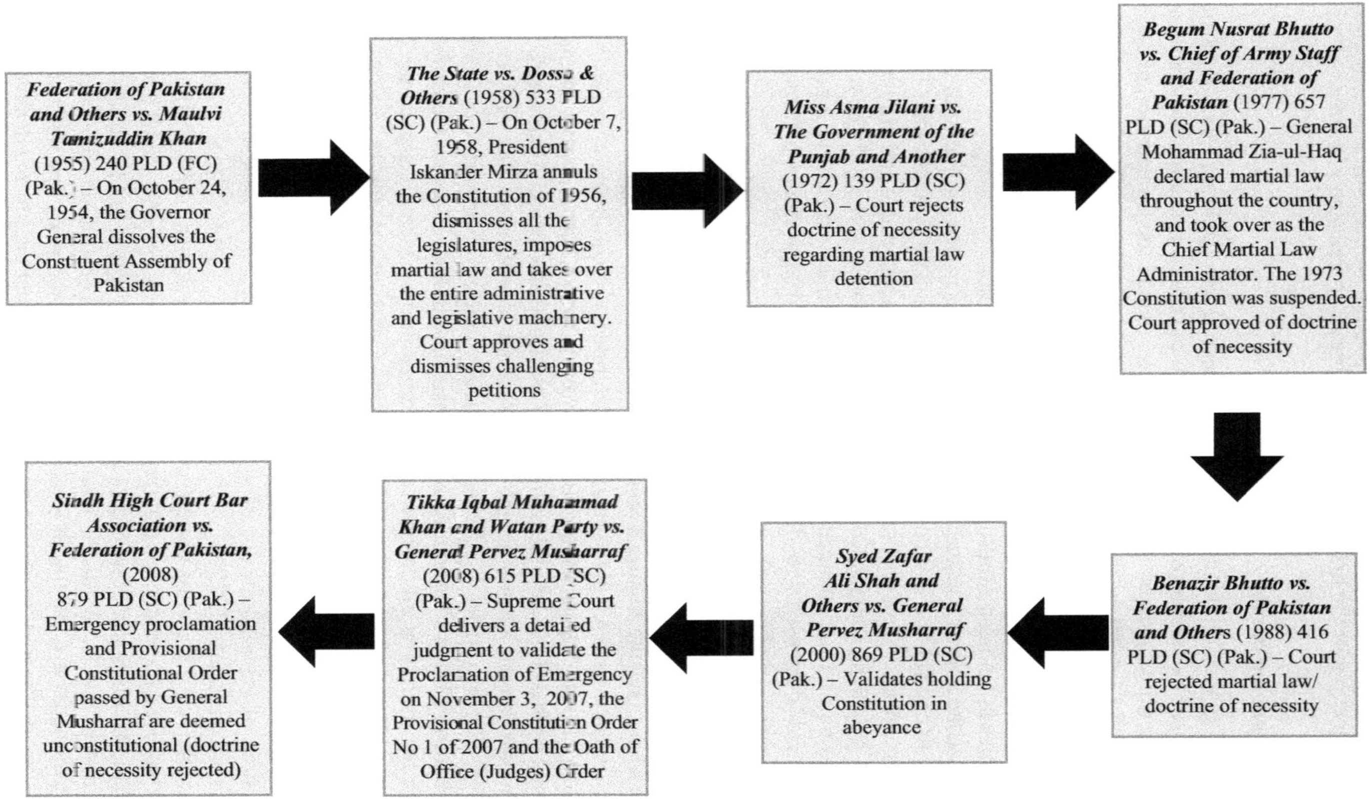

Figure 4.1 Pakistan: timeline for the doctrine of necessity

These struggles often cause such a breakdown that the constitution does not survive, and a new Constituent Assembly is tasked with creating a new constitution, which explains the many constitutional breaks in Pakistan's history.

B. Constitutional breaks

Two kinds of constitutional breaks can be identified in Pakistan. First, there are breaks caused by the imposition of martial law and the suspension of the constitution during military dictatorships. For example, though the Constitution of 1956 "established Pakistan as an Islamic republic . . . [with] a parliamentary form of government with a unicameral legislature,"[107] it was abrogated almost immediately after its ratification by President Iskander Mirza, who suspended the Constitution and disbanded the newly formed Parliament. This would happen several more times in Pakistan's turbulent democratic evolution.

The second kind of constitutional break that has taken place in Pakistan is when the current constitution is set aside in order to draft and ratify a new one. The first attempt came after the Constitution of 1956 had been suspended and military ruler General Ayub Khan demanded that a new constitution be drafted.[108] The resulting Constitution of 1962 changed the nation's parliamentary system to a presidential one and "dispensed with democratic representative government, fundamental rights, separation of powers, and provincial autonomy."[109]

The difference between the 1956 Constitution and 1962 Constitution was very great, considering "the former had a parliamentary structure based on the British model whereas the latter, framed under the martial law regime of Field Marshal Ayub Khan, gave the country a presidential system."[110] Even though this Constitution greatly empowered the executive branch ruled by the military, it was set aside in 1969 with the imposition of martial law by Yahyah Khan, who was appointed as Chief Martial Law Administrator by his predecessor, General Ayub Khan.[111]

Though Yahyah Khan attempted to pass a new constitution, this was accomplished after his ouster by the democratically elected government of Zulfiqar Ali Bhutto.[112] Bhutto "produced a consensus-based draft of a new Constitution which the leaders of all parliamentary groups in the Assembly signed on 20th October 1972."[113] Unlike the 1952 and 1964 Constitutions, the 1973 Constitution made significant achievements by introducing a bicameral legislature and empowering the Prime Minister as well as provincial governments.[114] The 1973 Constitution was partly a consequence of the dissolution of Pakistan and the formation of Bangladesh out of what was formerly East Pakistan, as will be discussed on pages 74–75.

Despite being the most current constitution for Pakistan, the Constitution of 1973 has been suspended several times, first in 1979 by General Zia Ul Haq, who claimed that his martial law orders and regulations "would not be challenged in any court of law."[115] While the suspensions of each constitution have been illustrated in Figure 4.1, the life of each of the three constitutions described above is illustrated in Figure 4.2, which chronologically lays out the life and death of each constitution.

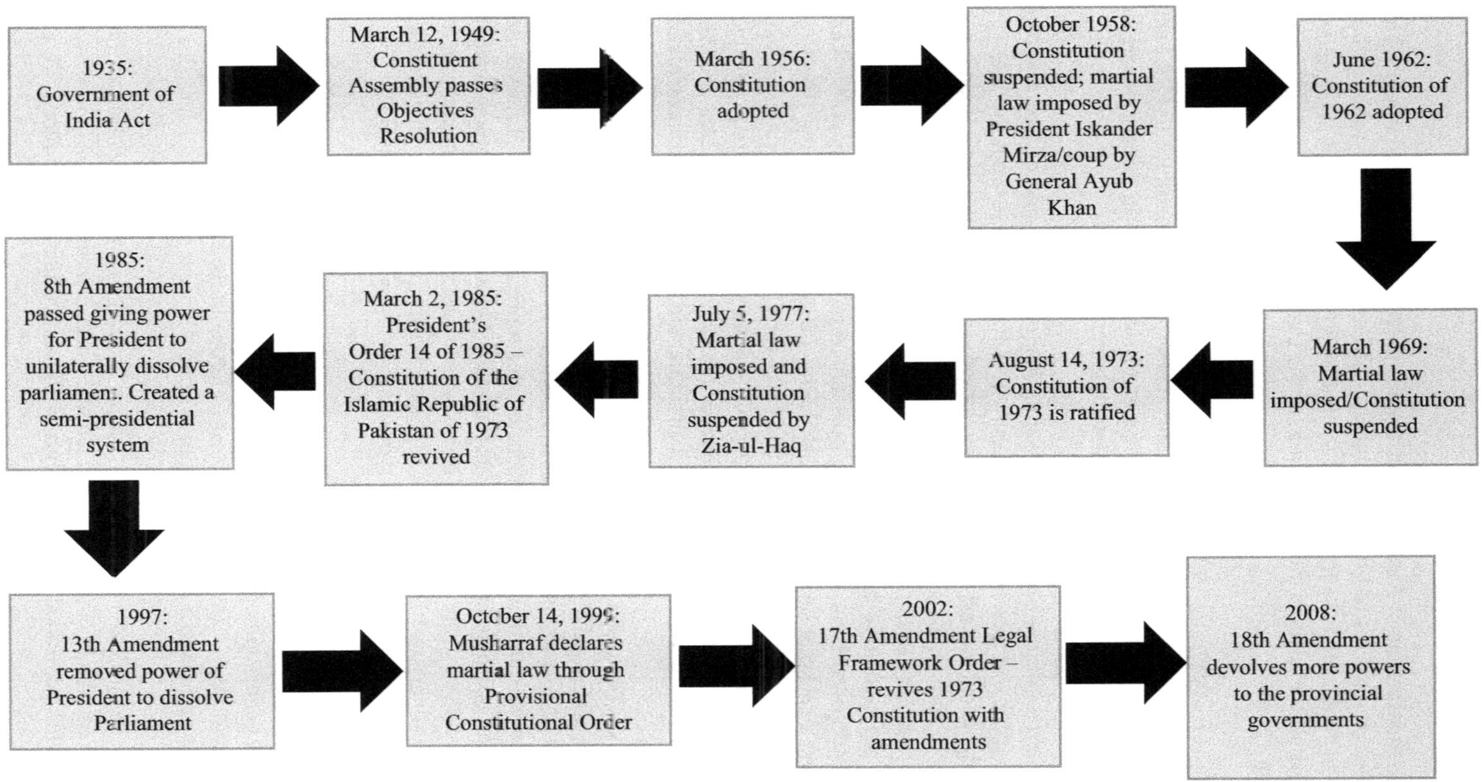

Figure 4.2 Constitutional chronology

C. Dissolution of Pakistan

The dissatisfaction in East Pakistan began under the One Unit policy, which was seen as a means to limit the autonomy of East Pakistan. Even though East Pakistan "contained the majority of the nation's population," they were "given only half of the seats in the upper house of the Central Legislative (In 1950)."[116] Further,

> between 1947 and 1971, West Pakistan's monopolization of control intensified until it had subjugated politically and exploited economically East Pakistan. The relationship between West and East Pakistan in this period can be characterized as internal or intrastate colonialism.[117]

This internal colonialism eventually "culiminat[ed] in the end of One Unit but also the civil war that led to the separation of East Pakistan from the West."[118] Political leaders in East Pakistan rejected the formation of "a strong federal government . . . headed by a strong executive, elected for a fixed term, and having little accountability to the federal legislature."[119] Instead, they called for "a directly elected representative government, a parliamentary system, limited powers for the federal government, and a greater quantum of provincial autonomy."[120] While they were somewhat successful in establishing a federal system in the 1956 Constitution, the 1962 Constitution was "forced on the East Wing under Ayub Khan's martial law that prevailed at the time."[121] The centralized presidential system set up by the 1962 Constitution only deepened the divisions between East and West Pakistan as it "made both the federal structure and its system of representation vulnerable."[122]

These developments increased the protests led by East Pakistanis, which were eventually addressed through the creation of the Legal Framework Order in 1970. This LFO dissolved "the One Unit Arrangement in West Pakistan" and "would give the more populous East Pakistan greater representation."[123] However, the LFO did not go far enough for the East Pakistanis, who continued their movement for independence from Pakistan. The response from West Pakistan came in the form of a military operation launched in East Pakistan predicated on an invocation of a state of emergency throughout the country.[124] Newberg explains that:

> The brutal war sustained images of an army terrorizing its own unarmed civilians, millions of refugees evacuating Bengal's cities, guerillas operating in the countryside, the intercession of foreign powers and intervention by the Indian army . . . In truth, the war was its coda to the two-winged state rather than a prelude to a new constitutional order.[125]

In the end, Bangladesh was permitted to declare its independence from Pakistan, which concluded decades of conflicts between the two wings, causing Pakistan to lose "more than half of its population" and "more than 54,000 square miles of its territory."[126]

Despite the conclusion of the civil war, "many complex and confused legal issues were left to the courts to resolve," creating the basis for a new generation of jurisprudence following the passage of the 1973 Constitution.[127]

D. Conclusions

The socio-political context for Pakistan must be understood in order to understand the distinctions between Pakistan and India's use of judicial review. Though the Indian Supreme Court once dealt with the imposition of emergency rule through Indira Gandhi, it did not have to deal with a constant cycle of military coups, followed by technocratic rule, followed by civil unrest, followed by the reemergence of the civilian government, followed by military coups. The Supreme Court has made decisions under military duress, and this influence has led the Court to make legal that which can never be legal: military coups that abrogated or suspended the Constitution. In many ways, one can consider the active use of judicial review by the Supreme Court from 2007 onwards as the Court repenting for its past sins of legitimizing illegal regimes.

As one can see, Pakistan lacks political continuity, and this has impacted the constitutional continuity as well: the country has gone through three constitutions in three decades. This lack of continuity cannot be found in either India or the United States, making Pakistan's Constitution the youngest, as it only dates back to 1973. The Supreme Court of Pakistan has thus had far less time to interpret its Constitution than India or the United States.

IV. Conclusion

By examining the differences in the structures established by the Constitution, one can see why judicial review has been used more actively in Pakistan and India than in the United States. While the United States Constitution limits the Supreme Court to decide "cases and controversies," the Pakistani and Indian Supreme Courts can take up any issues relating to a fundamental right of public importance. This creates a much wider area for the courts of the Indian subcontinent to exercise judicial review. This limitation has been the basis of American judicial restraint doctrines like political question and standing along with other justiciability requirements, which will be discussed in Chapter 5.

Further, the United States Constitution left many issues to be addressed by the first Congress, like the form and shape of the judicial branch. The Indian and Pakistani Constitutions are more explicit, especially in the creation of the provincial High Courts and the Supreme Court and the expansive delegation of their powers. While the U.S. Supreme Court had to interpret the authority for judicial review from various parts of the Constitution, the Indian and Pakistani constitutions explicitly provide for that authority.

Judicial review has also expanded in the Supreme Courts of Pakistan and India, because unlike the United States, Pakistan and India lack state Supreme Courts or state constitutions. This reflects the American form of federalism, which grants more authority to states than Pakistan or India's provinces. As a result, judicial review is more dispersed in the United States, as both state and lower federal courts can exercise judicial review. This is not the case of Pakistan and India, which is why the Supreme Courts and their subordinate High Courts have the exclusive right to exercise judicial review.

Finally, there are socio-political conditions that distinguish Pakistan from both India and the United States. The level of political control exercised by the military, the country's history of constitutional breaks through coups and declarations of martial law, and the dissolution of the country in 1971 are all the basis for the Supreme Court's use of judicial review today. This historical lack of stability can help explain the varying jurisprudence from the Supreme Court that legitimized and then invalidated various impositions of emergency rule. In many ways, the Supreme Court's active use of judicial review today can be attributed to the Court attempting to remedy its past missteps.

These elements combined create a modern environment in which the Pakistani Supreme Court is exercising judicial review more actively and with less restraint than the United States and India.

Notes

1 See generally Calvin R. Massey, *The Locus of Sovereignty: Judicial Review, Legislative Supremacy, and Federalism in the Constitutional Traditions of Canada and the United States*, 1990 Duke L.J. 1229 (1990).
2 Robert Alan Dahl, *How Democratic Is the American Constitution?* (2003), at 65.
3 Neals-Erik William Delker, *The House Three-Fifths Tax Rule: Majority Rule, the Framers' Intent, and the Judiciary's Role*, 100 Dick. L. Rev. 341, 351 (1996) citing Thomas Jefferson, *Jefferson's Manual of Parliamentary Practice* (1801), reprinted in Constitution, Jefferson's *Manual, and Rules of the House of Representatives of the United States One Hundred Third Congress s 283* (William Holmes Brown ed., 1993)
4 Dahl, *supra* note 2.
5 Id.
6 Id.
7 Id.
8 John C. Reitz, *Political Economy and Separation of Powers*, 15 Transnat'l L. & Contemp. Probs. 579, 595 (2006).
9 Id.
10 The Federalist, No. 52. (Publius) (Clinton Rossiter ed., New American Library) (1961).
11 James Leonard & Joanne C. Brant, *The Half-Open Door: Article III, the Injury-In-Fact Rule, and the Framers' Plan for Federal Courts of Limited Jurisdiction*, 54 Rutgers L. Rev. 1 (2001), at 51.
12 Id at 55.
13 The Federalist No. 48. (James Madison) (Clinton Rossiter ed., New American Library) (1961).
14 Jack Rakove, *Original Meanings: Politics and Ideas in the Making of the Constitution* (1997) at 53.
15 David W. Tyler, *Clarifying Departmentalism: How the Framers' Vision of Judicial and Presidential Review Makes the Case for Deductive Judicial Supremacy*, 50 Wm. & Mary L. Rev. 2215, 2248 (2009) ("if a President has an obligation to ensure the faithful execution of laws, and he faithfully executes an unconstitutional law, it would appear that he has simultaneously undermined the higher law (e.g., the Constitution) that he

must also faithfully enforce. To avoid a logical contradiction, then, the Framers must have intended presidential non-enforcement to include the power of constitutional review.")

16 Id.

17 The Federalist No. 73. (Alexander Hamilton) (Clinton Rossiter ed., New American Library) (1961). ("The Provision For The Support of the Executive, and the Veto Power, New York Packet, Friday, Mar. 21, 1788.")

18 Tyler, *supra* note 15, at 2248. ("Best characterized as 'departmental theory of government,' this idea best reflects the Framers' support for a system that empowered the executive and the judiciary to each make its own constitutional determinations.").

19 Gordon Wood, *The Creation of the American Republic: 1776–1787* (2011), at 304.

20 Id.

21 Scott Douglas Gerber, *A Distinct Judicial Power: The Origins of an Independent Judiciary, 1606–1787* (2011) at 331.

22 Rivka Weill, *Reconciling Parliamentary Sovereignty and Judicial Review: On the Theoretical and Historical Origins of the Israeli Legislative Override Power*, 39 Hastings Const. L.Q. 457, 458–9 (2012)

23 Tyler, *supra* note 15.

24 An Act to Establish the Judicial Courts of the United States, ch. 20, 1 Stat. 73 (1789).

25 United States Constitution Article III, Section 2.

26 Judiciary Act, *supra* note 24.

27 Mark A. Graber, *Establishing Judicial Review: Marbury and the Judicial Act of 1789*, 38 Tulsa L. Rev. 609, 612 (2003)

28 Id at 629.

29 Judiciary Act of 1789: An Act to establish the Judicial Courts of the United States, 1 Stat. 73.

30 *Marbury v. Madison*, 5 U.S. 137 (1803).

31 *Stuart v. Laird*, 5 U.S. 299, 2 L. Ed. 115; 1 Cranch 299

32 Bruce Ackerman, *The Failure of the Founding Fathers: Jefferson, Marshall and the Rise of Presidential Democracy* (2007), at 8–9.

33 Id.

34 Id.

35 See generally Daniel J. Elazar, *Contrasting Unitary and Federal Systems*, 18 Int. Polit. Sci. Rev. 237–51 (1997).

36 Compare U.S. Constitution Amendment X: "The powers not delegated to the United States by the Constitution, nor prohibited by it to the States, are reserved to the States respectively" to Article 248 of India's Constitution: "Parliament has exclusive power to make any law with respect to any matter not enumerated in the Concurrent List or State List."

37 *Examples include Marbury v. Madison*, 5 U.S. 137 (1803). Dredd Scott v. Sanford, 60 US 393 (1857) See Michael Grossberg & Christopher Tomlins, *The Cambridge History of Law in America* (2008) at 308 ("Chief Justice Roger Taney's infamous decision in *Dred Scott v. Sanford* represented only the second time to that point that the Supreme Court had overturned an act of Congress.") See also *Legal Tender Cases*, 79 U.S. 457 (1870) (Supreme Court upheld Legal Tender Act for contacts made after February 1862 but invalidated the Act for contracts made before that date).

38 See Randy J. Holland, *State Constitutions: Purpose and Function*, 69 Temp. L. Rev. 989 (1996) ("The interstitial model recognizes the rights afforded by the United States Constitution as minimal guarantees and seeks to ascertain if those federal protections are supplemented or enhanced by state constitutional provisions")

39 See David A. Schlueter, *Judicial Federalism and Supreme Court Review of State Court Decisions: A Sensible Balance Emerges*, 59 Notre Dame L. Rev. 1079 (1984).

40 Id at 1095.

41 Richard H. Fallon, Jr., *Marbury and the Constitutional Mind: A Bicentennial Essay on the Wages of Doctrinal Tension*, 91 Cal. L. Rev. 1, 55 (2003), ("The Supreme Court

itself had measured a state law against a state constitution in *Cooper v. Telfair* [4 U.S. (4 Dall.) 14 (1800)]")

42 U.S. Constitution, Article VI. "This Constitution, and the Laws of the United States which shall be made in Pursuance thereof; and all Treaties made, or which shall be made, under the Authority of the United States, shall be the supreme Law of the Land; and the Judges in every State shall be bound thereby, any Thing [sic] in the Constitution or Laws of any State to the Contrary notwithstanding.")

43 Wallace Mendelson, *The Judiciary Act of 1789: The Formal Origin of Federal Judicial Review*, 76 Judicature 133, 134 (1992)

44 Id.

45 Bradford R. Clark, *The Supremacy Clause as a Constraint on Federal Power*, 71 Geo. Wash. L. Rev. 91 (2003)

46 Mendelson, *supra* note 43.

47 U.S. Const. art III, Section2.

48 Leonard & Brant, *supra* note 11.

49 *Coleman v. Miller*, 307 U.S, at 460 (Frankfurter, J., concurring).

50 Id.

51 Id.

52 Leonard & Brant, *supra* note 11, at 13.

53 See generally Louis L. Jaffe, *Standing to Secure Judicial Review: Public Actions*, 74 Harv. L. Rev. 1265 (1961), Raoul Berger, *Standing to Sue in Public Actions: Is it a Constitutional Requirement?* 78 Yale L.J. 816 (1969), Bradley S. Clanton, *Standing and the English Prerogative Writs: The Original Understanding*, 63 Brook. L. Rev. 1001, 1005 (1997), Cass R. Sunstein, *What's Standing After Lujan? Of Citizen Suits, "Injuries," and Article III*, 91 Mich L. Rev. 163, 188–89 (1992)

54 Leonard & Brant, *supra* note 11, at 47.

55 Id at 5–6 ("the framers most likely viewed the courts as a place where individual litigants came to have actual and personal grievances resolved.")

56 Id at 63.

57 Id.

58 See Manik Lal Gupta, *Constitutional Development of India* (1989) ("The Government of India Act . . . provided for an extensive overhauling of the Central Legislature with a view to giving it a more representative character and enabling it to exercise a greater influence if not control over the government. For the first time, the bicameral system was introduced.")

59 Hamid Khan & Muhammad Waqar Rana, *Comparative Constitutional Law* (2nd ed., 2014), at 168.

60 Imtiaz Omar, *Emergency Powers and the Courts in India and Pakistan* (2002), at 2.

61 Khan & Rana, *supra* note 59.

62 India Const., art. 74 (2) ("There shall be a Council of Ministers with the Prime Minister at the head to aid and advise the President who shall, in the exercise of his functions, act in accordance with such advice.")

63 Khan & Rana, *supra* note 59.

64 Rabindra Kumar Sethy, *Political Crisis and President's Rule in an Indian State* (2003), at 37.

65 Khan & Rana, *supra* note 59, at 169.

66 Id at 170–1.

67 Paula Newberg, *Judging the State: Courts and Constitutional Politics in Pakistan* (2002) at 111.

68 Tayyab Mahmud, *Praetorianism and Common Law in Post-Colonial Settings: Judicial Responses to Constitutional Breakdowns in Pakistan*, 1993 Utah L. Rev. 1225, 1253 (1993). (The 1962 Constitution "established a model of praetorian 'guided democracy,' which promised at best a benevolent dictatorship.")

69 Nazir Hussain Chaudhri, *Chief Justice Muhammad Munir: His Life, Writings, and Judgements* (1973), at 546. ("Some Thoughts on the Draft Constitution")

70 Pakistan Const., art. 48.
71 Khan & Rana, *supra* note 59, at 172.
72 Id at 172. ("The President exercised his discretionary power to dissolve the National Assembly and to dismiss the Prime Minister on no less than four times, that is, in 1988, 1990, 1993, 1996.")
73 Newberg, *supra* note 67, at 27.
74 Mahmud, *supra* note 68, at 1253 (The 1962 Constitution "established a model of praetorian 'guided democracy,' which promised at best a benevolent dictatorship.")
75 *Synthesis of Parliamentary Sovereignty and Judicial Supremacy: Some Comparison,* Byjus, Available at http://byjus.com/free-ias-prep/synthesis-of-parliamentary-sovereignty-and-judicial-supremacy-some-comparison
76 Umama Moin, Parliament and the Supreme: The Indian Experience (2011) (Aligarh Muslim University). Available at http://shodhganga.inflibnet.ac.in/handle/10603/11379 (last accessed on Oct. 31, 2016), at 59.
77 The U.S. Supreme Court's only invalidation of federal laws during its first century of existence was in the cases of *Marbury v. Madison* and *Dred Scott v. Sandford,* as mentioned above.
78 Shah Nawaz, *Judicial Activism and the Problem of Governance in India* (Aligarh Muslim University, 2011). Available at http://shodhganga.inflibnet.ac.in/handle/10603/40573 (last accessed on Oct. 31, 2016), at 125.
79 Moin, *supra* note 76, at 56.
80 See generally Pakistan Const. Part VI: Judicature; India Const., Part V Chapter IV and Part VI Chapter V.
81 United States Constitution, Amendment 10. ("The powers not delegated to the United States by the Constitution, nor prohibited by it to the States, are reserved to the States respectively, or to the people")
82 India Const., art. 248. "(Parliament has exclusive power to make any law with respect to any matter not enumerated in the Concurrent List or State List")
83 Khan & Rana, *supra* note 59, at 201.
84 Id.
85 Katharine Adeney, *A Step Towards Inclusive Federalism in Pakistan? The Politics of the 18th Amendment,* 42 Publius Volume 4 (2013), at 538. See also Khan & Rana, *supra* note 59, at 182. ("The Preamble of the 1973 Constitution lays down that the territories of Pakistan shall form a federation, wherein the units would be autonomous with such boundaries and limitations on their own powers and authority as may be prescribed.")
86 Eighteenth Amendment Revisited, edited by Maqsudul Ali Khan, Muhammad Hanif, and Muhammad Nawaz Khan, Islamabad Policy Research Institute. Chapter I: Muhammad Hanif & Muhammad Nawaz Khan, *After 18th Amendment: Federation and Provinces*. See also Chapter IV, p. 141.
87 Mahmud, *supra* note 68.
88 Id. ("The vast majority of powers on the Concurrent List have now been allocated to the provinces, requiring the devolution of seventeen ministries from the center. Residual powers remain with the provinces.")
89 Khan & Rana, *supra* note 59, at 200.
90 Id at 201.
91 Maryan S. Khan, *Genesis and Evolution of Public Interest Litigation in the Supreme Court of Pakistan: Toward a Dynamic Theory of Judicialization,* 28 Temple J. Intl. & Comp. L. 284 (2015).
92 See generally Husain Haqqani, *Between Mosque and Military* (2005). Ayesha Siddiqa, *Military Inc.* (2007). Imtiaz Omar, *Emergency Powers and the Courts in Pakistan and India* (2002).
93 Mahmud, *supra* note 68, at 1228.
94 Pamela Constable, *Pakistan's Predicament,* 12 J. Democracy 1 (2001), at 15.
95 Id.
96 Newberg, *supra* note 67, at 9.

97 Leo E. Rose & D. Hugh Evans, *Pakistan's Enduring Experiment*, 8 J. Democracy 1 (Jan. 1997), at 83–96.

98 See Hans Kelsen, *Pure Theory of Law* (Max Knight trans., 2014), at 218. For a discussion about validity and legitimacy of legal regimes, see also Hans Kelsen and Albert A. Ehrenzweig, *Professor Stone and the Pure Theory of Law*, 17 Stan. L. Rev. 1128, 1139 (1965). See also Michael Freeman, ed., *Lloyd's Introduction to Jurisprudence* (8th ed., 2014). (Extract by Hans Kelsen)

99 T.C. Hopton, *Grundnorm and Constitution: The Legitimacy of Politics*, 24 McGill L. J. 72, 79 (1978).

100 *The State v. Dosso & Others* (1958) 533 PLD (SC) (Pak.)

101 Newberg, *supra* note 67, at 244.

102 *Id.*

103 *Id.*

104 Mahmud, *supra* note 68, at 1303.

105 See *Benazir Bhutto v. Federation of Pakistan and others* (1988) 416 PLD (SC) (Pak.); *Miss Asma Jilani v. The Government of the Punjab and Another* (1972) 139 PLD (SC) (Pak.); Library of Congress, *Suspension and Reinstatement of the Chief Justice of Pakistan: From Judicial Crisis to Restoring Judicial Independence?* Available at www.loc.gov/law/help/pakistan-justice.php. ("In Mar. 9, 2007, when the President of Pakistan, General Purvez Musharraf, met the Chief Justice of the Pakistan Supreme Court, Iftikhar Muhammad Chaudhry, and reportedly importuned him to resign, the Chief Justice's refusal unleashed an unprecedented revolt led by Pakistani lawyers in support of judicial independence and the rule of law in Pakistan.")

106 Newberg, *supra* note 67, at 244.

107 James Wynbrandt, *A Brief History of Pakistan* (2009), at 178.

108 See Pakistan Const (1962), notes on Pakistan, Available at http://notesonpakistan.blogspot.com/2009/05/constitution-of-1962.html (last accessed on Apr. 6, 2016.)

109 Mahmud, *supra* note 85, at 1253.

110 Khan, Hanif, Khan, *supra* note 86, at 11.

111 Newberg, *supra* note 67, at 112.

112 Khan, Hanif, Khan, *supra* note 86, at 22.

113 Id at 22–3.

114 Id at Razia Musrrat, *Chapter V, Constitutional Provisions on Creation of Provinces and Suggest Models*, at 162.

115 Mahmud, *supra* note 68, at 1274.

116 Wynbrandt, *supra* note 107, at 172.

117 Andrew M. Beato, *Newly Independent and Separating States' Succession to Treaties: Considerations on the Hybrid Dependency of the Republics of the Former Soviet Union*, 9 Am. U. J. Int'l L. & Pol'y 525, 545 (1994).

118 Newberg, *supra* note 67, at 53.

119 Mahmud, *supra* note 68, at 1232.

120 Id.

121 Wynbrandt, *supra* note 107, at 198.

122 Newberg, *supra* note 67, at 111.

123 Wynbrandt, *supra* note 107, at 198.

124 Omar, *supra* note 61, at 29.

125 Newberg, *supra* note 67, at 117.

126 Wynbrandt, *supra* note 108, at 202.

127 Newberg, *supra* note 67, at 120.

5 Modern justiciability standards and procedures

I. Introduction

As described in Chapter 4, there are constitutional distinctions that affect judicial review powers exercised by the Supreme Courts of Pakistan, India and the United States. There are also differences in the common law jurisprudence developed by the Supreme Courts over time, which have either limited or expanded the Court's judicial review powers depending on the country. While the United States Supreme Court has imposed relatively rigid locus standi limitations in cases like *Lujan v. Defenders of Wildlife* and precluded cases involving political questions in cases like *Baker v. Carr*, Pakistan and India have lowered the bar and eased access to seek relief at the Supreme Court through public interest litigation. This distinction has partially contributed to the mounting issue of backlog in the Supreme Courts of India and Pakistan.

Along with differing doctrines, the Indian and American courts employ a different procedure for case-selection. The justices of the United States Supreme Court meet regularly to determine which cases will be granted hearings, with the court taking notice of only 1% of the cases presented to it.[1] In India's Supreme Court, there is a biweekly procedure for the selection of cases, with the Court granting hearings to 12% of the petitions presented before it.[2] The Supreme Court of Pakistan lacks an analogous procedure, with each justice independently engaging in case-selection.[3]

The substantive and procedural differences in the pre-hearing writ of certiorari evaluation in America and maintainability-assessment in India are key in understanding the varied evolution of judicial review in the Supreme Courts of Pakistan, India, and the United States. For Pakistan, the lowering of standing requirements and the lack of pre-hearing justiciability procedures have exacerbated the Court's workload. The prescriptive part of this study addresses this issue by suggesting a justiciability standard and procedure for the Pakistani Supreme Court to adopt, which will be developed using the comparative examples of the United States and India.

II. United States

A. Case or controversy

The United States Supreme Court has narrowly interpreted the "case or controversy" language in the Article III of the Constitution to limit its jurisdiction. The

Supreme Court's interpretation of the "case or controversy" clause has produced barriers that plaintiffs must satisfy, including standing,[4] mootness,[5] and ripeness.[6]

Chief Justice Earl Warren explained in *Flast v. Cohen* that the phrase cases or controversies "define[s] the role assigned to the judiciary in a tripartite allocation of power to assure that the federal courts will not intrude into areas committed to the other branches of government."[7] Based on this respect for the separation of powers, the Court has explained that its justiciability requirements "limit the business of federal courts to questions presented in an adversary context and in a form historically viewed as capable of resolution through judicial process."[8] All of these doctrines limit "the jurisdiction of federal courts; when its requirements are not satisfied [as] courts are without power to proceed, regardless of the wishes of the parties."[9]

While standing deals with the issue of injury, ripeness and mootness deal with the timing of the suit. The United States Supreme Court has interpreted standing, ripeness and mootness in ways that limits the Court's exercise of judicial review powers, prohibiting the Court from adjudicating potentially hypothetical or moot legal issues.

i. Ripeness

In examining the ripeness of a claim, the Supreme Court has assessed whether the plaintiff has or will suffer an imminent harm. The Court explores whether the danger motivating the plaintiff is "real and immediate, rather than distant and speculative" and whether there is "concrete demonstration that some harm really will occur; it must be based on objective evidence and not merely his own assertions."[10] The policy behind the ripeness limitation to the Supreme Court's judicial review power is related to the separation of powers doctrine:

> to prevent the courts, through avoidance of premature adjudication, from entangling themselves in abstract disagreements over administrative policies, and also to protect the agencies from judicial interference until an administrative decision has been formalized and its effects felt in a concrete way by the challenging parties.[11]

Alexander Bickel explains that the Supreme Court avoids accepting cases where a governmental action is in its initial stages and will postpone litigation in order to assess the "full, rather than merely the initial, impact of the statute or executive measure whose constitutionality is in question."[12]

In *Abbot Laboratories*, the Supreme Court laid out competing considerations for its ripeness determination: "the fitness of the issues for judicial decisions and the hardship to the parties of withholding court consideration."[13] This formula has been used since *Abbott* was decided, although there is academic disagreement on whether ripeness is based on the Constitution or on prudential self-limitations on the Court's power.[14] Regardless of its foundation, the Court has used the test to weigh its ability to adjudicate an issue against the hardship that plaintiff would suffer without judicial remedy. While hardship has been important in the Court's analysis, the ripeness test from *Abbot Laboratories* has often been used to deny judicial relief to plaintiffs.

The analysis of ripeness is quite different in the Supreme Courts of Pakistan and India, as these Courts forego procedural waiting requirements and take notice of initial policy decisions by the Prime Minister. This is in part based on the constitutional provisions allowing the Supreme Court to provide advisory opinions when requested by the executive.[15] Nevertheless, utilizing the competing considerations laid out by the United States Supreme Court, the general trend in the Supreme Courts of Pakistan and India has focused more on the "hardship to the parties of withholding court consideration" in determining the boundaries of their jurisdiction than on the "fitness of the issues for judicial decisions."

ii. Mootness

Along with ripeness, mootness is also a consideration for the Supreme Court in assessing the justiciability of petitions. As mentioned earlier, the United States Supreme Court is not permitted to issue advisory opinions, and "the Supreme Court frequently explained the mootness doctrine [as being] derived" under this prohibition. The Court cannot provide remedies for a harm that no longer exists because "federal courts are without power to decide questions that cannot affect the rights of litigants in the case before them."[16]

The procedure for the Supreme Court after it has deemed that a case is moot is that the Court will "will vacate the lower court's decision and remand the case for dismissal."[17] The Court does this to ensure that the legal issue is left "unresolved" for future cases to decide, which is how the Court uses the mootness doctrine to protect the rights of future litigants who bring a claim to the Court at the proper time.[18]

In *DeFunis v. Odegaard*, the Supreme Court held that the mootness doctrine was founded in the "case or controversy" requirement from the Constitution.[19] While mootness may not have been mentioned specifically in the Constitution, it relates directly to the constitutionally mandated separation of powers and "avoids unnecessary federal court decisions, limiting the role of the judiciary."[20]

Regardless of its prudential or constitutional foundation,[21] the Supreme Court continues to use the mootness requirement to dismiss cases, which has led many commentators to "believe that the Court has manipulated standing rules based on its views of the merits of particular cases"[22] However, proponents of the justiciability rules argue that a strict adherence to the rules would counteract the "undesirable" scenario where federal courts are "able to manipulate justiciability doctrines to avoid cases or to make decisions about the merits of disputes under the guise of rulings about justiciability."[23]

There is one exception to the mootness doctrine: where an injury suffered by a plaintiff was "capable of repetition, yet evading review," and this kind of claim *could* be adjudicated by the Court.[24] This was used in *Roe v. Wade* to allow a woman to bring a claim concerning her pregnancy, even if the pregnancy could conclude before remedy could be provided by the Court.[25]

One focus for all the justiciability doctrines is to limit judicial review as a means to encourage inter-branch harmony. While inter-branch harmony is an important consideration for the Supreme Courts of India and Pakistan, the relationship between the judiciary and elected officials is more adversarial in South Asia than the United States. This has led to the Indian and Pakistani Supreme Courts taking up cases that would be deemed non-justiciable by the U.S. Supreme Court due to mootness or lack of ripeness.

iii. Locus standi

Ripeness and mootness are secondary determinations for the Court, which must first determine whether the plaintiff has locus standi, or standing. While the constitutional provision relating to "case or controversy" was discussed in Chapter 4, this section will examine the Supreme Court's interpretation of the provision.

Much like ripeness or mootness, standing is not mentioned in the Constitution, but the standing doctrines have been developed by the judiciary in interpreting the Constitution.[26] Generally, standing requires the plaintiffs to demonstrate that they have suffered harm caused by the defendant (causation) and that harm must capable of redress by judicial remedy (redressability). There are many reasons for this standing requirement, but the United States Supreme Court has primarily justified the requirement as being necessary to ensure respect for the separation of powers.[27]

Two cases from the United States that developed the standing requirements are especially significant when compared to either India or Pakistan. The first case was *Frothingham v. Mellon*, in which the Court concluded that

> the party who invokes the [judicial review] power must be able to show not only that the statute is invalid but that he has sustained or is immediately in danger of sustaining some direct injury as the result of its enforcement, and not merely that he suffers in some indefinite way in common with people generally.[28]

Frothingham eventually led to *Lujan v. Defenders of Wildlife*, in which non-governmental organizations were suing the Secretary (or Minister) of Interior for "wrongly" interpreting an endangered species statute. Justice Antonin Scalia wrote the opinion and rejected standing for the non-governmental organizations in order to respect "the separate and distinct constitutional role" of the judiciary, which is limited to "cases or controversies."[29] He further stated that "vindicating the public interest (including the public interest in Government observance of the Constitution and laws) is the function of *Congress* and the *Chief Executive*" (emphasis added).[30]

The Supreme Courts of Pakistan and India fundamentally disagree with such an absolute rejection of public interest litigation (PIL). Both Supreme Courts have taken up thousands of PIL cases, while the U.S. Supreme Court's jurisprudence generally rejects the justiciability of PIL based on rigid limitations on standing.[31]

Lea Brilmayer explains that the limitations on standing and the prohibition on PIL in the U.S. are not only meant to ensure inter-branch harmony, but are meant to protect the interests of future litigants. As the U.S. Supreme Court enforces stare decisis, giving binding effect to its prior decisions, the Court

> should be reluctant to permit [a] concerned citizen to assert the legal rights of his neighbor . . . We need to protect the neighbor's present and future interests; we do not want the concerned citizen to litigate abstract principles of constitutional law when the precedent established will govern someone else's first amendment rights. Similarly, even if the concerned citizen has his own claim, we should insist that he state it with specificity so that no overly broad precedent will threaten the rights of persons in different positions.[32]

Therefore, the United States Supreme Court has limited its exercise of judicial review through imposing standing requirements on litigants for a dual purpose: to maintain a cooperative relationship with the executive and legislative branches and to protect the right of future litigants who face actual harm from a law or state action.

B. Political question doctrine

The political question doctrine has also been used to dismiss claims at the Supreme Court to ensure that the Court does not preempt executive or legislative decisions. Despite setting out the judicial review power for the Supreme Court, Chief Justice Marshall explained in *Marbury* that "questions, by their nature political, or which are, by the constitution and laws, submitted to the executive, can never be made by this court."[33] Stated differently, "if the [executive or legislative] branch at issue has full discretion to act, then the Court will not second-guess or substitute its own judgment."[34] This is partially due to the unique position of the judiciary as an appointed and unelected body, which grants it legal power but vests most political power to the elected branches.[35]

In order to ensure that the judiciary does not infringe on the realm of the elected branches, the modern understanding of the political question doctrine has developed a great deal since its inception through *Baker v. Carr*. In *Baker*, the Supreme Court examined a claim challenging the redistricting of voting blocs in a state.[36] Several factors were listed for consideration of the political question doctrine in *Baker*: whether the Constitution assigned the issue to a political branch, whether there was a lack of legal standards to resolve the issue, whether the case forced the court to make an initial policy determination, whether the decision would express disrespect to the political branches, whether there was the potential for embarrassing conflict with policies from another branch on the issue.[37]

The *Baker* factors have been criticized as being "vague, confusing, and susceptible to misinterpretation."[38] The development of the political question doctrine has been also unclear, and as one scholar writes, "at least part of the explanation for this confusion is the largely unpredictable method in which the Supreme Court has chosen to invoke the doctrine over the years."[39] There has been so much confusion, in fact, that some argue that the political question doctrine is now "dead."[40]

Scholars have complained that "the Court has never used the "political question doctrine" as true "justiciability doctrine,"[41] but rather as a prudential consideration, which "is characterized by an attitude that could legitimately be called 'realpolitik': the Court must survive in an often hostile political world."[42]

Alexander Bickel, who pioneered the prudential vision of the political question doctrine, suggested that the real factors behind the Supreme Court's decisions to dismiss petitions based on the political question doctrine are:

> (a) the strangeness of the issue and its intractability to principled resolution;
> (b) the sheer momentousness of it, which tends to unbalance judicial judgment;
> (c) the anxiety, not so much that the judicial judgment will be ignored, as that perhaps it should but will not be;
> (d) ('in a mature democracy'), the inner vulnerability, the self-doubt of an institution which is electorally irresponsible and has no earth to draw strength from.[43]

Others disagree with this approach. Professor Herbert Wechsler has argued that the Court can only decline a remedy in a case based on political question when the Constitution explicitly vests that decision in a political branch.[44] The various elements proposed by the Supreme Court in *Baker* and by Professors Bickel and Wechsler will be examined in Chapter 7 during the prescriptive analysis.

The political question doctrine has been used by the Court to maintain a cooperative and deferential relationship with the elected branches. The Court's deference to the elected branches increases their legitimacy and effectiveness, and more importantly facilitates respect for the people's democratic will to control their nation's policy-making. On the other hand, advocates for judicial review argue that the Court must not relegate itself to deferentially approving executive action or legislative acts because

> only if the federal courts rule on the political branches' respective powers can a transparent debate occur about the limits of such power and whether any additional limitations are desired and necessary. This debate is central to protecting our democratic governing structure and the balance of power.[45]

While the political question doctrine has been recently used to dismiss petitions concerning foreign policy, it did not stop the Court from ultimately deciding the results of a presidential election in *Bush v. Gore*. In that case, "the United States Supreme Court, by a 5–4 vote, gave George Bush exactly the relief he sought – an order to stop the second, manual recount of the Florida ballots."[46] The Court took up a case that would ultimately decide the presidency of the United States, which many considered a purely political question.[47] Justice Stephen Breyer wrote a dissenting opinion to the case, stating that the selection of a president was a political question:

> of course, the selection of the President is of fundamental national importance. But that importance is political, not legal. And this Court should resist the temptation unnecessarily to resolve tangential legal disputes, where doing so threatens to determine the outcome of the election.[48]

Some argue that cases like *Bush* demonstrate a trend in the United States Supreme Court to set aside the political question doctrine analysis and has opened the door to a form of "judicial supremacy."[49]

While there are a few exceptional cases wherein the U.S. Supreme Court reviews political questions, Pakistan and India's Supreme Courts have, by comparison, greatly expanded their powers over time by often deciding politically sensitive issues. Therefore, at the justiciability and merits stage, Pakistan and India's Supreme Courts are far less willing to dismiss cases that might present political questions. This has led to clashes between the Court and the elected branches over disqualifications of the head of the government, which will be detailed in Chapter 6.

C. Writ of certiorari procedure

In a small number of cases, the United States Supreme Court has original jurisdiction for issues involving ambassadors, public ministers, or a state/province serving as a party before the Court. For all other cases, the Supreme Court acts as an appellate court. Most parties have previously litigated in a lower court before applying to the Supreme Court for a writ of certiorari or a command to the lower courts to submit documents for evaluation of their judgment. The United States Supreme Court has "virtually complete discretion over which cases to hear, and proportionally it chooses very few indeed."[50]

This was not always the case. Until 1925, many U.S. Supreme Court justices argued that the Court was overworked because its docket included too many cases due to the lack of case-selection discretion. Chief Justice William H. Taft pushed for reform in this area and argued that a new law was needed that would "enlarge the field in which certiorari" replaced obligatory jurisdiction, which would allow the Supreme Court to "be given sufficient control over the number and character of cases which come before it."[51] Therefore, the justices helped draft the Judiciary Act of 1925, also known as the Certiorari Act or Judges' Bill, which "rendered the majority of the Supreme Court's workload discretionary, by removing the possibility of direct appeal to the court in most circumstances."[52] The Act gave "the Court more discretion as to which cases to hear" and "greatly reduced the number of decisions in either state courts of last resort or federal appeals courts that parties could appeal to the Supreme Court as a matter of right."[53] Instead of granting hearings to most petitioners as it did in the past, after the Certiorari Act, the Supreme Court could "decide whether or not to grant the petition and hear the case":

> this authority made the single biggest difference in the Supreme Court's docket. No longer did the Court have to hear almost every case an unhappy litigant presented to it. Instead, for the most part, the Court could select only those relatively few cases involving issues important enough to require a decision from the Supreme Court.[54]

The Certiorari Act differentiates the United States Supreme Court from that of Pakistan or India, both of which often lack "case-selection discretion," for reasons that will be explained later.[55]

The case-selection process for the Court revolves around the cert pool and the Rule of Four.[56] The cert pool is a grouping of all the clerks working for the justices participating in the pool, and it reviews all the petitions before the Supreme Court. This pool

> was designed to reduce the workload by eliminating duplication of effort. Rather than have each chamber review every petition, the petitions are randomly assigned for evaluation among the six chambers in the pool . . . A clerk will review the petitions assigned to her and then write a cert. pool memo for each of her petitions.[57]

The pool memo will include the facts of the case, the decision by the lower court, and the recommendation by the clerk on whether writ should be granted, with the justices then making their own determination based on the memo. Some have complained that this vests too much power in the clerks. However, former Chief Justice Rehnquist wrote that "the individual justices are quite free to disregard whatever recommendation the writer of the pool memo may have made, as well as the recommendation of his own law clerks, but this is not a complete answer to the criticism."[58]

Nevertheless, once the pool memos have been drafted, the Chief Justice "prepares a list of those cases he believes to be worthy of discussion" for the conference of justices.[59] Any justice can add a case to the Discuss List, and "all cases not making the discuss list are automatically denied cert."[60] At the conference, each case is evaluated by the justices, and if a case receives four votes in favor of hearing, it will be granted cert and the litigants will be asked to prepare briefs and oral arguments for the court. Some cases will be summarily disposed by the Court, or rather relief will be granted to the petitioner without the scheduling of an oral hearing.

The certiorari process in the United States is far more discriminating than Pakistan or India. The average acceptance rate for cases in the U.S. Supreme Court ranges between 1 and 5% depending on the year and level of activism exercised by the Court.[61] For example, in 2001, 8,255 cases were filed but only 84 petitioners were granted writ, of which 79 cases were disposed of.[62]

Though there are ideological or perhaps political divisions in the Supreme Court that become apparent in the certiorari process, Chief Justice Rehnquist stated that

> several thousand of the petitions for certiorari filed with the Court each year are patently without merit; even with the wide philosophical differences among the various members of our Court, no one of the nine would have the least interest in granting them.[63]

In its recent history, the Supreme Court has limited its granting of cert to those cases involving a circuit split, which occurs when two federal circuit courts of appeal disagree on a point of law.[64] While it does not guarantee review, if the circuit court of appeals have split on a case, this increases "the likelihood that the case will be reviewed."[65] Nevertheless, the Court does grant cert in the absence of a circuit split in exceptional cases involving national importance.[66]

Therefore, the United States addressed the problem of an overworked Supreme Court early in the twentieth century by instituting discretionary jurisdiction and the writ of certiorari process. There are certain ideological, structural, and historical differences between the Supreme Courts of Pakistan and India and the United States that limit the applicability of American-style limited judicial review to the Indian subcontinent. Yet, the focus by the U.S. Supreme Court on developing standards for standing, limiting judicial involvement in political questions, and instituting a pre-hearing culling procedure for petitions might offer a comparative solution for the overwhelmed judiciaries of Pakistan and India.

III. India

The Supreme Court of India may exercise original, advisory and appellate jurisdiction.[67] For its original jurisdiction, the Court can act on matters of public importance relating to a fundamental right in the Constitution, transfer of cases from the High Courts, and legal disputes between one or more states and the national government.[68] There are also several types of appeals listed in the Constitution, including general appeals, statutory appeals, and appeals by special leave.[69]

A. Standing

The Supreme Court of India once had a similar view as the United States on creating high barriers for standing, as "early judgments [in the Supreme Court of India] adopted the traditional approach to standing, insisting that a person who challenged legislation or action on the basis of the Constitution must be personally affected."[70] However, this changed in 1976, "when the Supreme Court declared that the plea of 'no locus standi' would not necessarily . . . [disqualify] an interested public body which had brought a wrongdoer before court."[71] The Court held that

> whether a person has the locus to file a proceeding depends mostly and often on whether he possess a legal right and that right is violated. But in an

appropriate case, it may become necessary in the changing awareness of legal rights and social obligations to take a broader view of the question of locus to initiate a proceeding.[72]

This has led to the development of more active and plaintiff-friendly standards for standing than those imposed by the U.S. Supreme Court. This could be partially due to the colonial history described in Chapter 2, or to structural elements of India's constitution as described in Chapter 4. Yet, Chief Justice Balakrishnan offers a different explanation: the Indian Supreme Court's "dilution of the rules of standing . . . has allowed the Courts to recognize and enforce rights for the most disadvantaged sections in society through an expanded notion of 'judicial review'."[73] In this way, the Court downplays the significance of meeting technical legal requirements as a way to address the unwillingness or inability of political actors to deal with the concerns of poor or disenfranchised citizens.

The earlier judgments by the Supreme Court of India that contained traditional limits on standing were criticized because they "prevented the enforcement of the rights of the poor and disadvantaged, who were unable to approach the court."[74] The focus on disenfranchised groups reflects the second element of the *Baker v. Carr* test in the United States: difficulties posed to plaintiff if the Court refuses to provide relief or accept standing. In *Gupta v. Union of India*, the Court held that:

> in a country like India where access to justice being [sic] restricted by social and economic constraints, it is necessary to democratise judicial remedies, remove technical barriers against easy accessibility to Justice and promote public interest litigation so that the large masses of people belonging to the deprived and exploited sections of humanity may be able to realise and enjoy the socio-economic rights granted to them and these rights may become meaningful for them instead of remaining mere empty hopes.[75]

This opened the door for representational standing by someone other than the person who suffered the harm directly so that

> any member of the public could approach the court for relief where a legal wrong or legal injury had been caused to a person or class of persons by reason of violation of any constitutional or legal right and such person or class of persons was unable to approach the court personally because of poverty, helplessness, disability, or a socially or economically disadvantaged position.[76]

Eventually, this has led to the acceptance of public interest litigation (PIL) at the Supreme Court, which allows non-governmental organizations and groups to bring claims on behalf of individuals that are not able to bring the case themselves, something the U.S. Supreme Court directly rejected in *Lujan v. Defenders of Wildlife*. In *Gupta*, the Court stated that "any member of the public having sufficient interest can maintain an action for judicial redress for public injury arising from . . . violation of some provision of the Constitution or the law."[77] Therefore, one of the only justiciability questions asked by the Court concerning standing for plaintiffs is whether they have "sufficient interest" as a member of the public in stopping some sort of government misdeed.[78] This is strikingly dissimilar to the U.S. Supreme Court with its discretionary jurisdiction setting high barriers for plaintiffs to prove they have proper standing to argue the case before the court.

B. Public interest litigation (PIL)

Public interest litigation (PIL) cannot be found in the text of the Constitution, but has been interpreted into the Constitution as based on the spirit rather than the letter of India's Constitution. Chief Justice Balakrishnan argued that "even though the framers of our Constitution may not have thought of these innovations on the floor of the constituent assembly, most of them would have certainly agreed with the spirit of these judicial interventions."[79] Though PIL has "had mixed success at shrinking poverty or correcting injustices," it has reinforced the credibility of the democratic system by empowering "citizens marginalized by the corruptions of routine politics."[80]

While PIL is meant to empower poor or disenfranchised groups, it has been criticized by some for causing "new problems such as an unanticipated increase in the workload of the superior courts" and inter-branch conflict.[81] In fact, one scholar has categorized PIL at the Supreme Court of India as having three phases: the third and current phase "is a period in which anyone could file a PIL for almost anything," and "it seems that there is a further expansion of issues that could be raised as PIL."[82]

Yet, others argue that

> the Court was able to develop a degree of discretion following the expansion of standing doctrine in PIL; the Court was thus able to screen out a large number of PIL writ petitions that were not deemed to be meritorious or in the public interest.[83]

Regardless of the discretion exercised in the use of PIL, its very existence demonstrates an ideological difference between the United States and Indian Supreme Courts. While many of the U.S. Supreme Court's limitations on standing were developed to avoid inter-branch conflicts and judicial hyper-activity, the Supreme Court of India focuses on pursuing the "higher purpose" of remedying legal complaints from poor or disenfranchised citizens regardless of inter-branch discord.

C. Political question doctrine

Along with standing, the Supreme Court of India has interpreted the political question doctrine differently from the United States Supreme Court. In *Roy v. Union of India*, the Supreme Court of India held that "the doctrine of the political question was evolved in the United States of America on the basis of its Constitution which has adopted the system of a rigid separation of powers, *unlike ours*" (emphasis added).[84] In fact, a rigid separation of powers was directly rejected by the Constituent Assembly in India[85] and later by the Supreme Court in *Ram Jawaya Kapur v. State of Punjab*.[86]

Similarly, the Supreme Court held that that political question doctrine is "basically of American origin"[87] and cannot be transported to India "since that doctrine is based on, and is a consequence of, a rigid separation of powers in the U.S Constitution and our Constitution is not based on a rigid separation of powers."[88] While separation of powers is "an essential framework of the constitutional scheme," in India, the Supreme Court has interpreted the Constitution as requiring an "artistic blend" and "adroit mixture of judicial, legislative and executive functions."[89] Nevertheless, the Court also concluded that "[a]lthough the doctrine of separation of powers has not been recognized under the constitution in its absolute rigidity . . . the constitution-makers have meticulously defined the functions of various organs of the state."[90] Further, the Court has acknowledged the benefit of dismissing political cases and deferring to political branches through the political question doctrine, using it as "a tool for maintenance of governmental order."[91]

Unlike their American counterparts, the Supreme Court of India has adopted the idea that "there is no blanket rule for judicial reluctance," which means each case must be examined individually to understand whether it presents a non-justiciable question.[92] In a case where the Court examined the legality of constitutional amendments duly passed by Parliament, the Court concluded that "it is not possible to define what is a political question [sic]."[93] Further, the Court stated that it never decides political questions, but in this case the Court could "ascertain whether Parliament is acting within the scope of [its] amending power."[94]

Therefore, while separation of powers is a part of the basic framework of Indian constitutional democracy and the political question doctrine generally facilitates inter-branch harmony, neither have become rigid rules limiting the actions of the Court for cases with political implications.

D. Pendency and procedure for case selection

The cost for the Supreme Court of India setting aside the justiciability doctrines adopted by the U.S. Supreme Court has been an increasingly unsustainable workload for the Court. Much like the U.S. Supreme Court prior to the passage of the Judges' Bill in 1925, the Supreme Court of India currently lacks "case-selection discretion" for some issues, which means that the Court "hears thousands of cases each year, increasing dramatically since 1950."[95] Today, there are nearly 47,000 new petitions before the Supreme Court each year, with the Court granting hearings for over 8,000 cases.[96]

Part of this burst in litigation can be attributed to the increase in the number of Supreme Court judges over time,[97] which facilitated the creation of many different benches working on different cases at the same time in the Supreme Court of India.[98] However, there is a more substantive method the Court has used to dispose of such a high number of petitions. Despite lacking case-selection discretion along the lines of the United States Supreme Court, the Supreme Court of

India has adopted a " 'split-stage' process in which new "admission matters" are screened by designated benches on Monday and Friday."[99] These admission hearings "involve direct petitions and appeals to the Court," and the Court can dismiss the petition for lack of merit, issue a summary disposition with a final order, or refer the matter for oral hearing before another bench as a "regular matter."[100] In these meetings, the Court can evaluate the justiciability of any petition, including cases involving public interest litigation. The Court will review up to 60–65 cases in these admission hearings each week.[101]

The Supreme Court of India has also adopted a justiciability-evaluation procedure to dispose of cases without granting hearings to the petitioners: "most of the Court's caseload consists of review of routine civil and criminal appellate cases, of which thousands are summarily dismissed at the initial admission stage."[102]

Despite the existence of multiple benches and the pre-hearing justiciability analysis, delay remains a problem at the Supreme Court of India, with nearly 64,000 cases in backlog.[103] It has taken the Supreme Court over five years to issue a final order in 17% of those cases accepted for review.[104]

IV. Pakistan

Much like India, Pakistan's Supreme Court has three types of jurisdiction under the constitution: original, appellate, and advisory. The Court's original jurisdiction in Article 184 includes the duty to settle disputes between and among the provincial and national governments. Further, Subsection 3 of Article 183 is the basis for suo motu and public interest litigation. The Court's appellate jurisdiction in Article 185 lays out several instances when the Court may review judgments by the lower courts, including the High Courts. Further, under Article 186A the Court can transfer a case immediately from a High Court. Lastly, and perhaps least important in modern jurisprudence, the court's advisory jurisdiction is recognized in Article 186.

A. Standing/public interest litigation (PIL)

In the aftermath of the passage of the 1973 Constitution, the Supreme Court adopted some rigid requirements for standing and justiciability. Earlier, in *Asma Jilani v. Government of Punjab*, the Supreme Court held that "the Court's judicial function is to adjudicate upon a real and present controversy which is formally raised before it by a litigant" and that the Court could not "enter upon purely academic exercises or to pronounce upon hypothetical questions,"[105] mirroring the American approach. This followed a decision from 1959,[106] where the Pakistani Supreme Court had held that a "[petitioner] cannot move the Court pro bono public,"[107] much as in *Lujan v. Defenders of Wildlife* in the United States.

This changed with the decisions in *Bhutto v. Federation of Pakistan*[108] and *Darshan Masih v. State*,[109] in which the Court set aside the standing test in cases that presented an issue of public importance relating to a fundamental right in the Constitution.[110] *Masih* involved the use of suo motu powers of the Court, while

Bhutto was an issue of public interest litigation. The difference between the two cases was merely the format of approaching the Court – petitioners in *Bhutto* filed proper petitions, while the petitioners in *Masih* simply sent a telegram to the Chief Justice.

In *Bhutto*, the Supreme Court acknowledged that it could not decide abstract or hypothetical matters, but dispensed with formal standing requirements in the case. The Court critiqued the rigid standing doctrine as employed by the U.S. Supreme Court as essentially an "outgrowth of Anglo-Saxon jurisprudence" that gives "protection to the affluent or to serve in aid for maintaining the status quo of vested interests."[111] The Court further concluded that its interpretation of its jurisdiction under Article 184(3) of the Constitution[112] "should not be ceremonious" in its observance of rules but should be flexible in order to "extend the benefits of socio-economic change through this medium of interpretation [of the Constitution by the Supreme Court] to all sections of the citizens."[113]

Article 184 (3) of the Constitution allows for the Court to examine cases that present a "question of public importance," which was interpreted as allowing for PIL. Though the Court had historically accepted petitions from "next friends," the Court went one step further in *Bhutto* by further relaxing "the rule on locus standi so as to include a person who bona fides makes an application for the violation of any constitutional right of a determined class of persons whose grievances go unnoticed and un-redressed."[114] Therefore, claims on behalf of poor or underrepresented minorities could be made by non-governmental organizations, civic groups, or political parties. The Court would dispense with "the traditional rule of locus standi" wherever there was a violation of fundamental rights for "a class or group of persons" who are underrepresented or disenfranchised by the state.[115]

Around the same time as *Bhutto*, the Supreme Court narrowed its interpretation of public importance in *Medhi v. Pakistan International Airlines Corp*, where the Court stated that:

> The issues arising in a case, cannot be considered as a question of public importance, if the decision of the issues affects only the rights of an individual or group of individuals. The issue in order to assume the character of public importance must be such that its decision affects the rights and liberties of people at large . . . Therefore, if a controversy is raised in which only a particular group of people is interested and the body of the people as a whole or the entire community has no interest, it cannot be treated as a case of "Public Importance".[116]

Despite this limiting analysis in *Medhi*, the Court's decision in *Bhutto* set the precedent for a long-term evolution of PIL in Pakistan. Though the Supreme Court only accepted 39 PIL cases in the first decade after *Bhutto* and *Medhi*,[117] this has now drastically changed, with PIL petitions skyrocketing. In 2010 alone the Supreme Court handled 27 suo motu cases, 135 human rights cases, 81 constitutional petitions, and 60,000 Human Rights Cell applications (all of which are categorized as PIL).[118] While most of the human rights cell applications were handled or dismissed without hearing, the cumulative amount of public interest litigation the Court faces today is unprecedented in Pakistan's judicial history.

Maryam Khan's study on PIL illustrates that the Supreme Court has experienced three waves of PIL activism: 1988–2005, 2005–2009, and 2009–2015.[119] Each wave of activism has shown "that there are alternating periods of judicial activism on the one hand and judicial retreat from political questions on the other."[120] The third wave was led by Chief Justice Iftikhar Chaudhry, after he led the Lawyers' Movement for the restoration of democracy and the ouster of General Pervez Musharraf. Under Chaudhry, the court took on political questions "under the ever-expanding umbrella of PIL" and determined

> matters such as regime legitimacy, law reform, economic policy and deregulation, regulation of electoral processes, eligibility of elected representatives to hold office, validity of constitutional amendment processes, intervention in executive appointments, conflict management, and even some issues bearing on foreign policy . . . Most, if not all, of these [are] political questions.[121]

Political questions will be discussed later in this chapter, but there is also the issue of suo motu, which has produced waves of activism in the Court, especially after 2009 and the Lawyers' Movement.

B. Suo motu

The most significant example of Pakistan's Supreme Court setting aside justiciability requirements is through suo motu cases. Suo motu litigation allows the Supreme Court to adjudicate cases before the concerned parties have formally requested judicial remedy. Suo motu was not "expressly granted in the Constitution, but was rather developed over a series of judgments" that analyzed Article 184(3) of the Constitution.[122]

As mentioned earlier, in the *Masih* case[123] brick kiln workers "managed to send a telegram to the Chief Justice claiming that they were being unlawfully detained by the brick kiln owner."[124] The Chief Justice instituted the case for hearings, despite lacking any submission from legal counsel, and concluded that the Court would "dispense with the traditional requirements of locus standi" in order to provide justice to the majority of Pakistanis who lacked education and resources.[125]

Later, the Court began taking suo motu notice through newspaper articles, letters from concerned citizens, and other informal sources. The institution of cases through suo motu is directly controlled by the Chief Justice. While all justices can recommend a case for suo motu, a rule was created in 2006 to require the Chief Justice to individually approve of any suo motu use.[126] Further, because the Chief Justice controls the bench assignments of junior justices, he could "assign the [suo motu case] to himself and two other judges of his liking" and ensure that there is no dissent from his decision on the bench.[127]

i. Role of the Chief Justice in suo motu

The Chief Justice plays a main role for the exercise of suo motu and can initiate a case based on a few scenarios that would seem completely non-justiciable in the U.S. Supreme Court. The Chief Justice can initiate a case and schedule hearings if he or she i) reads about a story involving fundamental rights and public interest in the media, ii) receives an informal letter or telegram from individuals alleging a violation of their fundamental rights or iii) receives a request from the Human Rights Cell of the Court (which will be described below.)

The frequency of suo motu depends greatly on the judicial philosophy of the serving Chief Justice. While Chief Justice Sheikh Riaz only took six suo motu cases from 2002 to 2003, Chief Justice Chaudhry took up 123 cases between 2005 and 2013.[128] This number is especially striking because Parliament was only able to pass 131 laws during that same time.[129] It should not be surprising that these cases led to a breakdown in inter-branch harmony and temporarily put the Court on a collision course with the elected branches of government.[130]

However, Chaudhry represented an aberration for use of suo motu at the Supreme Court, because the Chief Justice usually exercises restraint and limits the use of this kind of litigation. Chaudhry's successors Tassaduq Jillani and Nasirul Mulk collectively used suo motu fewer than ten times each in their respective tenures lasting 2013–2014.[131] Chief Justice Jillani, through his judgment in *Dossani Travels*, explained that the Supreme Court must adopt "judicial restraint displayed in deference to the principle of trichotomy of powers" going forward.[132]

In 2014, an international judicial conference attended by Chief Justice Jillani set forth a declaration that requested the Pakistani Supreme Court to "exercise its suo motu jurisdiction under a structured and regulated scheme" that respected the trichotomy of branches "so that the exercise of judicial powers neither hampers nor stunts policies of the executive."[133] However, as of yet, the Court lacks a legal standard to bind future Chief Justices and regulate the use of suo motu by the Supreme Court.

ii. Human Rights Cell

While the Chief Justice can use suo motu himself, the Chief Justice receives thousands of letters and informal complaints each year from common citizens. To handle these kinds of petitions, the Human Rights Cell (HRC) was created to assist the Office of the Chief Justice. The HRC receives an average of 250 informal complaints and letters from citizens per day.[134] After receiving the complaint, the staff "prepares a brief summary of the grievances for the benefit of and in accordance with the orders of the Hon'ble Chief Justice."[135] Then, the Cell uses informal means to resolve the dispute, working with executive and legislative agencies at the federal and provincial level by allowing them to issue comments on the complaint. Finally, "if it appears that a genuine grievance of the applicants has not been sufficiently redressed in the reports and comments then the case is fixed and heard in Court as [an] HR Cell case."[136]

From November 2009 until December 2013, the HRC instituted 209,882 claims and disposed of 188,857, leaving pendency of 21,000 petitions.[137] Of these petitions, the Chief Justice only assigned 343 for hearings and formal proceedings before the court.[138]

C. Procedure for case selection and role of Registrar

Outside the realm of suo motu, there may be an informal procedure for the Court's exercise of its original jurisdiction. While the procedure for the Human Rights Cell has been made public, there is little information concerning the case-selection procedure of the Supreme Court of Pakistan itself. Much like India today and the United States prior to the passage of the Judges' Bill, Pakistan's Supreme Court lacks case-selection discretion in some instances. Under Article 185(2) of the Constitution, "the Supreme Court is obliged to hear thousands of cases in appeal" when an appeal involves over $500 and the lower courts have disagreed on the case.[139]

In addition, the Court lacks a justiciability standard to apply to each petition before the Court. While there are some general principles that have emerged from the Court evaluating the justiciability of petitions, "matters of public importance may be deduced on a case-by-case basis."[140] This piecemeal approach has left the Court without limitations to its exercise of judicial review, which has directly affected its ability to dispose of cases efficiently.

Further, unlike the Indian Supreme Court, which grants oral hearings only after filtering petitions through the admissions stage, the Supreme Court of Pakistan

> conventionally . . . grants an oral hearing to most, if not all, appeals and petitions fixed before it. It should thus come as no surprise that even as a court of 17 justices hears various cases in smaller benches of three judges or at times only two judges, it may take years before a particular action is heard.[141]

There is no publication that explains the Supreme Court's practical internal process of selecting petitions, but there are a few important rules in the Rules of the Supreme Court, adopted in 1980. According to the Rules, a formal application for relief is filed with the Registrar of the Court, who must recommend any technical changes that petitioners may need to make to ensure their petition accords with Supreme Court practices.[142] The Registrar is also tasked with keeping "a list of all the cases pending before the court . . . [and] prepar[ing] the list of cases ready for hearing."[143] If directed by a Judge in Chambers, a Registrar may "adjourn any matter" and "the Judge in Chambers may at any time refer any matter to the [full] Court."[144]

A Judge in Chambers, meaning an individual judge on the Supreme Court, has the right to address the following matters independently:

> (1) Application for leave to compromise or discontinue a pauper appeal . . . (5) Rejection of plaint . . . (6) Application for setting down for judgment in default of written statement . . . (10) Application for withdrawal of suit,

appeal or petition, for rescinding leave to appeal and for dismissal for non-prosecution.[145]

While one justice may exercise control over these issues, litigants can challenge the decision of the justice by requesting a two- or three-justice bench to reconsider the question.[146] However, "after the final disposal of the first application for review no subsequent application for review shall lie to the Court and consequently shall not be entertained by the Registry."[147]

For petitions concerning criminal appeals, the Court "may, upon perusal of the papers, reject the petition summarily without hearing the petitioner in person, if it considers that there is no sufficient ground for granting leave to appeal."[148] The Court must grant a hearing for petitions involving the death penalty.

There are several actions that one justice or a bench of justices can do after receiving a petition from the Registrar: they can dismiss the petition (unless the subject matter is covered by the mandatory jurisdiction of the Supreme Court in the Constitution), grant summary judgment, or accept the petition for hearing. There is little information regarding the dismissal or acceptance rate, but the general trend is to schedule hearings for most petitions cleared by the Registrar.[149]

The Supreme Court of Pakistan has not only set aside many of the doctrines underlying justiciability and judicial deference to political branches, but it has avoided developing a formal bifurcated process or institution to first assess the justiciability of claims before granting a time-consuming hearing to the litigants. This has produced an overworked court with a seemingly unending backlog of cases.

D. Ripeness

While the Supreme Court of Pakistan has relaxed the requirements for standing, it has still evaluated the issue of ripeness in its decisions. In challenges to the validity of laws, the question for the Supreme Court has been whether petitioners must wait to be harmed or whether they can preemptively challenge legislation. In *Hakim Muhammad Anwar Babri v. Pakistan (1973)*, the Court held that it can only exercise judicial review when "some legal or constitutional question presents itself for judicial determination."[150] In *Rolling Mills v. Province of West Pakistan (1968)*, the Court found that "there was no present injury but a mere anticipation of a penal action by the Government, and hence it was held that this did not constitute a cause of action for invoking the writ jurisdiction of the Court.[151]

The Court altered this rule through its holding in *Bhutto*, asserting that if a law ex facia violates fundamental rights enumerated in the Constitution, then the parties challenging the law need not wait until they suffered an injury through the law's enforcement.[152] The Court found that establishing formal barriers to judicial review like ripeness would violate the "the object and intention of the framers of the Constitution," which was to "to keep the Fundamental Rights at a high pedestal and to save their enjoyment from legislative infractions."[153] Any governmental acts that would violate those fundamental rights are void ab initio, which is why citizens need not wait to suffer an actual injury to challenge those acts.

E. Political question doctrine

The political question doctrine has been used flexibly by the Supreme Court of Pakistan much like India, and unlike the United States. The Supreme Court of Pakistan is different from the United States in that the instinct in Pakistan's judiciary is to take on political cases rather than refuse to adjudicate them. In 1993, the Court acknowledged that it is not easy to determine whether a case presents a non-justiciable issue relating to a political question. However, the Court asserted that its "function is to enforce, preserve, protect and defend the Constitution," and it would exercise its judicial review power "irrespective of the fact that it is a political question" to address "any action taken, act done or policy framed which violates the provisions of the Constitution"[154] or any "abuse, excess or nonobservance" of the Constitution by governmental actors.

The Court has acknowledged that the political question doctrine was created in order to ensure the balance and separation of powers between branches of government,[155] which aligns with Professor Wechsler's theory[156] that the Supreme Court should only defer to the political branches when those branches have been given constitutional authority to control a certain subject.[157] If the subject of a case is not delegated to another branch in the Constitution, the Court can almost always exercise judicial review. In a similar vein, the Supreme Court of Pakistan has stated that:

> This "political question doctrine" is based on the respect for the Constitutional provisions relating to separation of powers among the organs of the State. But where in a case the Court has jurisdiction to exercise power of judicial review, *the fact that it involves [a] political question, cannot compel the Court to refuse its determination.*[158]

Stated more simply, "while exercising such powers, the Court will not abdicate its jurisdiction merely because the issue raised has a political complexion or political implication."[159]

The *Memogate* controversy is the most striking recent example of the Pakistani Supreme Court exercising its judicial review powers, in a case to which the U.S. Supreme Court would almost certainly deny writ of certiorari and defer to the decision-making of the political branches.[160] In this case, Pakistan's Ambassador to the United States allegedly sent a memo on behalf of the civilian government asking for the U.S. military to intervene and stop a potential military coup if it happened. The memo was challenged by political parties in Pakistan at the Supreme Court and the Ambassador was recalled to Islamabad. In the Court's view, the justiciability of the case would hinge on whether the Ambassador was working as a potentially treacherous rogue agent or was operating under the instruction of the ruling administration. If the latter were true, the case would be based on an administration's foreign-policy decisions, which would likely be deemed non-justiciable if presented before the United States Supreme Court. However, Pakistan's Supreme Court stated that along with the foreign policy issues, there were also issues relating to the fundamental rights of citizens that could be litigated if the accusations were true. Justice Jawad Khawaja wrote a concurring opinion, in which he concluded that:

> I would only add that the conduct of a government's foreign policy is indeed, by and large, a political question. But the fact is that the present petitions do not require us to devise the country's foreign policy or to direct the government in that regard. These petitions only seek to enforce the People's right to know the truth about what their government, and its functionaries, are up to. And that is by no means, a political question.[161]

Therefore, the rule from the *Memogate* decision seems to be that despite the fact that cases may pose political issues, this "cannot compel the Court to refuse its determination," and the Court must separate the legal from political issues and limit its decision to the legal issues raised by the plaintiff.[162]

The cumulative impact of the Pakistani Supreme Court's "slowly disappearing" restrictions of justiciability relating to standing, ripeness, and the political question doctrine is that "the Court has adjudicated upon all kinds of political, foreign policy, large scale law and order issues, economic matters, highly complicated policy issues and socio-cultural problems."[163] The limits on justiciability were especially ignored in the post-2009 tenure of Chief Justice Iftikhar Chaudhry, who is attributed with "a radical judicialization of the state and societal issues."[164] Since 2009, the Supreme Court has taken cognizance of "a broad swath of political questions,"[165] oftentimes through its use of the suo motu powers adopted by the Supreme Court of Pakistan.

F. Pendency and backlog

The Supreme Court of Pakistan publishes an annual report that lays out the rate of institution, disposal, and pendency of cases. In 2014, 18,000 cases were instituted, 16,000 were disposed of, and 22,000 cases were in pendency.[166] To compare, in 2002, 11,000 fresh cases were instituted, 8,000 were disposed of by the court, and there was a backlog of 14,000 cases.[167] The Court has predicted that it would take 14.8 months to remove the cases from the pendency list.[168] Along with the backlog on petitions for original jurisdiction, the Court currently is deciding around 3,000 appeals cases per year, with 4,000 new appeals being instituted and a backlog of 11,000.[169]

These figures do not take into account the separate work of the Human Rights Cell, which has a backlog of 19,000 petitions and receives nearly 90,000 new petitions each year.[170]

V. Conclusion

As explained in the first part of this study, the Supreme Courts of India and Pakistan were designed to be more active than their American counterpart. This difference can be found in the jurisprudence of the Supreme Courts of India and Pakistan,

Table 5.1 Comparative justiciability standards and statistics

	Pakistan	*India*	*United States*
Standards for the exercise of judicial review	– Matter of public importance – For the "enforcement of a fundamental right" – Supreme Court Chief Justice exercises suo motu powers to call parties to the court – Public interest litigation removes standing requirements	– Matter of public importance – For the "enforcement of a fundamental right" – Sufficient interest test – Public interest litigation removes standing requirements	– "Case or controversy" – Ripeness/Mootness – Standing – Political question doctrine
Procedure	– No formal procedure, judges decide internally with little room for rejecting petitions that would otherwise fail to meet justiciability standards	– Two days per week Court meets to conduct admissions hearings. Admission hearings "involve direct petitions and appeals to the Court" – The Court can dismiss the petition for lack of merit, issue a summary disposition with a final order, or refer the matter for oral hearing before another bench as a "regular matter"[171]	– One day per week the Court meets to determine which cases will be granted hearings through writ of certiorari – Rule of Four applies where if four justices agree the case presents a justiciable issue, it is scheduled to be litigated in front of the Court[172]
Petitions per year	18,000 (not including 1.2 million Human Rights Cell requests)[173]	47,000	8,000
Percentage of hearings granted	Most petitions are eventually scheduled for hearings[174]	15–26%[175]	1%
Disposal rate per year	16,000[176]	8,000	8,000
Number of cases in pendency	22,000[177]	64,000	Nearly 0

which have set flexible requirements for standing and justiciability. This has been justified not only through the Constitution empowering the Supreme Courts with expansive jurisdiction, but also on the Court's objective to provide justice to the masses, many of whom have historically lacked such access. Accordingly, while the

U.S. Supreme Court has created rigid limitations on justiciability, India and Pakistan have lowered standing requirements to allow more petitioners to seek relief at the Supreme Court. As a result, the Court in Pakistan lacks a substantive standard to use in order to critically examine its use of judicial review in a particular case.

The lack of a standard is exacerbated by the fact that unlike the Indian and American Supreme Courts, Pakistan's Court does not regularly meet as a group to filter petitions based on justiciability as depicted in Table 5.1. In the United States, the justices meet each week to determine which cases will be granted a writ of certiorari, with the Court taking only 1% of the cases. In India, the Supreme Court employs a similar strategy, meeting twice a week to discuss the justiciability of petitions, granting hearings to only 12% of petitions. Pakistan's Supreme Court lacks this weekly justiciability-assessment process and this can at least partially explain why the Court is often overworked. More significantly for the purposes of this study, the Court's failure to reject petitions challenging policy matters allows the Court to infringe on the territory of the Prime Minister or Parliament, which is prohibited under the Constitution's separation of powers doctrine.

The lack of standard and process has led to an excess of Supreme Court cases in Pakistan, with the Court struggling to keep pace with the rate of submissions while simultaneously attempting to conclude older cases. By comparatively examining the bifurcated justiciability-assessment procedures in India and the United States, the study attempts to contextualize the need for a standard and process, which will be proposed in Chapter 7. The proposed standard and process will take the American and Indian examples into account to provide Pakistan's Supreme Court with a method of providing justice while also respecting the boundaries of its power.

Notes

1 See generally H. W. Perry Jr, *Deciding to Decide: Agenda Setting in the United States Supreme Court* (1994).

2 Nick Robinson, *A Quantitative Analysis of the Indian Supreme Court's Workload*, 10 Journal of Empirical Legal Studies 570, at Table 11 (2013). Available at http://ssrn.com/abstract=2312974 or http://dx.doi.org/10.1111/jels.12020.

3 See Pakistan Supreme Court Rules (1980), Order V. ("The power of the Court in relation to the following matters may be exercised by a Single Judge, sitting in Chambers.")

4 Erwin Chemerinsky, *Constitutional Law: Principles and Policies* (4th ed., 2011), at 55 ("the standing requirement that a plaintiff demonstrate that he or she has suffered or imminently will suffer injury is crucial in determining whether there is an actual dispute that the federal courts can adjudicate.")

5 Id at 55. ("the mootness requirement states that federal courts should dismiss cases where there no long is an actual dispute between the parties, eve, though such a controversy might have existed at one time. ")

6 Id at 55. ("the ripeness doctrine determines whether a dispute has occurred yet or whether the case is still premature for review.")

7 *Flast v. Cohen*, 392 U.S. 83, 95 (1968).

8 Id.

9 Lea Brilmayer, *The Jurisprudence of Article III: Perspectives on the "Case or Controversy" Requirement*, 93 Harv. L. Rev. 297 at 297–98 (1979).

10 Id at 299.

11 *Abbott Labs. v. Gardner*, 387 U.S. 136, 148–49, 87 S. Ct. 1507, 1515, 18 L. Ed. 2d 681 (1967).
12 Alexander M. Bickel, *The Least Dangerous Branch: The Supreme Court at the Bar of Politics* (2nd ed., 1986), at 123–24.
13 Abbot Labs, *supra* note 11.
14 See Gene R. Nichol, Jr., *Ripeness and the Constitution*, 54 U. Chi. L. Rev. 153 (1987).
15 See Pakistan Const., art 186 and India Const. art. 143.
16 *North Carolina v. Rice*, 404 U.S. 244, 246, 92 S.Ct. 402, 404, 30 L.Ed.2d 413 (1971).
17 Chemerinsky, *supra* note 4, at 115.
18 Chemerinsky, *supra* note 4, at 115.
19 *DeFunis v. Odegaard*, 416 U.S. 312, 316, 94 S. Ct. 1704, 1705–06, 40 L. Ed. 2d 164 (1974).
20 Chemerinsky, *supra* note 4, at 114.
21 Id at 50. ("It must be emphasized that both constitutional and prudential limitations on justiciability are the product of Supreme Court decisions.")
22 Id, at 61. Citing Gene Nichol, Jr, *Abusing Standing: A Comment on Allen v. Wright*, 133 U. Pa. L. Rev. 635, 650 (1985); Mark Tushnet, *The New Law of Standing: A Plea for Abandonment*, 62 Cornell L. Rev. 663 (1977).
23 Id at 52.
24 *S. Pac. Terminal Co. v. Interstate Commerce Comm'n*, 219 U.S. 498, 515, 31 S. Ct. 279, 282, 55 L. Ed. 310 (1911).
25 *Roe v. Wade*, 410 US 113 (1973).
26 Chemerinsky, *supra* note 4, at 50. ("Each of these justiciability doctrines was created and articulated by the United States Supreme Court. Neither the text of the Constitution, nor the framers in drafting the document, expressly mentioned an of these limitations on judicial power.")
27 Linda Sandstrom Simard, *Standing Alone: Do We Still Need the Political Question Doctrine?* 100 Dick. L. Rev. 303, 304 (1996). ("Rather, the Court has relied heavily upon separation of powers principles to interpret the requirements of standing. Thus, the adoption of the causation and redressability elements and the incorporation of separation of powers principles have broadened the reach of standing and made judicial review more restrictive.")
28 *Frothingham v. Mellon*, 262 U.S. 447 (1923), at 488.
29 *Lujan v. Defenders of Wildlife*, 504 U.S. 555 (1992), at 576.
30 Id.
31 There are exceptions to this rule in the United States that allow for "third party standing"; see Gwendolyn McKee, *Standing on a Spectrum: Third Party Standing in the United States, Canada, and Australia*, 16 Barry L. Rev. 115 (2011). McKee explains that taxpayers can have standing to challenge a Congressional violation of the Taxing or Spending Clause in relation to the Establishment Clause, Id at 121. See *Flast v. Cohen*, 392 U.S. 83 (1968) and *Hein v. Freedom from Religion Foundation, Inc.*, 551 U.S. 587 (2007). Further, third party standing can be granted in challenges that a law is overbroad, especially in relation to freedom of speech or abortion rights.
32 Brilmayer, *supra* note 9, at 308.
33 *Marbury v. Madison*, 5 U.S. (1 Cranch) 137, 170 (1803).
34 Gwynne Skinner, *Misunderstood, Misconstrued, and Now Clearly Dead: The "Political Question Doctrine" as a Justiciability Doctrine*, 29 J.L. & Pol. 427, 456 (2014).
35 Stephen R. Alton, *From Marbury v. Madison to Bush v. Gore: 200 Years of Judicial Review in the United States*, 8 Tex. Wesleyan L. Rev. 7, 26 (2001). ("Recall that one of the major disputes about judicial review centered around the proper role of an unelected judiciary in a democracy.")
36 *Baker v. Carr*, 369 U.S. 186 (1962).
37 Id.

38 Skinner, *supra* note 34, at 430.
39 Martin H. Redish, *Judicial Review and the 'Political Question'*, 79 Nw. U. L. Rev. 1031 (1984).
40 See Rachel E. Barkow, *More Supreme Than Court? The Fall of the Political Question Doctrine and the Rise of Judicial Supremacy*, 102 Colum. L. Rev. 237 (2002) and Skinner, *supra* note 34.
41 Skinner, *supra* note 34, at 431.
42 Redish, *supra* note 39, at 1032.
43 Bickel, *supra* note 12, at 184.
44 Herbert Wechsler, *Toward Neutral Principles of Constitutional Law*, 73 Harv. L. Rev. 1, 6–9 (1959)
45 Skinner, *supra* note 34, at 431.
46 Alton, *supra* note 35, at 26.
47 See Id.
48 *Bush v. Gore*, 531 U.S. 98, at 153.
49 Barkow, *supra* note 40, at 336. ("Whatever one thinks of the Bush cases on their merits, the Court's belief that it had a constitutional duty to decide the cases before the state and federal political branches even had a chance to weigh in on the questions – let alone conclusively resolve them – is disconcerting. It belies a level of judicial immodesty that threatens to undermine the delicate constitutional balance of power. Thus, while the Supreme Court has made much of its role in preserving and protecting the separation of powers, it is blind to its own aggrandizement at the expense of the other branches.")
50 Perry Jr, *supra* note 1, at 22.
51 William Howard Taft, *Three Needed Steps of Progress*, 8 A.B.A.J. 34 (Address to the Chicago Bar Association) (Jan. 1922).
52 Id.
53 William Rehnquist, *The 2003 Year-End Report on the Federal Judiciary*. Available at www.supremecourt.gov/publicinfo/year-end/2003year-endreport.aspx (last accessed on Oct. 17, 2016).
54 Perry Jr, *supra* note 1, at 42.
55 Manoj S. Mate, *The Variable Power of Courts: The Expansion of the Power of the Supreme Court of India in Fundamental Rights and Governance Decisions* (2010) (University of California, Berkley) Available at http://escholarship.org/uc/item/3f1640wm (last accessed on Oct. 31, 2016), at 10, Footnote 11.
56 James F. Fagan, Jr., *When Does Four of a Kind Beat a Full House? The Rise, Fall and Replacement of the Rule of Four*, 25 New Eng. L. Rev. 1101, 1105–06 (1991). ("Whether to grant a petition for writ of certiorari is determined by a rule of four, that is, the vote of at least four Justices to grant such writ.")
57 Perry Jr, *supra* note 1, at 42.
58 William H. Rehnquist, *The Supreme Court* (Rev Upd ed., 2002), at 233.
59 Perry Jr, *supra* note 1, at 43.
60 Id.
61 Id at 22.
62 2003 Year End Report, *supra* note 53.
63 Rehnquist, *supra* note 58, at 233
64 Kermit L. Hall, James W. Ely & Joel B. Grossman, *The Oxford Companion to the Supreme Court of the United States* (2005), at 155.
65 Id.
66 Eugene Gressman, et al., *Supreme Court Practice* (2007), at 262. ("The importance of the issues involved in the case as to which review is sought is of major significance in determining whether the writ of certiorari will issue.")
67 *Supreme Court of India: Practice & Procedure (A Handbook of Information)*, (3rd ed., 2010.) at 11.

68 Id at 14. Citing India Const., arts 32 and 131.
69 India Const., arts 132, 133 and 134 (establishing general appeals from High Court judgments that involve a substantial question of law concerning the interpretation of the constitution. Statutory Appeals are included in various statutes like Pak. Code Crim. Proc, Sec. 370 and Customs Act (Pak.) Section 130E, etc. Appeals by special leave are enumerated in Article 136 of the Constitution of India.)
70 *Constitutional Law of South Africa*, (Stuart Woolman ed., 2nd Revised & enlarged ed.) (2008). Cheryl Loots, Chapter 8: Access to the Courts and Justiciability.
71 *Id.*
72 *Fertilizer Corporation Kamgar Union (Regd.) Sindri v. Union of India*, 1981 AIR 344, 1981 SCR (2) 52. (India)
73 Hon'ble Mr. K.G. Balakrishnan, Chief Justice of India, Address at the Trinity College of Dublin. (Oct. 14, 2009).
74 Constitutional Law of South Africa, *supra* note 70.
75 *S.P. Gupta v. President of India and ORS.* AIR 1982 SC 149, 1981 Supp (1) SCC 87, 1982 2 SCR 365 (India).
76 Constitutional Law of South Africa, *supra* note 70.
77 Gupta, *supra* note 75, at 30.
78 See generally *Dr. D.C. Wadhwa & ORS v. State of Bihar & ORS*, 1987 AIR 579, 1987 SCR (1) 798 (1986). (India).
79 Balakrishnan, *supra* note 73.
80 Pratap Bhanu Metha, *The Rise of Judicial Sovereignty*, 18 J. Democracy 70 (2007) at 71.
81 Surya Deva, *Public Interest Litigation in India: A Critical Review*, 28 Civ. Justice Q. 1 (2009), at 33.
82 Id at 28.
83 Mate, *supra* note 55.
84 *A. K. Roy, Etc v. Union of India and ANR*, 1982 AIR 710, 1982 SCR (2) 272 (India).
85 Rekha Kumari R Singh, *An Analytical and Critical Study on Judicial Activism vis vis Judicial Overreach With Respect to Legislative Function of the Indian Parliament* (Veer Narmad South Gujarat University) (2015) at 124.
86 *Ram Jawaya Kapur v. State of Punjab*, AIR 1955 SC 549. (India). ("The Indian Constitution has indeed not recognized the doctrine of separation of powers in its absolute rigidity. . . [however] it can very well be said that our Constitution does not contemplate assumption, by one organ or part of the state, of functions that essentially belong to another.")
87 *Gurudevdatta VKSSS Maryadit & ORS v. State of Maharashtra & ORS*, AIR 2001 SC 1980 (India).
88 *A. K. Roy, Etc v. Union of India and ANR* 1982 AIR 710, 1982 SCR (2) 272 (1981) (India). Citing *Constitutional Law of India* (2nd ed., Volume III pages 1795 and 1797).
89 Singh, *supra* note 85, at 130.
90 *Asif Hamid v. State of Jammu and Kashmir* (1989) AIR (SC) 1899. (India).
91 *Marydit*, *supra* note 87.
92 Id.
93 *I. C. Golaknath & ORS v. State of Punjab & ANRS*, 1967 AIR 1643, 1967 SCR (2) 762 (India).
94 Id.
95 Mate, *supra* note 55, at 13.
96 Id.
97 See Supreme Court (Number of Judges) Amendment Act 2008, Bill 41 of 2008. Available at www.prsindia.org/uploads/media/1209532839/1209532839_The_Supreme_Court__Number_of_Judges__Amendment_Bill__2008.pdf (last accessed on Oct. 17, 2016). (There are now 31 justices serving on the Supreme Court of India)

98 Mate, *supra* note 55, at 14. ("The Central government responded by increasing the number of judges on the bench from 8 in 1950 to 11 in 1956, 14 in 1960, 18 in 1978 and 26 in 1986. . . As the Court expanded in size, judges increasingly adjudicated matters, even politically significant ones, in smaller benches of 2 or 3 judges, with higher rates of unanimous decisions.")
99 Id.
100 Id.
101 Id.
102 Id.
103 Pratap Bhanu Mehta, *The Oxford Handbook of the Indian Constitution* (2016), at 414.
104 Robinson, *supra* note 2, at 573.
105 *Asma Jilani v. Government of Punjab* (1972) 139 PLD (SC) (Pak.)
106 This decision was based on the 1956 Constitution, which mirrors the language of the 1973 Constitution, making the analysis valid for the subsequent constitution.
107 *Province of East Pakistan v. Mehdi Ali Khan* (1959) 387 PLD (SC) (Pak.) Available at www.uniset.ca/islamicland/PLD1959SCPak387.html (last accessed on Dec. 27, 2016).
108 *Benazir Bhutto v. Federation of Pakistan* (1998) 416 PLD (SC) (Pak.)
109 *Darshan Masih v State* (1990) 513 PLD (SC) (Pak.)
110 Jona Razzaque, *Public Interest Environmental Litigation in India, Pakistan, and Bangladesh* (2004), at 27–8.
111 *Bhutto*, *supra* note 108.
112 Pakistan Const., art.184(3) ("Original Jurisdiction of Supreme Court. ("Without prejudice to the provisions of Article 199, the Supreme Court shall, if it considers that a question of public importance with reference to the enforcement of any of the Fundamental Rights conferred by Chapter I of Part II is involved have the power to make an order of the nature mentioned in the said Article.")
113 *Bhutto*, *supra* note 108.
114 Id.
115 Id.
116 *Medhi v. Pakistan International Airlines Corp* (1998) 793 PLD (SC) (Pak.) Available at Wen Chen Chang, Li-ann Thio, Kevin Y.L. Tan & Jiunn-rong Yeh, *Constitutionalism in Asia: Cases and Materials* (2014), at 254.
117 Moeen Cheema & Ijaz Shafi Gilani, *The Politics and Jurisprudence of the Chaudhry Court 2005–2013* (2015), at 84. Faisal Siddiqi, Chapter 3, Public Interest Litigation: Predictable Continuity and Radical Departures.
118 Id.
119 Maryam S. Khan, *Genesis and Evolution of Public Interest Litigation in the Supreme Court of Pakistan, Toward a Dynamic Theory of Judicialization*, 28 Temp. J. Intl. & Comp. L. 284 (2015).
120 Id at 286–7.
121 Id a.
122 Moeen Cheema & Ijaz Shafi Gilani, *The Politics and Jurisprudence of the Chaudhry Court 2005–2013* (2015). Asher A. Qazi, Chapter 9: Suo Motu: Choosing Not to Legislate Chief Justice Chaudhry's Strategic
123 Masih, *supra* note 109.
124 Cheema & Gilani, *supra* note 122, at 286.
125 Id.
126 Id at Footnote 12.
127 Id at 289.
128 Id at 290.
129 Id at 289.
130 See generally, Nirupama Subramanian, *In Clash of Institutions, Pakistan's Supreme Court Sets the Pace*, The Hindu, Apr. 4, 2012. Available at www.thehindu.com/

opinion/op-ed/in-clash-of-institutions-pakistans-supreme-court-sets-the-pace/article2858006.ece (last accessed on Oct. 17, 2017).

131 For suo motu decisions by Chief Justices Jilani, and Nasir ul-Mulk see Sabir Shah, *History of Voluntary Court Initiatives in Pakistan, India, US,* The News, Aug. 25, 2015. Available at www.thenews.com.pk/print/58421-history-of-voluntary-court-initiatives-in-pakistan-india-us (last accessed on May 23, 2016).

132 *Dossani Travels v. Federation of Pakistan*, Civil Appeal Nos 800-L, 801-L & 802-L OF 2013 & Civil Petition Nos 1148/2013 & 1348/2013. (SC) (Pak.)

133 Nasir Iqbal, *SC Urged to Regulate Use of suo motu Powers*, Dawn, Apr. 20, 2014. Available at www.dawn.com/news/1100999 (last accessed on May 23, 2016).

134 Supreme Court of Pakistan, Annual Report 2010–2011, Available at www.supremecourt.gov.pk/Annual_Rpt/Human%20Rights%20Cell.pdf (last accessed on Oct. 17, 2016), at 129.

135 Id.

136 Id.

137 Press Briefing of District General for the Human Rights Cell, Supreme Court of Pakistan, Feb. 20, 2014. Available at www.supremecourt.gov.pk/web/user_files/File/pb_dg_hrcell_dt_20.02.2014.pdf (last accessed on Oct. 17, 2016).

138 Cheema & Gilani, *supra* note 117, at 85.

139 Cheema & Gilani, *supra* note 122, at 293–94.

140 Menski, Werner, Alam, R. & Raza, *Public interest in litigation in Pakistan* (2000). ("[the] Supreme Court has decided [in], *Shahida Zahir Abbasi v. President of Pakistan* (1996) PLD (SC) 632 (Pak.), at 659, per Saiduzzaman Siddiqui J, that matters of public importance may be deduced on a case-by-case basis . . . However, even on a case-by-case basis, some general principles still emerge.")

141 Cheema & Gilani, *supra* note 122, at 293–94.

142 Pakistan Supreme Court Rules, 1980, Order III, Article 10a.

143 Id at Order III, Article 9.

144 Id at Order V, Article 5

145 Id at Order V, Article 2

146 Id at Order V, Article 2

147 Id at Order XXVI, Article 9.

148 Id at Order XXIII, Article 4.

149 Cheema & Gilani, *supra* note 122, at 293–94. ("[The Supreme Court] conventionally . . . grants an oral hearing to most, if not all, appeals and petitions fixed before it. It should thus come as no surprise that even as a court of 17 justices hears various cases in smaller benches of three judges or at times only two judges, it may take years before a particular action is heard.")

150 *Hakim Muhammad Anwar Babri v. Pakistan* (1973) 817 PLD (Lah.) (Pak.).

151 *Bhutto, supra* note 108. (Explaining the holding in Rolling Mills v. Province of West Pakistan (1968) 318 SCMR (SC) (Pak.).

152 Id.

153 Id.

154 Muhammad Nawaz Sharif v. Federation of Pakistan (1993) 433 PLD (SC) (Pak.) Available at https://pakistanconstitutionlaw.com/p-l-d-1993-sc-473/

155 Watan Party and Others v. Federation of Pakistan and Others (2012) 292 PLD (SC) (Pak.) at 59–60. Available at www.supremecourt.gov.pk/web/user_files/File/Const.P.77-78-79%20[Memogate]DetailedOrder.pdf (last accessed Oct. 16, 2016). ("This 'political question doctrine' is based on the respect for the Constitutional provisions relating to separation of powers among the organs of the State.")

156 See Herbert Wechsler, *Toward Neutral Principles of Constitutional Law*, 73 Harv. L. Rev. 1, 9 (1959). ("[T]he only proper judgment that may lead to an abstention from decision is that the Constitution has committed the determination of the issue to another agency of government than the courts.")

157 Id.
158 *Watan Party*, *supra* note 155, at 59.
159 Id.
160 Id.
161 Id at 4. (Justice Jawad S. Khawaja's concurring opinion.)
162 Id at 59–60.
163 Cheema & Gilani, *supra* note 117, at 86.
164 Id at 99.
165 Khan, *supra* note 119, at 286–7.
166 Pakistan Supreme Court Annual Report, 2014–2015. Available at www.supremecourt.gov.pk/links/sc-a-rpt-2014-15/index.html (last accessed on Oct. 17, 2016).
167 Id at 112–14.
168 Id at 113.
169 Id at 112.
170 Press Briefing, *supra* note 137.
171 Mate, *supra* note 55, at 14.
172 Fagan, Jr., *supra* note 56, at 1105–6. ("Whether to grant a petition for writ of certiorari is determined by a rule of four, that is, the vote of at least four Justices to grant such writ.")
173 Annual Report, *supra* note 166, at 113.
174 Cheema & Gilani, *supra* note 111, at 293–94. ("[The Supreme Court] conventionally . . . grants an oral hearing to most, if not all, appeals and petitions fixed before it. It should thus come as no surprise that even as a court of 17 justices hears various cases in smaller benches of three judges or at times only two judges, it may take years before a particular action is heard.")
175 Robinson, *supra* note 2, at 590. ("one finds that since 1996 the Court's acceptance rate of admission matters has been between 15% and 26%.")
176 Annual Report, *supra* note 166, at 113.
177 Id.

6 Executive disqualification and judicial review

I. Introduction

In order to understand the practical power-sharing relationship between the judiciary and the executive branch, one must understand judicial involvement in disqualification or impeachment proceedings for the executive. This has differed drastically between the United States, India, and Pakistan. The cases of *Gilani*,[1] *Nixon v. United States*,[2] and *Indira Gandhi v. Raj Narian*[3] demonstrate a difference between the relative restraint exercised by the Supreme Courts of India and the United States when it comes to removing prime ministers or presidents, and the hyper-activism of Pakistan's Supreme Court in 2012.

At the height of Pakistan's Supreme Court's hyper-activity, the Court took suo motu notice of a contempt of court case against Prime Minister Yousaf Raza Gilani, who was accused of refusing to implement a Supreme Court order.[4] Though the Court had the right to hold the Prime Minister in contempt of court, the right to disqualify the Prime Minister was constitutionally delegated to the Speaker of the House. However, when the Speaker of the House refused to disqualify Gilani after his conviction for contempt of court, the Court unilaterally demanded the retroactive ouster of Prime Minister Gilani in a short order.[5] This came as the final straw in a long-running conflict between the judiciary and the executive branch and demonstrated an overreach by the Court that could potentially impact future jurisprudence if left unexamined.[6] The judgment of this case was reaffirmed in 2017 when the Supreme Court formed a Joint Investigation Team to investigate allegations that Prime Minister Nawaz Sharif and his family were engaged in tax evasion and corruption.[7]

In comparison, the Supreme Court of India overturned a 1975 decision by the High Court of Allahabad[8] that convicted then-Prime Minister Indira Gandhi of election fraud and banned her from Parliament for six years.[9] Immediately after the High Court decision, Gandhi imposed emergency rule, suspended all fundamental rights, and passed a constitutional amendment that eliminated the jurisdiction of the judiciary in election matters concerning the Prime Minister.[10] The case was then submitted to the Supreme Court which established a compromise: the justices invalidated Gandhi's criminal conviction, allowing the Prime Minister to finish her term in office,[11] while also invalidating her administration's constitutional amendment that eliminated the jurisdiction of the judiciary in election matters. The Court overturned the Amendment as the justices concluded that it violated the basic structure of India's Constitution, which guarantees judicial independence.[12]

The United States Supreme Court did not deal with the possible removal of President Richard Nixon, but focused on whether presidential immunity could be applied to suppress certain audio tapes after they were subpoenaed by the Special Prosecutor for use by a grand jury.[13] It is important to note that unlike in Pakistan, there was no petitioner in Nixon that requested for the Court to unilaterally remove or impeach President Nixon. This allowed the U.S. Court to concentrate on the much narrower legal question and avoid a discussion of the impeachment duties constitutionally delegated to the Senate.[14] Accordingly, the U.S. Supreme Court never attempted to unilaterally remove an elected President, not unlike the Indian Supreme Court's treatment of Prime Minister Gandhi.

The Supreme Courts of the United States and India exercised relative restraint when faced with the possibility of disqualifying or impeaching a potentially corrupt president or prime minister, while Pakistan's Supreme Court involved itself in this politically sensitive topic. By unilaterally disqualifying the Prime Minister, the Supreme Court of Pakistan endangered its own credibility by appearing to disrupt Pakistan's fragile democratic administration, rather than acting cooperatively with Parliament as designated by the Constitution.[15]

This chapter will explore the reasons for the unwillingness of the Supreme Courts of the United States and India to engage in unilateral removal of a sitting chief executive in relation to the practical use of judicial review and power in the modern era. There are connections between the restraint doctrines described in Chapter 5 and the reasoning in these cases. A comparison of the *Gilani, Gandhi*, and *Nixon* cases demonstrates the need for Pakistan's Supreme Court to structuralize and restrain its judicial review process, especially when it relates to the disqualification of a democratically elected prime minister.

The deference shown to the legislature by the Supreme Courts of India and the United States when dealing with the impeachment of the chief executive is the product of jurisprudence that restrains a country's Supreme Court from infringing on the constitutionally delegated duties of the other branches. With the proper structure, the Supreme Court of Pakistan could rightly refuse to review cases that involve matters of impeachment or disqualification, which are best left to elected officials and the democratic will of the electorate. At the same time, emulating the position of India and the United States Supreme Court, the Supreme Court of Pakistan could set out a position to exercise judicial review over narrow legal questions that are tangentially related to the impeachment proceedings.

II. Pakistan

A. Timeline of events for Prime Minister Gilani's disqualification

The timeline for the events leading up to Prime Minister Gilani's disqualification by Pakistan's Supreme Court is complex, as can be seen in Figure 6.1. Gilani was

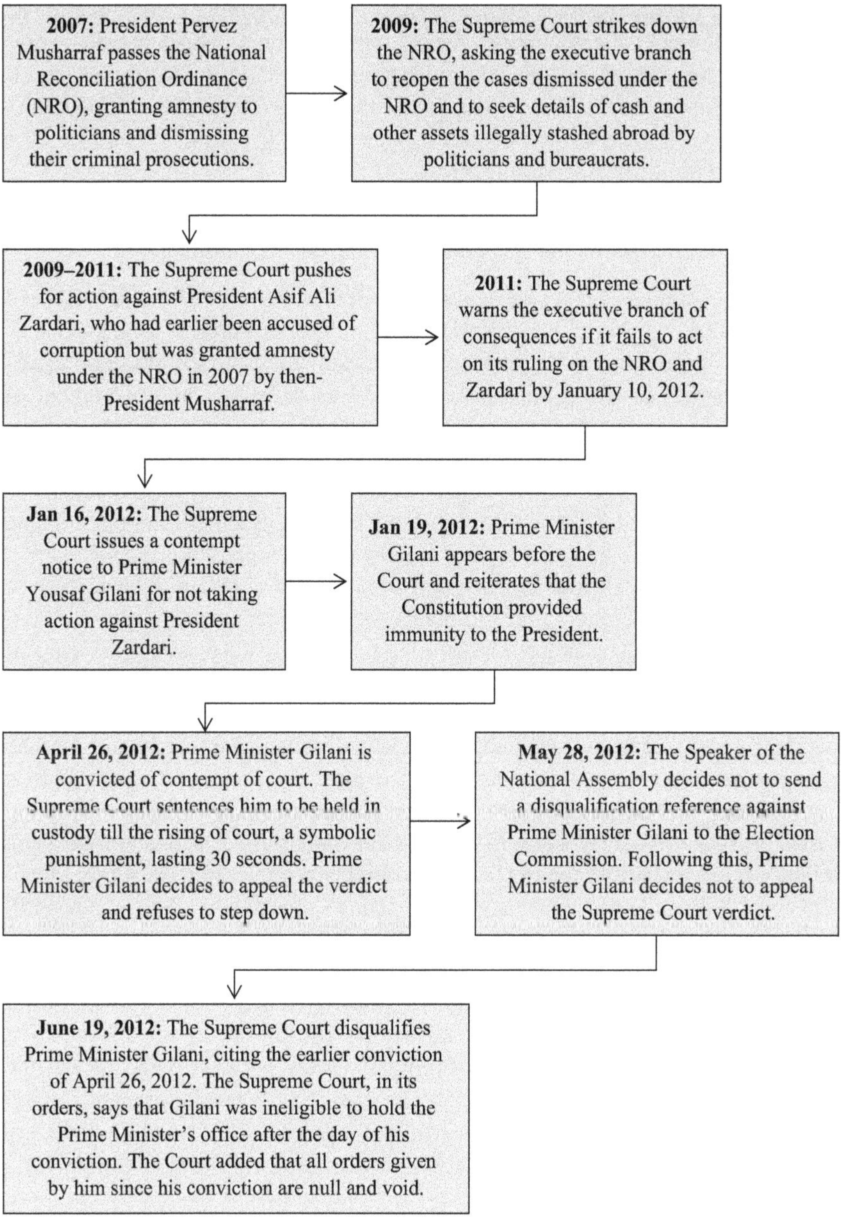

Figure 6.1 Events leading to Prime Minister Gilani's removal

held in contempt of court for refusing to implement a Supreme Court order to reopen a money laundering case against President Asif Ali Zardari in Switzerland.[16] President Zardari was alleged to have engaged in corrupt criminal acts in 1998, but his case was one of the thousands that were dismissed through the passage of the National Reconciliation Ordinance (NRO). The Supreme Court invalidated this Ordinance and called upon the Gilani administration to reopen criminal cases against beneficiaries of the NRO. In order to understand Prime Minister Gilani's refusal to implement the Court's order, and the Court's response of unilaterally dismissing the Prime Minister, one must understand the domino effect of events that started with the passage of the NRO.

B. President Zardari and the National Reconciliation Ordinance

Switzerland initiated a legal case against President Zardari in 1997 when "Geneva judicial authorities" began investigating allegations that Zardari "took kickbacks from Swiss cargo inspection companies and channeled some $12 million via offshore companies in Swiss bank accounts."[17] Subsequently, the government of Pakistan asked Swiss authorities to "be made a civil party in those proceedings so that in the event the payments of commissions and kickbacks were proven the amount be returned to the Government of Pakistan being its rightful claimant."[18] However, "Pakistan did not pursue corruption allegations against Zardari at home after Pakistan's Supreme Court in 2001 annulled a 1999 conviction against him."[19]

Zardari's other legal cases in Pakistan were later dismissed after the passage of the 2007 National Reconciliation Ordinance (NRO) under the presidency and military rule of Pervez Musharraf. The NRO automatically dismissed "thousands of criminal cases including corruption charges" against many key politicians, including Zardari.[20] The stated purpose of the NRO was to dismiss politically motivated criminal cases that were originally pursued to weaken politicians and thereby strengthen military rule. However, because the NRO granted "immunity to a number of PPP (Pakistan People's Party) leaders from long-standing corruption cases," it was viewed by some as a political power-sharing agreement between military (i.e. Musharraf) and the leading political party (i.e. PPP) in which Musharraf would "be allowed to serve another term as president while . . . [the PPP] would be enabled to contest relatively free and fair general elections and form the next government if successful."[21]

However, this political compromise was challenged before the Supreme Court, which reviewed the NRO in 2009 and held it void ab initio, or void from its creation.[22] There were several constitutional issues with the NRO. First, the law substituted "the judicial forum with an executive authority granted blanket immunity"; it was "contrary to the principle of the independence of the judiciary mentioned in Article 2A of the Constitution."[23] Stated differently, by granting a blanket immunity, the NRO deprived the Supreme Court of its right to deal with criminal suspects on a case-by-case basis. Secondly, the Supreme Court held that the NRO violated the principle of equality among citizens, as only leading political figures were able to have criminal cases dismissed, while other citizens did not have that option.

For the reasons laid out above and others set out by the Supreme Court, in 2009, the Supreme Court ordered the reopening of all criminal corruption cases, including the case against Zardari, who had become President of the nation in

2008.[24] The impact of the decision was substantial: "with legal cover stripped away from the unpopular president, and more than 248 officials barred from leaving the country, the government was thrown into chaos."[25]

C. Non-implementation of Supreme Court's NRO verdict

The manner of reopening the cases was left to the executive branch, led by the Prime Minister, whose affected subordinates involved the Law Minister and Attorney General.[26] Despite the Court's order, none of these individuals or institutions moved towards reopening the case against Zardari. Prime Minister Gilani explained that despite the Supreme Court's NRO judgment, his understanding was that any currently serving President was entitled to immunity[27] according to Article 284 of the Constitution.[28] Some alleged that there was an inherent conflict of interest that would prevent the Prime Minister from prosecuting the President, as both men were from the same political party (PPP). In fact, President Zardari was the de facto leader of the PPP, while Gilani was a more junior member, so the President could practically order the Prime Minister to continually refuse implementation of the Supreme Court's order based on the power of his higher position in the party structure.[29]

While it is unclear whether Gilani faced intra-party pressure to refrain from prosecuting the President, it became evident that he would not implement the Supreme Court's decision. This led to Chief Justice Iftiqar Chaudry exercising suo motu jurisdiction, and a seven-member bench framed a charge against Gilani for contempt of court.[30] Through a short order on April 26, 2012, Gilani "was convicted under Article 204(2)[31] of the Constitution read with section 3 of the Contempt of Court Ordinance, 2003[32] and sentenced under section 5 of the Ordinance to undergo imprisonment till rising of the Court."[33] The symbolic imprisonment lasted thirty seconds.

D. Supreme Court overrides constitutional provision for disqualification of Prime Minister

In its original decision, the Supreme Court did not consider whether this contempt of court conviction would automatically disqualify Gilani from serving in Parliament because the Constitution leaves the disqualification decision to the National Assembly and its Speaker. The Constitution of Pakistan does not designate a specific process for disqualifying or impeaching the Prime Minister. Rather, the Prime Minister is subject to the same disqualification procedure as any other member of the national Parliament. Along with the Speaker, the Election Commission of Pakistan could initiate an investigation and recommend the Prime Minister's disqualification from Parliament.

According to Article 63 of Pakistan's Constitution, the Prime Minister, as a member of the Parliament, can be disqualified on the following grounds:

> (g) he has been convicted by a court of competent jurisdiction for propagating any opinion, or acting in any manner, prejudicial to the ideology of

> Pakistan, or the sovereignty, integrity or security of Pakistan, or the integrity or independence of the judiciary of Pakistan, or which defames or brings into ridicule the judiciary or the Armed Forces of Pakistan, unless a period of five years has elapsed since his release; or h) he has been, on conviction for any offence involving moral turpitude, sentenced to imprisonment for a term of not less than two years, unless a period of five years has elapsed since his release.[34]

The decision to begin the disqualification proceedings against the Prime Minister is vested in the Speaker of the National Assembly according to Article 63(2) of the Constitution. The Speaker of the National Assembly "shall, unless he decides that no such question has arisen, refer the question to the Election Commission within thirty days," and if the Election Commission finds grounds for disqualification, the Prime Minister "shall cease to be a member and his seat shall become vacant."[35]

In Gilani's case, on May 24, 2012, Speaker Fehmida Mirza announced that she saw no grounds for disqualifying the Prime Minister.[36] Many believed the matter should have ended there, according to the Constitution, as the Election Commission was not invoked by the Speaker. However, in response to the Speaker's refusal, the Supreme Court passed an order on June 19, 2012 that

> declared that Syed Yousaf Raza Gillani *had become disqualified* from being a Member of the Majlis-e-Shoora (Parliament) in terms of Article 63(1)(g) of the Constitution on and *from the date and time of pronouncement of the judgment of this Court dated 26.04.2012* with all consequences, i.e. *he also ceased to be the Prime Minister of Pakistan with effect from the said date and the office of* ***the Prime Minister shall be deemed to be vacant accordingly.*** The Election Commission of Pakistan was required to issue notification of disqualification of Syed Yousaf Raza Gillani from being a Member of the Majlis-e-Shoora (Parliament) with effect from 26.4.2012.[37]
>
> (emphasis added)

This judgment was lauded by some as a check on corruption in Pakistan's top-most political ranks,[38] but other commenters termed the decision as a "legal coup."[39] As Rasjee Jatlee points out, "the judgment raised questions about the powers of the executive, the sovereignty of Parliament and the role of the judiciary . . . and created immediate political ripples for the beleaguered government."[40]

E. Critics of the Court emerge

In the aftermath of the decision, three kinds of critiques emerged from jurists and legal experts. The first set of complaints was about the problem with unelected justices on the Court circumventing the democratic will of the people, whose embodiment was the duly elected Prime Minister. Chaudhry's defenders argued that the Chief Justice and other judges who led the Lawyers' Movement[41] embodied the public will: "the entire basis of judicial power and legitimacy went through a radical transformation from judicial power being based only on constitutional guarantees of security of tenure and moral legitimacy to *judicial power being based on public legitimacy*" (emphasis added).[42]

While Chaudhry's decisions generally increased the Court's public profile and credibility, some cautioned that Chaudhry should have exercised restraint in this case. Saroop Ijaz pointed out that the Supreme Court "should be cognizant that, even relying on their own deepest convictions, they may err, especially when the decisions entails overturning the consensus of the people."[43] Others, like Supreme Court Bar President Asma Jahagir, argued that the decision by the Court set a very dangerous precedent as it is " 'not a good tradition to disqualify the prime minister under Article 63,' and that no Prime Minister would survive in future if that same tradition continued."[44] Dr. Hasan Askari Rizvi explained that the decision damaged Pakistan's tumultuous democratic history as "once again, non-elected institutions are trying to re-formulate the elected institutions . . . previously the military was doing it, now it is the judiciary."[45]

Further reviewing the Court's legal reasoning, Dr. Osama Siddique concluded that the case was a "non-starter" during which the

> Chaudhry Court consistently skirted around the clear-cut immunity . . . persisted and eventually sent one Prime Minister packing in 2012 by holding him in contempt for not doing what it thought required to pursue the case; [and] came close to also bringing down his successor.[46]

The second set of complaints related to how the judgment "weakened democratic institutions"[47] by strengthening the military. As described in Chapter 4, Pakistan's fourth branch of government, the military, has continually projected the narrative of corrupt or inept politicians to justify military coups. As Najam Sethi explained, the continual embarrassment of the executive by the Supreme Court under Chief Justice Chaudhry served "the Army's purposes" because the Army wanted "the politicians to fight amongst themselves and remain discredited."[48] Such infighting could facilitate the military solidifying "its control over foreign policy and national security, and limits the civilian government's attempts to control the military."[49]

The third complaint about the judgement was that it failed to demonstrate judicial impartiality: "there is also concern that the judiciary 'may have implicitly played politics by trying to determine not just the legal issues but to influence the preferred political outcome in Pakistan'."[50] Moeen Cheema explains that

> the Supreme Court appeared to be playing a significant role in undermining the electoral prospects of the incumbent government. In a whole host of cases, including most prominently the NRO saga the court had brought issues of governmental corruption to the forefront and helped shape a narrative of failures of governance.[51]

It is important to note that many of the petitioners requesting to have the NRO stricken and Zardari cases reopened were political opposition parties such as the Watan Party, Pakistan's Tehreek-i-Insaaf, and Pakistan Muslim League (Nawaz). All these parties stood to gain political power and votes in the subsequent election if the Supreme Court continued to embarrass the PPP's executive regime, which should have raised red flags for the Supreme Court in assessing the justiciability of their purely political claims. Ironically, five years following this decision, Nawaz Sharif himself was disqualified by the Court after his main political opponent was able to successfully petition the Supreme Court for his removal.

F. Legitimacy lost by the Court

The damage was not limited to the PPP administration under President Zardari and Prime Minister Gilani. In fact, the Court damaged much of its own "credibility and public perception" as "the more prominent High Court and Supreme Court bar associations became increasingly critical of the exercise of judicial power and accused the court of having over-stepped its constitutional bounds thereby intruding on the domain of the executive."[52]

The critique of the Chaudhry Court went beyond the *Gilani* case as "the post 2009 judiciary has increasingly been ridiculed and criticized for its apparent overreach into political questions which have historically been considered to be the exclusive domain of the political executive."[53] By its actions, the Supreme Court

- i destabilized the relationship between the judiciary and executive,
- ii weakened a democratically elected government allowing the military to expand its control over policy-making,
- iii skirted the constitutionally designated disqualification process for the Prime Minister, and
- iv diminished public support for Supreme Court judicial review.

The absence of an effective justiciability standard allowed the Chief Justice of the Supreme Court to lead the apex court into questionable political scenarios, although some scholars have rejected a binary view of non-justiciable political questions and justiciable legal questions.[54]

G. Nawaz Sharif and Panamagate

Despite the overall restraint exercised by successors to Chief Justice Chaudhry, the Gilani decision was reaffirmed in 2017 when the Supreme Court took up petitions against Prime Minister Nawaz Sharif. Starting in 2014, allegations surfaced that Prime Minister Sharif illegally used government funds and evaded taxes, which resulted in protestors calling for his resignation.[55] These allegations were based on information disclosed in the Panama Papers, which were leaked documents that exposed thousands of politicians globally for owning off-shore accounts and possessing illicit funds.[56] The revelations resulted in Prime Minister Nawaz Sharif "being asked to account for the sources of income that have allowed his family members to buy expensive property in London."[57] Critics raised concerns about how the Sharif family "made enough money for Sharif's children to set up large offshore companies in 1993 and 1994," especially when "Sharif's political career was booming at the time."[58] In response, Sharif attempted to form an inquiry commission led by a former Supreme Court justice. However, when asked to legitimize this commission, the Chief Justice of the Supreme Court refused to accept the formation of a "toothless commission."[59]

As a result, the leading political opposition party (Pakistan Tehreek-i-Insaaf, or PTI) filed a petition calling for the Supreme Court to disqualify the Prime Minister for corruption. The party's leader stated, "I don't think the Supreme Court will deviate from its earlier judgments, wherein it disqualified the parliamentarians including ex-prime minister Yousef Raza Gilani."[60] This is ironic considering Nawaz Sharif himself once welcomed the Supreme Court decision in 2013 disqualifying Gilani, stating that "this is real accountability."[61]

At the outset, the Court dismissed PTI's claims against Prime Minister Sharif as being frivolous and concluded that the petitioners had improperly invoked Article 184(3).[62] A prior attempt to petition the Supreme Court for Sharif's disqualification was also rejected in 2014. In accordance with his judicial restraint policies, Chief Justice Nasirul Mulk rejected four pleas claiming Sharif should be disqualified because he had lied to Parliament in a session concerning mediation with the political opposition.[63] The Court determined that the petitions were not justiciable and that the Court would not exercise its review powers over the alleged statements of the Prime Minister on the floor of Parliament.[64]

However, petitions calling for Sharif's dismissal based on allegations of corruption continued to be filed at the Supreme Court and eventually Chief Justice Asif Saeed Khan Khosa allowed petitions to be heard by the Court starting in October 2016.[65] Rather than dealing with Sharif's remarks in Parliament, these petitions focused on the issues relating to tax evasion, money laundering, and off-shore accounts.[66]

In a decision passed on April 20, 2017, the Court upheld its holding from the *Gilani* case but did not unilaterally dismiss Prime Minister Sharif.[67] While the Court reasserted its right to unilaterally disqualify members of the executive branch based on proven or conceded allegations, the Court held that allegations against Sharif had not been proven yet.[68] Therefore, the Court formed a Joint Investigation Team that was tasked with scrutinizing Sharif's financial records in order to evaluate his guilt and report their findings to the Supreme Court thereafter.

During the Joint Investigation Team's inquiries, it was discovered that Nawaz Sharif had failed to report un-withdrawn assets from his company in the United Arab Emirates, Capital FZE.[69] Once the Joint Investigation Team presented these findings to the Supreme Court, the Court held that Prime Minister Nawaz Sharif was "not honest in terms of . . . Article 62(1)(f) of the Constitution of the Islamic Republic of Pakistan, 1973, therefore, he is disqualified to be a Member of the Majlis-e-Shoora (Parliament)."[70] The Court ordered the Election Commission to immediately inform the Prime Minister of his disqualification and directed the

National Accountability Bureau to submit a case against him before the Accountability Court within six weeks of the decision's publication.[71]

The Supreme Court went further to grant the Chief Justice of Pakistan the ability to appoint a Supreme Court judge "to supervise and monitor implementation of this judgment in letter and spirit and oversee the proceedings conducted by the NAB and the Accountability Court in the above matters."[72] This involvement by the Supreme Court not only in the disqualification of the Prime Minister but his subsequent trial before an Accountability Court has been criticized as an attack on the independence of the Accountability Court itself: Babar Sattar rhetorically asked how any Accountability Court judge could feel unaffected by "such a definitive and damning judgment by five [SC] judges, a time frame to complete a case, an implementation bench for the case . . . [where] and the prime minister involved"?[73]

Further, many have criticized the decision as violating Nawaz Sharif's right to a fair trial and right to appeal. While legal experts were divided over whether Nawaz Sharif had the right to appeal the Supreme Court's decision,[74] his legal team has initiated proceedings to do just that through three petitions before the Court.[75] However, after scheduling oral hearings, the Supreme Court decided to dismiss all three of Sharif's review petitions, solidifying and affirming their earlier decision calling for his disqualification.[76]

The decision in this case reaffirmed the Supreme Court's holding in *Gilani*, and perhaps more importantly, has caused an outburst of petitions to the Court seeking disqualification of politicians based on allegations of "dishonesty" or corruption. This outburst should have been expected when the Court has continuously wielded "a very dangerous sword" of Article 62, the constitutional grounds for disqualification, seemingly without hesitation.[77]

In fact, the lead petitioner in the case to disqualify Prime Minister Sharif was Imran Khan, leader of the PTI, who is himself currently refuting petitions before the Supreme Court calling for his disqualification.[78] Khan has been accused of seeking foreign funding for his political party and contempt of court; further, he is being investigated by the Election Commission of Pakistan for alleged corruption.[79]

This means that the shadow of the *Gilani* case has extended from one administration to the next, hanging a judicial Sword of Damocles over all future democratically elected leaders in the country. In comparison to Pakistan's Supreme Court's cases of the *Gilani* and *Sharif*, the Supreme Courts of India and the United States have handled similar issues with allegedly corrupt executive branch leaders very differently.

III. United States

For comparative purposes, the U.S. Supreme Court jurisprudence demonstrates how the detailed and structuralized evaluation of justiciability has been used to restrain the Court from unilaterally disqualifying or impeaching the head of the executive branch. While the focus of this section will be President Nixon's impeachment, there have been other impeachments in U.S. history. President Andrew Johnson was the first to be impeached, and President Bill Clinton was the last president to face impeachment; however, neither were convicted by the Senate.[80]

The case of *Nixon v. United States* in 1973 demonstrated that the Supreme Court would step in to answer narrow legal questions surrounding subpoenas of the President for a grand jury criminal investigation, but left the act of impeaching the President to the two houses of Congress. As mentioned earlier, unlike in Pakistan, none of the parties in the *Nixon* case requested the Court unilaterally remove the President. Instead, each focused on addressing the legal issues underlying presidential immunity and justiciability.

A. The constitutional impeachment clause

In the United States' Constitution, the "impeachment power grants expressly to Congress the judicial power to try the President and others for 'Treason, Bribery, or other high Crimes and Misdemeanors.'"[81] In an impeachment case, the House of Representatives serves as a prosecutorial chamber,[82] the Senate serves as a decisional chamber, and the Chief Justice of the Supreme Court presides over the impeachment trial.[83] Stated differently, "the question is for the House in determining whether to impeach and for the Senate as the final adjudicative body."[84]

While the Chief Justice is included in the impeachment trial as a symbolic representative of the judiciary, the real work is done by both houses of the legislature, as the power to impeach is "granted to one branch" but there is a division of "power within that branch."[85] The Supreme Court recognized that this system created four inherent checks and balances that would eliminate the need for the Supreme Court to exercise judicial review over the impeachment process:

> the division of impeachment authority between the House and the Senate, a two-thirds vote in the Senate for a conviction, the members of the Senate must be under oath, and the chief justice shall preside in a presidential impeachment trial.[86]

These four elements "prevent the Senate from "usurp[ing] judicial power"[87] and also prevent the Court from intervening in a constitutional process that inherently excludes judicial review.

Since the Constitution vests exclusive powers for impeachment in the legislature, it has been argued that "impeachment was a *political* not a *judicial* process and therefore the Senate did not have to decide whether the president had committed an indictable offense but only whether he was fit to continue in office" (emphasis added).[88] One scholar argues that impeachment is a partisan process because the only presidents subject to impeachment proceedings are those who faced "hostile opposition" from political rivals in control of the legislature.[89] This may be an overstatement, but it can explain why certain presidents can avoid impeachment proceedings for "clear violations of the Constitution" while others are threatened with impeachment for "illegal personal behavior."[90] Arnold Leibowitz argues that the partisan nature of the impeachment process has damaged the office of the President and democratic institutions generally.[91]

One example of this was the attempted impeachment of Bill Clinton, which was regarded by some as a politicized impeachment purportedly punishing him for his personal conduct.[92] On the other hand, the initiation of impeachment proceedings against Richard Nixon was more of a bipartisan affair with some Republicans voting in favor of his articles of impeachment in Congress,[93] so there have been both non-partisan and partisan impeachments in American history.

Despite the critiques of the partisan nature of the impeachment process, the Supreme Court has exercised restraint relative to the Supreme Court of Pakistan regarding judicial involvement in impeachments, because "the critical problem is that allowing any level of judicial review of this unique [impeachment] mechanism is incompatible with both the judicial function and the framers' objectives in designing the judicial impeachment process."[94]

B. Framers' intent

In relation to the framers' objectives, the Court in the *Walter Nixon v. United States* recognized that "judicial review over impeachment procedures frustrates the original constitutional scheme" for impeachment.[95] Though the Walter Nixon case was not about presidential impeachment, the Supreme Court concluded that Nixon's counsel was unable to prove that the framers had ever considered giving the judiciary any role in the impeachment process outside of the Chief Justice's involvement in the Congressional impeachment proceedings. This was because the framers "wanted the body empowered to try impeachments to be sufficiently numerous and to have sufficient fortitude and public accountability to make necessary policy choices," which required impeachment to be conducted exclusively by elected legislature officials.[96]

Framers like Alexander Hamilton believed that the Supreme Court would never possess "the degree of credit and authority" that "might be indispensable to reconcile the people to a decision in an impeachment proceeding contrary to the views of the people's representatives."[97] Setting aside the inability of the Court to adjudicate impeachment, there were also questions about the unwillingness of judges to do so; Michael Gerhardt explains that "the Framers also believed, not insignificantly, that judges might be influenced by the difficult conflict of interest of impeaching the person who had appointed them or their fellow judges."[98] Therefore, judicial review or involvement of the judiciary in the impeachment process was a non-starter for the framers of the Constitution, and this perspective has been affirmed by the Supreme Court in various cases.

C. Judicial function

Along with respecting "the Framer's objectives,"[99] the Supreme Court has also exercised restraint regarding judicial review of impeachments in order to foster "effective functioning of the judicial branch."[100] Justice Joseph Story argued that "limits on justiciability exist in part to protect the courts themselves."[101] He stated that the Court should embody a "spirit of moderation and exclusive devotion to judicial duties," which can be achieved by restraining judicial review over "the acts of political men and their official duties."[102]

The legitimacy and credibility of the Supreme Court is established as much by what the Court does as what it refuses to do. The caveats from Justice Story were ignored by Pakistan's Supreme Court under Chief Justice Chaudhry, so the Court failed to "protect itself" from engaging in a purely political matter and damaged its credibility by unilaterally disqualifying Prime Minster Gilani.

D. Nixon v. United States

While the Supreme Court justices may have known the impact of their decision might lead to the removal of President Nixon,[103] the word impeachment cannot be found anywhere in the Court's decision. In fact, Chief Justice Burger in footnote 19 of the case concluded

> We are not here concerned with the balance between the President's generalized interest in confidentiality and the need for relevant evidence in civil litigation, nor with that between the confidentiality interest and congressional demands for information, nor with the President's interest in preserving state secrets. We address only the conflict between the President's assertion of a generalized privilege of confidentiality and the constitutional need for relevant evidence in criminal trials.[104]

Therefore, the Court made it clear that regardless of the political aftermath of its decision, the only question it was concerned with was the production of evidence before a grand jury[105] from a sitting President. The Court concentrated on the narrow legal question of presidential immunity rather than declaring that President Nixon had violated his constitutional duty, because "such a declaration would have come very close to being an advisory opinion, which the judiciary, limited by the Constitution to deciding cases and controversies, has no power to render."[106]

In this case, a grand jury named the President, among others, as an unindicted co-conspirator to various crimes, including defrauding the United States and obstructing justice. Subsequently, the Special Prosecutor requested that the President turn over evidence, including audiotapes, under Rule 17(c) of the Federal Rules of Criminal Procedure. When the President resisted, the federal District Court ordered the President to turn over the evidence despite his claim of presidential immunity.[107] The President continued to fight the implementation of the order and eventually submitted a petition for certiorari[108] at the Supreme Court.

President Nixon's broad claim was that his case presented a non-justiciable political question that was outside the realm of judicial review.[109] The Court dismissed this argument, affirming its right to interpret provisions of the Constitution like those relating to presidential immunity.[110] The Court rejected the claim to non-justiciability as well as to presidential immunity, ordering President Nixon to release the tapes to the Special Prosecutor so that the potential criminal trial of the President as a co-conspirator could proceed. This never took place as Congress preempted the criminal investigation by filling three articles of impeachment against Nixon, beginning on July 28[111] after the Supreme Court's decision was delivered on July 24, which led to his resignation on August 8.[112] The following month, President Gerald Ford pardoned Nixon.

By exercising judicial review over the real and narrow legal issue of the scope of presidential immunity, the Court accomplished two goals: it deferred to the legislature to handle the impeachment itself, but exercised judicial review to assist the grand jury in conducting investigations into the President's potential crimes. It is important to note that unlike Pakistan's Supreme Court, which ran roughshod over the Parliamentary Speaker's decision not to disqualify Prime Minister Gilani, the Supreme Court in President Nixon's case was not impeding Congress's proceedings, as those proceedings were initiated *after* the Court's decision. By requiring the President to turn over incriminating evidence to the grand jury in a criminal investigation, the Supreme Court likely assisted Congress in agreeing to impeach the President immediately after the evidence was revealed.

If a similar analysis had been used in Prime Minister Gilani's case in Pakistan's Supreme Court, the Court would have narrowly tailored its analysis to the question of presidential immunity, which was being raised by Gilani as justification for his failure to comply with an order to prosecute the president. In reality, the Court skirted the immunity issue altogether, and circumvented the sole disqualification power vested in the National Assembly or the Election Commission by the Constitution to dismiss the Prime Minister.

Pakistan's Supreme Court could have even found that immunity did not apply for foreign crimes committed before the president assumes office. If that were to happen, the Court could have ordered the Gilani administration to prosecute President Zardari, after it definitively decided that presidential immunity did not apply to him. If Prime Minister Gilani continued to refuse, the Court could have then held him in contempt of Court and sent notice of this conviction to the Speaker of the National Assembly.

The decision regarding Prime Minister Gilani's status by Pakistan's Speaker of the National Assembly, much like the outcome of impeachment proceedings in the United States' House or Senate, would have been non-justiciable if Pakistan's Supreme Court had adopted a structuralized and critical analysis of justiciability before engaging in politically sensitive cases.

E. Theory on expanding American Supreme Court judicial review to impeachments

The *Gilani* case in Pakistan does not necessarily shed a positive light on judicial review of impeachment proceedings. However, American theorists like Raoul Berger have argued in favor of the U.S. Supreme Court exercising judicial review over impeachments.[113] While he recognizes that "it has been thought that in the domain of impeachment the Senate has the last word . . . because the trial of impeachments is confided to the Senate alone," Berger argues that the case of *Powell v. McCormack* calls for "reconsideration of the scope of the Senate's 'sole' right to try impeachments."[114]

In *Powell v. McCormack* the House of Representatives dismissed Congressman Adam Clayton Powell from the House for misconduct. The House circumvented the Constitution's impeachment requirements of a two-thirds majority by "excluding" the Congressman rather than "expelling" him (as the two-thirds requirement only applies for expulsions). The Court held that "(1) that judicial review of Congressman Powell's exclusion was not precluded by the 'political question' doctrine, and (2) that the House of Representatives was without power to *exclude*, as distinguished from *expel*, a member for misconduct" (emphasis added).[115]

However, this case was unlike any other impeachment, as it concerned the legislature circumventing legal requirements for expulsion under the Constitution, which the Supreme Court found was justiciable as a legal matter. This was not the case in President Nixon's impeachment, nor was it applicable to the case of Prime Minister Gilani in Pakistan, neither of which included circumvention of constitutional impeachment or disqualification requirements by the legislature.

While some scholars have made the case in favor of judicial review over the impeachment process, much of the scholarship concludes that "the legal reasoning in support of judicial review of impeachment cases is dubious, at best."[116]

F. Comparative conclusions

As discussed above, the restrained use of judicial review in the impeachment process by the U.S. Supreme Court is based on: i) respect for the Framer's intent in the impeachment clause, ii) judicial self-interest in preserving its legitimacy and public credibility, and iii) respect for a critical assessment of the justiciability of claims. These three buffers allow the U.S. Supreme Court to defer to the political branches to conduct impeachments, but also allow the U.S. Supreme Court to take action when there is an underlying legal issue: for example, if the scope of presidential immunity needs to be defined in relation to grand jury indictments. If such a multilayered analysis was implemented by Pakistan's Supreme Court, Prime Minister Gilani would likely not have been unilaterally disqualified by the Court, and the Court might have staved off the critiques that came in the wake of the *Gilani* decision.

IV. India

While President Nixon and Prime Minister Gilani's cases concerned the disqualification of the head of the executive branch due to misdeeds they committed during their term in office, the case of *Indira Nehru Gandhi v. Raj Narain* was about potential electoral crimes committed by Gandhi during the election period. Despite this difference, the tempered decision by India's Supreme Court in *Gandhi v. Narain* is significant for comparison to Pakistan because the Court was able to exercise judicial review powers by evaluating the legality of a constitutional amendment while also overturning a decision by a lower court to disqualify the Prime Minister. Much as in President Nixon's case, where the Court narrowly focused on the legal question of presidential immunity in relation to a grand jury indictment but deferred the impeachment decision to the elected branches, India's Supreme Court was able to strike a similar compromise.

Further, in a more recent case involving the disqualification of a Supreme Court Justice, the Supreme Court of India rejected a petition to review the impeachment decision by the Parliament, citing non-justiciability of the claim.[117] Again, as in the United States, the critical evaluation of the justiciability or maintainability of petitions that is missing in Pakistan allows the Supreme Courts of India and the United States to avoid overactive use of judicial review in the impeachment process and other areas of law.

A. Timeline of events

The *Indira Gandhi* Supreme Court case was the culmination of a long-simmering conflict between the judiciary and the Prime Minister.[118] This started with the Supreme Court's ruling in *I. C. Golaknath v. State of Punjab*, in which "the Supreme Court took an extreme view . . . that Parliament could not amend or alter any fundamental right."[119] Then, the Supreme Court delivered another blow to the Gandhi administration in 1974 through *Kesavananda Bharati v. State of Kerala* decision, which laid out the "basic structure doctrine" and invalidated constitutional amendments passed by Parliament under Gandhi's leadership.

The following year, Gandhi's election was challenged in the High Court of Allahabad by "socialist leader" Raj Narain.[120] The High Court ruled that Gandhi had violated election laws (namely the Representation of People Act) by using government officials to administer partisan campaign rallies and functions.[121] Due to these violations, "the High Court held the appellant to be disqualified for a period of six years."[122] According to the High Court, Gandhi "was thus guilty of a corrupt practice . . . accordingly [she] stands disqualified for a period of six years from the date of this order."[123]

The decision was appealed to the Supreme Court, with Gandhi's lawyers asking for an unconditional stay of the High Court decision. The Supreme Court granted a conditional stay on June 24, 1975, allowing "Indira Gandhi to attend Parliament as a member and PM without a vote, pending the final decision in the election appeal."[124] During this interim period, the High Court "debarred [Gandhi] from taking part in parliamentary proceedings and to take salary as an MP."[125] This decision was "was considered an affront to the prime minister by her advisors."[126] Therefore, two days after the interim order, the Prime Minister Gandhi declared Emergency Rule, suspending constitutional rights.

During the emergency period, Parliament passed the Thirty-Ninth Amendment, which inserted Article 329A into the Constitution. This article "prohibited any challenge to the election of the President, Vice-President, Speaker and Prime Minister, irrespective of the electoral malpractice"[127] before a court of law. Further,

"Parliament was also made to pass the Election Laws Act, 1975 – an ordinary legislation by which the electoral offences for which Indira Gandhi was disqualified by the Allahabad HC [High Court] were retrospectively nullified."[128]

Therefore, the final case before the Supreme Court revolved around three basic questions: i) whether Parliament could amend the Constitution to prohibit judicial review of elections for the Prime Minister, President, and Speaker of Parliament, ii) whether Parliament could change the Election Laws to prohibit disqualification of parliamentarians, and iii) whether Gandhi could be removed from her post as Prime Minister through judicial order.

B. Constitutional provisions for disqualification

According to India's Constitution, when it comes to the Prime Minister, the impeachment rules are not directly enumerated. As the Prime Minister is chosen by whichever party holds the greatest majority in Parliament, he or she remains a member of Parliament and subject to disqualification under Articles 101, 102, and 103. According to Article 101, no Parliamentarian may be a member of both houses of Parliament. Articles 102 and 191 designate grounds for disqualification, which include "unsound mind," lack of citizenship, or any law duly passed by Parliament. Article 103 states that whenever there is an issue of disqualification, "the question shall be referred for the decision of the President and his decision shall be final," but the President must seek the advice of the Election Commission.

Therefore, the President and Election Commission hold a great deal of power in the impeachment proceedings of parliamentarians, including the chief parliamentarian, the Prime Minister.[129] However, Parliament itself still retains a great deal of power according to Subsection 3 of Article 102, as it can pass any law that would have the effect of disqualifying parliamentarians.

Further, when it comes to disqualifications based on a parliamentarian's defection from their original political party, Schedule X of the Constitution controls.[130] In those cases, any question relating to "whether a member of a House has become subject to disqualification" should be referred to the decision of the Speaker of such house, "and this decision shall be final."[131] Therefore, along with Subsection 3 of Article 102, Parliament, through its speaker, retains exclusive control over disqualifications based on political defection.

Though it is unrelated to constitutional analysis, a no-confidence vote is a political tool that can serve as a form of disqualification of the Prime Minister exercised exclusively by Parliament.[132] The response by Parliament to the Prime Minister committing crimes can take place through this no-confidence vote, unlike in the United States where actual impeachment is the only option of removing the head of government. However, upon a vote of no-confidence, "the Prime Minister must resign but may advise the President to dissolve the Lok Sabha (lower house) and call for new elections."[133] The process of new elections is daunting to many parliamentarians, which is why there have been very few calls for no-confidence,[134] and of those, most have been unrelated to criminal allegations against the executive. Another limitation of the no-confidence vote is that it only leads to the Prime Minister resigning from his post;

he retains his membership in Parliament. If the Prime Minister has been accused of criminal or corrupt acts, the only means to remove them from Parliament completely is through disqualification as specified under Articles 101–103.

Finally, in order to understand the decision in *Gandhi v. Narain*, one must also understand the two major changes to the constitution instituted through the Thirty-Ninth Amendment and the changes to the Representation of People Act. First, the Amendment altered Article 71 of the Constitution to prohibit judicial review of election matters concerning the President or Vice President, leaving the matter to Parliament, "including the grounds on which such election may be questioned."[135] Second, Article 329A was added to the Constitution with the aim of depriving the judiciary of the ability to review the election issues concerning the Prime Minister or Speaker. The new article prohibited "any court" from taking action on cases concerning the "doubts and disputes in relation to such election including the grounds on which such election may be questioned."[136] Finally, the Election Laws Act changed the trigger point for the election rules to apply only once a person "has been duly nominated as a candidate in her election."[137] As Gandhi's conviction was based on actions she took predating her official candidacy, according to the amended election rules, the Supreme Court vacated the High Court's conviction.

The provisions of the Thirty-Ninth Amendment in Gandhi's case were similar to Pakistan's NRO, as both attempted to oust the jurisdiction of the courts from hearing cases involving certain political figures. Both of these ouster clauses were rejected by the Supreme Court, as discussed earlier for Pakistan and explored for India below.

C. Legal aspects of **Gandhi v. Raj Narain**

The Supreme Court of India constituted a bench presided by Chief Justice A.N. Ray to review the High Court of Allahabad's conviction of Indira Gandhi for violating election laws, with additional questions concerning the legality of the Thirty-Ninth Amendment and the Election Laws Act. In order to assess Gandhi's conviction, the Court first focused on the question of when election laws were triggered for a candidate. To that end, the Court upheld the Election Laws Act, concluding that the validity of such statutes depend "entirely on the existence of the legislative power" and that "it is within the powers of Parliament to frame laws with regard to elections."[138] While counsel for Narain alleged that "if a candidate is free to spend as much as a candidate likes before the date of nomination a great premium would be placed on free use of money before the date of the nomination," the Supreme Court upheld the Election Laws Act, deferring to the fact that "the Legislature has now set the matter at rest."[139] As the Act altered the triggering date for an individual to be considered a candidate subject to election spending rules, the Court was able to review the High Court's conviction of Gandhi, which was based on an earlier triggering date.

Accordingly, the Supreme Court set aside

> the finding of the High Court that the appellant held herself out to be a candidate from December 29, 1970. . . because the law is that the appellant became a candidate. . . [on] February 1, 1971.[140]

Based on the new election laws, the Court also overruled the High Court's finding "that the appellant committed corrupt practices," and set aside the High Court's disqualification of the Prime Minister.[141]

Scholarship on this decision focuses the final question for the Court: whether the Thirty-Ninth Amendment passed by Gandhi's administration, which eliminated judicial power to disqualify the Prime Minister, was valid. The Supreme Court "struck down this amendment under the basic structure doctrine as violating the separation of powers and judicial review, both core principles of the Indian Constitution."[142] The Court concluded that the Thirty-Ninth Amendment violated three principles of India's Constitution: "fair democratic elections, equality, and separation of powers."[143] However, the focus for the purposes of this study is to highlight the fact that despite the Court insisting that it had the right to review jurisdiction-ouster clauses in constitutional amendments, the Indian Court restrained its use of this power when evaluating election statutes passed by Parliament and disqualifying the de facto head of the executive branch.

Nick Robinson explains that "in a politically pragmatic maneuver that also followed an existing line of precedent, the Court found Indira Gandhi's election valid by upholding legislation that had retroactively removed the legal basis for her original conviction."[144]

Along with being politically pragmatic, the Supreme Court was able to overrule the disqualification of the Prime Minister at the High Court by focusing on a narrow legal question concerning the power of Parliament to create election laws through statutes. Even if such election laws were being used to retrospectively shield the Prime Minister from prosecution, the Court focused on the constitutional delegation of authority to Parliament to establish election laws, and restrained its use of judicial review in that arena. This legal approach adopted by the Court fostered the politically pragmatic decision of the Court to avoid the oncoming collision between the Gandhi administration and the apex court.

The approach taken by India's Supreme Court poses a compromise between the deference of the U.S. Supreme Court for impeachment issues and the interference of Pakistan's Supreme Court. For the U.S., the political question doctrine played a significant role in the Court's decision to leave impeachment untouched by judicial review.[145] However, this kind of blanket deference was not accepted by India's Supreme Court, which stated that "the function of the parliament is to make laws, not decide cases . . . the Indian Parliament will not direct that an accused in a pending case shall stand acquitted or that a suit shall stand decreed."[146] Justice Chandrachud went on to state that

> the political usefulness of the doctrine of separation of powers is now widely recognized, though a satisfactory definition of the three functions is difficult to evolve . . . the concentration of powers in any one organ may, by upsetting that fine balance between the three organs, destroy the fundamental premises of a democratic government to which we are pledged.[147]

The Supreme Court of Pakistan cited this quotation to legitimize its dismissal of the Prime Minister, which the Supreme Court of India resolutely refused to do.[148] Unlike the Supreme Court of India, Pakistan's Supreme Court took unilateral action to terminate a prime minister, overriding the constitutional provisions delegating disqualification decisions to the Speaker of the National Assembly and the Election Commission.

The decision by India's Supreme Court "did not end the Emergency or remove Prime Minister Gandhi from power, but it did show the Court was willing to be an independent voice."[149] So, while the Court compromised to allow Gandhi to continue her term in office, it also set out its position to review constitutional amendments that limit the jurisdiction of the Court on issues regarding disqualification of elected officials and elections.

The decision has been criticized by some,[150] yet in the end, Gandhi lost political support in the country due to this case, while the Supreme Court's social status was elevated.[151] This was the culmination of a "protracted struggle to establish its [the Supreme Court's] credibility and independence in the face of repeated attempts to diminish its standing as a significant force in Indian politics," with Gandhi serving as a "looming presence" over that struggle.[152]

D. Comparative conclusions

When it came to the potential disqualification of Prime Minister Indira Gandhi, India's Supreme Court compromised. By overturning the Allahabad High Court's conviction of Gandhi for corrupt practices, the Supreme Court allowed her to retain her position as Prime Minister. However, in the same case, the Supreme Court overturned an amendment passed by the Gandhi administration, concluding that the ouster of jurisdiction for the judiciary over executive malfeasance violates the basic structure of the Constitution, which guarantees the independence of the judiciary.

By doing so, the Court was able to stave off a further breakdown in democratic institutions in India. A verdict confirming the Allahabad High Court's conviction of Gandhi would likely have led to an ultimate clash between the judiciary and executive, which could have resembled Pakistan's scenario under Musharraf's military dictatorship when "non-compliant" judges were removed from the bench and sometimes placed on house arrest or monitored by state agencies. By refusing to disqualify the Prime Minister, the Supreme Court of India lived to fight another day, with its public legitimacy and activism increasing greatly after emergency rule was lifted.

The Gandhi case demonstrates how the Supreme Court's restraint in exercising judicial review of impeachments or disqualifications can:

i Avoid a complete breakdown of executive-judicial relations through compromise such that the compromise

  a must on the one hand allow the Court to set out its own duties to interpret the law, and
  b on the other hand, allow the Court to defer issues like impeachment and disqualification of elected officials to the elected branches as mandated by the Constitution.

ii Strengthen democratic institutions by

 a avoiding breakdowns of checks and balances, and
 b maintaining or increasing the Supreme Court's legitimacy in the public.

iii Address criminal or corrupt practices by the executive.

If one were to apply the methods of India's Supreme Court to the *Gilani* case, a different result would have been likely. According to *Indira Nehru Gandhi v. Raj Narain*, the Supreme Court of India declined its potential use of judicial review of laws passed by Parliament under Article 124(5), just as the Supreme Court of Pakistan could have done by addressing the constitutional provisions relating to presidential immunity, which were key to Gilani's defense. Beyond this point, the Pakistani Supreme Court would need to defer to the decision of Parliament based on the Constitution.

Notes

1 *Muhammad Azhar Siddique v. Federation of Pakistan*, Const. Petition No. 40 of 2012 & CMA No.2494/12 etc. (SC) (Pak.)
2 There are two pertinent cases by the name of Nixon: *Richard M. Nixon v. United States*, 418 U.S. 683 (1974) (1973) and *Walter Nixon v. United States*, 506 U.S. 224 (1993).
3 *Indira Nehru Gandhi v. Shri Raj Narain* (1976) AIR 1975 SC 2299, 1975 (Supp) SCC1, 2 SCR 347 (India).
4 *Siddique*, *supra* note 1. (Contempt proceedings against Syed Yousaf Raza Gillani, the Prime Minister of Pakistan regarding non-compliance of this Court's order dated 16.12.2009)
5 Pakistan Const., art. 63(2): ("if any question arises whether a member of the Majlis-e-Shoora (Parliament) has become disqualified from being a member, the Speaker or, as the case may be, the Chairman shall, unless he decides that no such question has arisen, refer the question to the Election Commission within thirty days.")
6 For an example of overextension analysis see *A Judicial Coup*, Express Tribune, June 12, 2012. Available at http://tribune.com.pk/story/396001/a-judicial-coup/ (Accessed on June 20, 2016).
7 *Imran Ahmad Khan v. Miam Muhammad Nawaz Sharif*, Const. Petition No. 29 of 2016 (SC) (Pak.)
8 *The State of Uttar Pradesh v. Raj Narain*, AIR 1975 SC 865 (1975) 3 SCR 333 (India).
9 See generally G. G. Mirchandani, 320 Million Judges (2003) about Indira Gandhi's dissolving of Lok Sabha (lower parliamentary house), holding of elections, accusations of election fraud, and the Allahabad High Court's decision.
10 Satya Prakash, *The Court Verdict that Prompted Indira Gandhi to Declare Emergency*, Hindustan Times, June 26, 2015. Available at www.hindustantimes.com/india/the-court-verdict-that-prompted-indira-gandhi-to-declare-emergency/story-uaDsy0j3B-0vSdiPn2md9WO.html (last accessed on June 20, 2016).
11 Gandhi, *supra* note 3, at Para 158. ("For the foregoing reasons the contentions of the appellant succeed and the contentions of the respondent fail. The appeal is accepted. The judgment of the High Court appealed against is set aside the cross objections of the respondent is dismissed.")
12 Id., at Para 213 ("As a result of the above, I strike down clause (4) of Article 329A on the ground that it violates the principle of free and fair elections which is an essential postulate of democracy and which in its turn is a part of the basic structure of the Constitution.")

13 See generally Larry A. Van Meter, *United States V. Nixon: The Question of Executive Privilege* (2007).
14 Impeachment proceedings are in fact not mentioned anywhere in the judgment, *United States v. Nixon*, 418 U.S. 683 (1974).
15 Jon Boone, *Pakistan's Prime Minister Yousuf Raza Gilani Disqualified by Supreme Court*, The Guardian, June 19, 2012, www.theguardian.cmom/world/2012/jun/19/pakistan-prime-minister-yousuf-gilani-disqualified (last accessed on June 20, 2016). ("The supreme court has edged one step closer to a judicial dictatorship of sorts," said Cyril Almeida, a journalist. "The constitution is very clear about how the disqualification process is supposed to work and the court has quite extraordinarily brushed all of that aside and is making up new rules of the game as it goes along.")
16 *Muhammad Azhar Siddique v. Federation of Pakistan etc.*, Const. Petition No. 40 of 2012 & CMA No.2494/12 at 68 (Justice Arif Hussain Khilji) ("Mr. Yusuf Raza Gilani, former Prime Minister of Pakistan, hereinafter referred to as 'the respondent', was charged by a 7-member bench of this Court under Article 204 (2) of the Constitution of Islamic Republic of Pakistan, 1973 read with section 3 of the Contempt of Court Ordinance (Ordinance V of 2003).")
17 *Swiss Close Case Against Zardari; $60 mln Unfrozen*, Reuters, Aug. 26, 2008, www.reuters.com/article/us-swiss-pakistan-zardari-idUSLQ17107020080826 (last accessed on June 20, 2016).
18 *Contempt Proceedings Against Syed Yousaf Raza Gillani*, Suo Motu Case No. 04 of 2010, Criminal Original petition No. 06 of 2012. (SC) (Pak.) (regarding non-compliance of this Court's order dated 16.12.2009) at Para 2 (Nasir Ul Mulk Judgment).
19 *Swiss Close Case Against Zardari. supra* note 17.
20 Moeen Cheema, *Back to the Future: The Pakistan Supreme Court's NRO Judgment*, Juris-Forum, Jan. 14, 2010. Accessed on June 21, 2016.
21 Moeen Cheema & Ijaz Shafi Gilani, *The Politics and Jurisprudence of the Chaudhry Court* (2015), at 187. (Moeen Cheema: The Chaudhry Court: Rule of Law or Judicialization of Politics).
22 *Dr. Mobashir Hassan v. Federation of Pakistan* (2010) 256 PLD (SC) (Pak.)
23 Id at Para 81.
24 Cheema, *supra* note 20.
25 Pamela Constable, *Playing With Fire: Pakistan at War With Itself* (2011), at 235.
26 Hassan, *supra* note 22. *Dr. Mobashir Hassan v. Federation of Pakistan, at* Para 174 ("The Federal Government, all the Provincial Governments and all relevant and competent authorities including the Prosecutor General of NAB, the Special Prosecutors in various Accountability Courts, the Prosecutors General in the four Provinces and other officers or officials involved in the prosecution of criminal offenders are directed to offer every possible assistance required by the competent Courts in the said connection.")
27 Boone, *supra* note 15. ("When Chaudhry ordered Gilani to ask the Swiss authorities to reopen the case the government refused, arguing the president enjoyed immunity as head of state.")
28 Pakistan Const., art. Article 248 (2) ("No criminal proceedings whatsoever shall be instituted or continued against the President or a Governor in any Court during his term of office.")
29 *Gilani Family's Predicament Remains Unexplained*, Dawn, Nov. 15, 2012. Available at www.dawn.com/2012/11/15/gilani-familys-predicament-remains-unexplained/ (last accessed on June 21, 2016). ("[Gilani] throughout [the conflict with the Supreme Court over Zardari's prosecution] followed the party guidelines and even sacrificed his job.")
30 Syed Yusuf Raza Gillani Contempt of Court, Criminal Original No. 06/2012, Suo Motu Case No. 04 of 2010. (Contempt proceedings against Syed Yousaf Raza Gillani, the Prime Minister of Pakistan regarding non-compliance of this Court's order dated 16.12.2009)

31 Pakistan Const., art. 204(2) ("A Court shall have power to punish any person who – a. abuses, interferes with or obstructs the process of the Court in any way or disobeys any order of the Court; b. scandalizes the Court or otherwise does anything which tends to bring the Court or a Judge of the Court into hatred, ridicule or contempt; c. does anything which tends to prejudice the determination of a matter pending before the Court; or d. does any other thing which, by law, constitutes contempt of the Court.")
32 Contempt of Court Ordinance, Article 3 ("Whoever disobeys or disregards any order, direction or process of a Court, which he is legally bound to obey; or commits a willful breach of a valid undertaking given to a court; or does anything which is intended to or tends to bring the authority of a court or the administration of law into disrespect or disrepute . . . is said to commit 'contempt of court'. The contempt is of three types, namely, the 'civil contempt', 'criminal contempt' and 'judicial contempt'.")
33 *Baz Mohammad Kaker v. Federation of Pakistan*, Constitution Petition No.77 of 2012 & CMA No.3057/2012. (SC) (Pak.) at Para 2.
34 Pakistan Const., art 63(1).
35 Id at Article 63 (2).
36 Nasir Jaffry, *Speaker Backs Gilani*, The Telegraph, May 24, 2012. Available at www.telegraphindia.com/1120525/jsp/foreign/story_15530347.jsp (last accessed on June 21, 2016).
37 Baz Mohammad Kaker, *supra* note 33, at Para 3.
38 *Pakistani Judicial System Groans Under Corruption, Volume of Cases*, Public Radio International, www.pri.org/stories/2012-02-03/pakistani-judicial-system-groans-under-corruption-volume-cases (last accessed on June 22, 2016).("Jilani said that Chaudhry is only doing what needs to be done to hold government to account. 'Where he feels things are going out of control and the government is unable to handle the situation, he intervenes,' Jilani said. 'He has this knack of grabbing and realizing the right opportunity. You can say, he has his hand on peoples' pulse and he knows what people want.'")
39 Omar Waraich, *Pakistan's Supreme Court v. Everybody, But Most of All the Prime Minister*, Time, 2012, http://content.time.com/time/world/article/0,8599,2106725,00.html (last acccessed on June 21, 2016). ("For the government and its supporters, the Supreme Court's actions amount to little more than a judicial coup in slow motion.")
40 Rajshree Jetly, *Pakistan's Judicial Renaissance: A New Phase?* 166 Institute of South Asia Studies 1 (2012), at 5.
41 Cheema, *supra* note 21, at 185–9. ("The Lawyer's Movement began in March 2007, when General Musharraf, Pakistan's president and military chief, suspended the Chief Justice of the Supreme Court, Iftikhar Muhammad Chaudhry, on charges of misconduct . . . Then in March 2009, thousands marched towards Islamabad demanding the reinstatement of Justice Chaudhry, the PPPP government buckled under the threat of a violent confrontation with the protestors and the pressure of the military command. In March 2009, Iftikhar Chaudhry once again became the Chief Justice of Pakistan. The restoration of the chief justice was formally effected through an executive notification and without the need for a fresh oath, thereby acknowledging the strength of the claim that Justice Chaudhry and the other judges had never legally removed from office.")
42 Moeen Cheema & Ijaz Shafi Gilani, *The Politics and Jurisprudence of the Chaudhry Court 2005–2013* (2015), at 95. Faisal Siddiqi, *Public Interest Litigation: Predictable Continuity and Radical Departures*.
43 Saroop Ijaz, *The Case for Judicial Minimalism in Pakistan*, Jurist-Forum, Oct. 11, 2010, http://jurist.org/forum/2010/10/the-case-for-judicial-minimalism-in-pakistan.php.
44 *'Pakistan's Supreme Court and the National Reconciliation Ordinance: What now for Pakistan?'* ISAS Brief no. 147, Dec. 22, 2009, at 6. (Citing Jamaluddin Jamali, 'PPP lawyers, Asma Jahangir rant against SC verdict', Pakistan Today (27 Apr. 2012) www.

pakistantoday.com.pk/2012/04/27/news/national/ppp-lawyers-asma-jahangir-rant-against-sc-verdict/?printType=article) (Accessed 20 June 2016.)

45 Qasim Nauman & Chris Allbritton, *Pakistan PM Charged With Contempt in Case That Could Drag on*, Reuters, Feb. 13, 2012, www.reuters.com/article/us-pakistan-politics-idUSTRE81C0D820120213 (last accessed on June 22, 2016).

46 Osama Siddique, "Judicialization of Politics: Pakistan Supreme Court's Jurisprudence After the Lawyers' Movement," in Mark Tushnet & Madhav Khosla, eds., *Unstable Constitutionalism: Law and Politics in South Asia* (2015).

47 Jetly, *supra* note 40, at 5.

48 Nauman & Allbritton, *supra* note 45.

49 Id.

50 Rajshree Jetly, *Pakistan's Supreme Court and the National Reconciliation Ordinance: What now for Pakistan?*' INST. S. ASIAN. STUD. BRIEF No. 147 (Dec. 2009.) Available at www.files.ethz.ch/isn/110966/148.pdf (last accessed on Oct. 31, 2016) at 3.

51 Cheema, *supra* note 21, at 199.

52 Id, at 199–200.

53 Moeen Cheema & Ijaz Shafi Gilani, *The Politics and Jurisprudence of the Chaudhry Court 2005–2013* (2015) at 226. Syed M. Ghazenfur, *Politics, Power, and the Crisis of Jurisprudence*.

54 Id at 226. ("It is here that an arbitrary division is struck between the legal and political question, which restricts the vision of the legal question to the domain demarcated by the words of law through the concept of justiciability. The urban popular media of Pakistan have asserted the critique of the contemporary Supreme Court within this binary, whereby judicially discovered legal truths are limited by the overbearing discourse of the legal and the political.")

55 PM says 'few thousand' chanting 'Go Nawaz Go' can't make him leave, Pakistan Today, Sep. 17, 2014. Available at www.pakistantoday.com.pk/2014/09/17/pm-says-few-thousand-chanting-go-nawaz-go-cant-make-him-leave/ (last accessed on October 14, 2017).

56 The International Consortium of Investigative Journalists, The Panama Papers, Available at https://panamapapers.icij.org (last accessed on Oct. 14, 2017).

57 Marvin Weinbaum & Nasir Naveed, *Fallout in Pakistan from the Panama Papers*, Middle East Institute. May 17, 2016. Available at www.mei.edu/content/article/fallout-pakistan-panama-papers (last accessed on July 30, 2016.)

58 Najma Minhas, *The Panama Papers and Pakistan: Beyond Nawaz Sharif*, The Diplomat, Apr. 11, 2016. Available at http://thediplomat.com/2016/04/the-panama-papers-and-pakistan-beyond-nawaz-sharif/ (last accessed on July 30, 2016.)

59 Raza Khan, *CJP Declines to Form 'toothless commission' on Panama Leaks*, Dawn, May 13, 2016. Available at www.dawn.com/news/1258127 (last accessed on July 30, 2016.)

60 *Plea in SC: PTI Finally Decides to Seek PM's Disqualification*, Express Tribune, July 29, 2016. Available at http://tribune.com.pk/story/1151524/plea-sc-pti-finally-decides-seek-pms-disqualification/ (last accessed on July 30, 2016.)

61 Declan Walsh, *Political Instability Rises as Pakistani Court Ousts Premier*, New York Times, June 19, 2012. Available at www.nytimes.com/2012/06/20/world/asia/political-instability-rises-as-pakistani-court-dismisses-prime-minister.html?_r=0 (last accessed on July 30, 2016).

62 Hasnaat Malik, *SC Office Returns Imran's 'frivolous' Plea Against PM*, Express Tribune, Aug. 31, 2016. Available http://tribune.com.pk/story/1173204/sc-office-returns-imrans-frivolous-plea-pm/ (last accessed on Oct. 15, 2016).

63 *Supreme Court Rejects Petitions in PM Disqualification Case*, Express Tribune, Dec. 9, 2014. Available at http://tribune.com.pk/story/804091/sc-rejects-petitions-in-pm-disqualification-case/ (last accessed on July 30, 2016).

64 *Id.*

65 Hasham Cheema, *How Pakistan's Panama Papers Probe Unfolded*, Dawn, July 29, 2017. Available at www.dawn.com/news/1316531 (last accessed on Oct. 14, 2017).
66 *Imran Ahmad Khan v. Miam Muhammad Nawaz Sharif*, Const. Petition No. 29 of 2016 (SC) (Pak.) at 160, Para 97. Available at www.supremecourt.gov.pk/web/user_files/File/Const.P._29_2016.pdf (last accessed on Oct. 14, 2017.) ("Surely, respondent No. 1 is not being proceeded against for making that speech and the said speech is being utilized in the present proceedings only for a collateral purpose to determine as to whether the said respondent had been making divergent statements on the same issue at different occasions or not and as to whether he had been honest in the matter or not.")
67 *Imran Ahmad Khan v. Miam Muhammad Nawaz Sharif*, Const. Petition No. 29 of 2016 (SC) (Pak.)
68 Id at pg 236 Para 23.
69 *Imran Ahmed Khan v. Mian Muhammad Nawaz Sharif*, C.M.A. No. 4978/2017 in Constitutional Petition No. 29/2016 and C.M.A. No. 2939/2017 in Constitutional Petition No. 29/2016. (SC) (Pak.) (July 28, 2017.) at Para 14. Available at www.supremecourt.gov.pk/web/user_files/File/Const.P._29_2016_28072016.pdf (last accessed on Oct. 14, 2017).
70 Id. at Para 15.
71 Id at Para 14.
72 Id at Para 16.
73 *Nawaz's Disqualification: What Legal Experts Say*, Geo News, July 29, 2017. Available at www.geo.tv/latest/151531-legal-heavyweights-weigh-in-on-scs-decision-on-panama-case (last accessed on Oct. 14, 2017).
74 Id.
75 Haseeb Bhatti, *Nawaz Sharif Files 3 Petitions Challenging Panamagate Verdict in SC*, Dawn, Aug. 15, 2017. Available at www.dawn.com/news/1351705 (last accessed on Oct. 14, 2017).
76 *Supreme Court Dismisses Sharif Family's Review Petitions in Panama Case*, The News, Sep. 15, 2017. Available at www.thenews.com.pk/latest/230142-Supreme-Court-concludes-hearing-in-Panama-case-review-petitions (last accessed on Oct. 14, 2017).
77 Bhatti, *supra* note 73.
78 Ineligibility case: Imran Khan submits reply in Supreme Court, Dunya News, May 29, 2017. Available at http://dunyanews.tv/en/Pakistan/390506-Ineligibility-case-Imran-Khan-submits-reply-in-Su (last accessed on Oct. 14, 2017).
79 Mohammad Bilal, ECP to hear PTI's foreign funding, Imran Khan's alleged contempt of court cases separately, Dawn, May 08, 2017. Available at www.dawn.com/news/1331825 (last accessed on Oct. 14, 2017).
80 For a legal historical version of presidential impeachments, See Arnold H. Leibowitz, *An Historical-Legal Analysis of the Impeachments of Presidents Andrew Johnson, Richard Nixon, and William Clinton: Why the Process Went Wrong* (2011).
81 Paul R. Verkuil, *Separation of Powers, the Rule of Law and the Idea of Independence*, 30 Wm. & Mary L. Rev. 301, 309–10 (1989) (Citing U.S. Const. Article II, Section 4.)
82 U.S. Const., Article I, Section 2.
83 Id at Article I, Section 3, Clause 5 & 6.
84 John R. Labovitz, *Presidential Impeachment* (1978) at 244.
85 Verkuil, *supra* note 81, at 309–10.
86 Michael J. Gerhardt, *The Federal Impeachment Process: A Constitutional and Historical Analysis* (2000), at 124.
87 Id at 123. Citing *Nixon v. United States*, 506 U.S. 224 (1993) at 235.
88 Jody C. Baumgartner & Naoko Kada, *Checking Executive Power: Presidential Impeachment in Comparative Perspective* (2003). William B. Perkins, *Chapter 2: The Political Nature of the Presidential Impeachment in the United States* at 28.
89 Id at 32.

90 Id at 30.
91 Leibowitz, *supra* note 80.
92 Geoffrey R. Stone, *Constitutional law* (2001), at 414. ("All of the relevant votes were highly partisan, with Democrats overwhelming voting against impeachment and conviction, and Republicans voting overwhelming in favor.")
93 David E. Rosenbaum, *Rodino Unit Issues Report Describing Case Against Nixon*, New York Times, Aug. 23, 1974. (Only ten Republicans voted against Nixon's Articles of Impeachment, and even they critiqued Nixon stating that Nixon "impeded the F.B.I.'s investigation of Watergate" and tried to withhold evidence of "terrible import.")
94 Gerhardt, *supra* note 86, at 123.
95 Id.
96 Id.
97 The Federalist No. 65 (Alexander Hamilton). (Clinton Rossiter ed., 1961).
98 Michael J. Gerhardt, *Rediscovering Nonjusticiability: Judicial Review of Impeachments After Nixon*, 44 Duke L.J. 231, 255 (1994) citing *Records of the Federal Convention, Volume II (*Max Farrand, ed., 1911), at 398–9.
99 Gerhardt, *supra* note 86, at 123.
100 Labovitz, *supra* note 84, at 243.
101 Id.
102 Joseph Story & Thomas M. Cooley, *Commentaries on the Constitution of the United States: With a Preliminary Review of the Constitutional History of the Colonies and States Before the Adoption . . . notes and Additions by Thomas M. Cooley* (2008), at 543.
103 Stone, *supra* note 92, at 413. (The expected impact of the decision can be seen in how quickly Nixon resigned after the Supreme Court's decision: "two days after the Supreme Court handed down its decision in Nixon, the House Judiciary Committee adopted an article of impeachment.")
104 *United States v. Nixon*, 418 U.S. 683, 712 (1974)
105 Charles Doyle, Cong. Research Serv., RL95–1135, *Federal Grand Jury* (2010), at 1–4 ("The federal grand jury exists to investigate crimes against the United States and to secure the constitutional right of grand jury indictment . . . The Fifth Amendment right to grand jury indictment is only required in federal cases . . . The grand jury may begin its examination even in the absence of probable cause or any other level of suspicion that a crime has been committed with its reach. In the exercise of jurisdiction, the grand jury may "investigate merely on suspicion that the law is being violated.")
106 Labovitz, *supra* note 84, at 244.
107 *United States v. Mitchell*, 377 F.Supp. 1326 (DC 1974).
108 CERTIORARI, Black's Law Dictionary (10th ed., 2014). An extraordinary writ issued by an appellate court, at its discretion, directing a lower court to deliver the record in the case for review. The writ evolved from one of the prerogative writs of the English Court of King's Bench, and in the United States it became a general appellate remedy. The U.S. Supreme Court uses certiorari to review most of the cases that it decides to hear.
109 Nixon, *supra* note 2 (1974) ("The first contention is a broad claim that the separation of powers doctrine precludes judicial review of a President's claim of privilege.").
110 Id at 684. ("The dispute between the Special Prosecutor and the President presents a justiciable controversy.")
111 Richard Lyons & William Chapman, *Judiciary Committee Approves Article to Impeach President Nixon, 27 to 11, 6 Republicans Join Democrats to Pass Obstruction Charge*, Washington Post, July 28, 1974 at A01.
112 Carroll Kilpatrick, *Nixon Resigns*, Washington Post, Aug. 9, 1974, at A01.
113 Raoul Berger, *Impeachment: The Constitutional Problems* (1974).
114 Id at 109.

115 Jules B. Gerard, *Review of "Impeachment: The Constitutional Problems,"* By Raoul Berger, 1974 Wash. U. L. Q. 179 (1974). Available at: http://openscholarship.wustl.edu/law_lawreview/vol1974/iss1/14

116 Labovitz, *supra* note 84, at 178.

117 *Sub-Committee on Judicial Accountability v. Union of India and ORS*, Etc (1992) AIR 320, 1991 SCR Supl. (2) 1. (India) at Para 35. ("In view of the above findings this Court cannot pass any order whether permanent or temporary on the prayer that the respondent No. 3 should not be allowed to exercise his judicial powers. In the result all the F writ petitions are dismissed.")

118 Arvind P. Datar, The case that saved Indian democracy, The Hindu, Apr. 24, 2013. Available at www.thehindu.com/opinion/op-ed/the-case-that-saved-indian-democracy/article4647800.ece (last accessed on July 5, 2016.)

119 Id. *Explaining I.C. Golaknath v. State of Punjab* (1967 AIR 1643, 1967 SCR (2) 762) (India) ("The Kesavananda Bharati case was the culmination of a serious conflict between the judiciary and the government, then headed by Mrs. Indira Gandhi.")

120 Prakash, *supra* note 10.

121 Priyadarshi, Divyanshu. *Case Study: Smt. Indira Nehru Gandhi v. Shri Raj Narain and ANR. on 7 November, 1975*, Symbiosis Law School, Sept. 13, 2012. Available at http://ssrn.com/abstract=2146120 (last accessed on Nov 6, 2016). (Explaining the decision in *The State of Uttar Pradesh v. Raj Narain* (1975 AIR 865, 1975 SCR (3) 333) (India) "The High Court held that Smt. Gandhi had procured assistance of Shri Yashpal Kapoor, a Gazetted Officer of the Government of India, the District Magistrate and Superintendent of Police, Rae Bareli, the Executive Engineer, PWD, and the Engineer, Hydel Department, for her election campaign and had thus committed corrupt practices under Section 123 (7) of the Representation of the People Act, 1951.")

122 Gandhi, *supra* note 3, at Para 1.

123 Prakash, *supra* note 10.

124 T. R. Andhyarujina, *When the Bench Buckled*, The Indian Express, July 8, 2015. Available at http://indianexpress.com/article/opinion/columns/when-the-bench-buckled/ (last accessed on Jul 5, 2016).

125 Prakash, *supra* note 10.

126 Andhyarujina, *supra* note 124.

127 Datar, *supra* note 102.

128 Andhyarujina, *supra* note 124.

129 *Sub-Committee On Judicial Accountability*, *supra* note 117. Justice Sharma Dissent at Para 11. ("The decision on such a dispute is left to the President, and he is not to act on the advice of the Council of Ministers but in accordance with the opinion of the Election Commission.")

130 Jenna Narayan, *'Defect-Shun': Understanding Schedule X to the Constitution of India*, 3 India L. J. Available at http://indialawjournal.com/volume3/issue_1/article_by_jenna.html (last accessed on July 7, 2016).

131 India Const., Schedule X, art. 6 (1)

132 N. Jayapalan, *Constitutional History of India* (1998), at 187. ("A reference may be made to the control of the Parliament over the Union executive. It has already been pointed out that the Union Cabinet is responsible to the House of the People. That means that the Ministry must resign if a vote of no confidence is passed against it in Parliament . . . All these methods can be adopted by parliament to enforce the responsibility of the executive to the legislature").

133 Stanley A. Kochanek & Robert L. Hardgrave, *India: Government and Politics in a Developing Nation* (Cengage Learning, 2007).

134 *Id.* ("On Nov. 7, 1990, V.P. Singh's government became the first to be voted out of office by a vote of no confidence. As mentioned before, in 1979, Prime Minister Desai had resigned before the vote was taken, and Charan Singh who succeeded him lasted only 24 days, never had a chance to even face Parliament.")

135 India Const. art 71, amended by The Thirty-Ninth Amendment Act, 1975.
136 Id at art. Article 329A.
137 Gandhi, *supra* note 3, at Para 91–3.
138 Divyanshu, *supra* note 121.
139 Gandhi, *supra* note 3, at Para 147.
140 Id at 157.
141 Id.
142 Nick Robinson, *Expanding Judiciaries: India and the Rise of the Good Governance Court*, 8 Wash. U. Global Stud. L. Rev. 1, 31–32 (2009)
143 Yaniv Roznai, *Unconstitutional Constitutional Amendments: A Study of the Nature and Limits of Constitutional Amendment Powers, London School of Economics* (2014) Available at http://etheses.lse.ac.uk/915/1/Roznai_Unconstitutional-constitutional-amendments.pdf (last accessed on July 11, 2016), at 57.
144 Robinson, *supra* note 142, at 32.
145 *Nixon, supra* note 2, at 240. (White, J. concurring). ("The majority states that the question raised in this case meets two of the criteria for political questions set out in *Baker v. Carr*, 369 U. S. 186 (1962).")
146 Gandhi, *supra* note 3. Chandrachud J. (concurring), at Para 686
147 Id at Para 687.
148 Baz Mohammad Kaker, *supra* note 33, at Para 61
149 Robinson, *supra* note 142, at 32.
150 Khaled Ahmed, *Restraint Must Follow Activism*, Friday Times, Feb. 3, 2012. Available at www.thefridaytimes.com/beta2/tft/article.php?issue=20120203&page=2 (last accessed on July 9, 2016). ("Just like Pakistan's Supreme Court with its background of bending like a reed to military's provisional orders (PCOs), the Indian Supreme Court submitted before the political power expressed through Prime Minister Indira Gandhi's emergency.)
151 Robinson, *supra* note 142, at 32. ("Public opinion, though, was shifting against the Prime Minister. The abuses of the Emergency and Indira Gandhi's subsequent loss in the polls when the Emergency ended in 1977 would be seared into the Indian collective conscious. Parliament had discredited itself, and the Court's basic structure doctrine seemed an increasingly sensible control.") See also P. P. Rao, "The Constitution, Parliament, and the Judiciary," in Pran Chopra, ed., *The Supreme Court Versus the Constitution: A Challenge to Federalism* (Sage Publications, 2006), at 73. ("The Supreme Court has emerged as the strongest wing of the state with unlimited and illimitable power.")
152 Gary J. Jacobsohn, *Constitutional Identity* (2010), at 52.

7 A proposed solution

Justiciability Council and four-element justiciability test

I. Challenges and opportunities for establishing repeatable restraint in Pakistan's Supreme Court

Each of the three countries in this study have varying colonization experiences with the law that impacted the delegation of judicial duties in their respective constitutions. Pakistan and India's Constitutions grant great power to the judiciary, while the U.S. Constitution makes the judiciary the least powerful of all the branches.[1] Accordingly, the jurisprudence of each country's Supreme Court concerning the scope of judicial review and the value of judicial restraint procedures and doctrines in the case-selection process varies greatly.

The judiciaries in Pakistan and India had historically adopted similar relaxed standards for justiciability, but this changed when Pakistan's Supreme Court was led by Chief Justice Iftikhar Chaudhry, as the Court entered uncharted territory with its expansion of judicial power. This was demonstrated by the Court's treatment of the legal phenomena of judges disqualifying the Prime Minister, as discussed in Chapter 6.

Since Chaudhry's retirement in 2013, the Court has adopted an informal policy of restraint under the leadership of three subsequent Chief Justices. While these Chief Justices have attempted to pull back from the Chaudhry era of "judocracy"[2] or "dictatorship of the judicial branch,"[3] the Court still lacks a case-selection process and discerning justiciability standard.

This chapter focuses on formulating a solution to fill this gap in Pakistan's judicial review process through a comparative analysis of the judicial review in Pakistan, India, and the United States. However, before presenting the solution, one must identify the historical challenges to adopting self-restraint doctrines and the opportunities presented by the Pakistani Supreme Court's current disposition towards restraint.

A. Challenges

i. General lack of standards

Before presenting a justiciability standard, it is important to note the lack of standards adopted by Pakistan's Supreme Court in general. Zeeshan Hashmi, former clerk for the Supreme Court of Pakistan, explained that while the Court is open to academic critiques, it is hard-pressed to adopt repeatable standards.[4] Former Chief Justice Tassaduq Jillani echoed these sentiments when explaining that the Chief Justice "cannot bind his successors nor is he bound by precedent which to his understanding of law is not tenable . . . the Supreme Court is not bound by the principle of stare decisis generally."[5] This is why "there is no objective test of the use of suo motu and Article 184(3) powers."[6] In relation to the justiciability or maintainability of petitions, the Supreme Court itself has held that

> no yardstick could be fixed as to who could file review petition against a judgement of the court nor any embargo could be placed on the right of an ordinary litigant to file a review petition for the redress of his grievance, which would always be decided on the basis of the facts and circumstances of each case.[7]

The Court also explained in *Muhammad Azhar Siddique v. Federation of Pakistan* that in "almost every petition filed before this Court under Article 184(3) of the Constitution, objection regarding maintainability is raised and dealt with by the court on the facts and circumstances of each case."[8]

The reluctance to adopt binding standards is partially related to the political tumult that Pakistan has experienced in the past with military coups and suspensions of the Constitution. Babar Sattar explained that even the "good judges have a lot of faith in their ability to do good and when you have unguided or excessive power, you can use it to repel dictators."[9] However, he argues that judges who are "visionary enough with enough conviction" would do a great service by establishing a binding standard for the exercise of judicial review under Article 184(3).[10]

ii. Role of Chief Justice

Without a standard, each Chief Justice is free to determine the level of the Court's exercise of judicial review, which some have concluded vests far too much power in the office of the Chief Justice. As Chief Justice Jillani stated, "the imprint of the Chief Justice is always present."[11] Following Chief Justice Iftiqhar Chaudhry, Pakistan's Supreme Court has been led by three Chief Justices who have adopted a policy of restraint.[12] As it relates to Chief Justice Jillani, "unlike his predecessor, who was accused of meddling in government affairs, Justice Jillani's term is credited with adopting the policy of 'judicial restraint' and bringing to a close years of judicial activism."[13]

The problem is that "if [the] distribution of power within an institution makes it susceptible to ready abuse, the institution remains at the mercy of the individual," or a Chief Justice.[14] The Court's reluctance to adopt standards allows the Chief Justice to exert control over the Court's use of judicial review; it also allows the Chief Justice to take cases based on the recommendations of other justices.[15] Interviews with justices and clerks of the Supreme Court indicated that the Chief Justice (with the assistance of the Registrar) would arrange hearings for any case that was deemed justiciable by any of his "brother judges." While the exercise of suo motu litigation through Article 184(3) of the Constitution is under the exclusive control of the Chief Justice, any justice could submit an issue to the Chief Justice, and Chief Justice would customarily accept the junior justice's recommendation to take up a case.

Cooperation among the judges and the diffusion of the Chief Justice's control over the Court's use of suo motu can be positive elements, but the informality of this system should be reconsidered. If there is no discussion and debate that critically examines the justiciability of every petition within the Court itself, then such a screening process should be carried out by an outside council. The United States and Indian Supreme Courts conduct their own regularly scheduled certiorari or maintainability assessments, as described in Chapter 5. However, due to the Pakistani Supreme Court's reluctance to adopt standardized procedures, as well as an increasingly unmanageable caseload and backlog, the best solution may be the establishment of an outside council to act as a filter for the Supreme Court, as will be explained below and as illustrated in Figure 7.1 later in this chapter. The establishment of such a council will be a key component to the evolution of a discerning justiciability standard.

B. Opportunities

i. Historical restraint doctrines

In adjusting the Court's justiciability standards, the Court can rely on its own judgments and dicta from past judges who were part of the Supreme Court's restraint policy in its first few decades of existence. Justice A. R. Cornelius, known as one of Pakistan's premier jurists, emphasized in one judgment that the Court should always keep in mind that "the will of the people is sovereign and is to be exercised through representative institutions as the essential feature of the constitutional order."[16] One commentator argued that "the tradition of judicial restraint may have ended in this country with the retirement of Judge A. R. Cornelius,"[17] but the Court can rely on his and other justice's judgments to revive restraint. Although the interventionism of the Supreme Court under Chief Justice Chaudhry and its overuse of judicial review ignored these considerations, restraint doctrines can be found in the history of the Court's jurisprudence.[18]

ii. Restoring public credibility

The Court's relationship with public opinion and credibility has been dynamic, because judges were once seen as stewards for the anti-democratic policies of various military-led governments. With the campaign launched by the Lawyers' Movement, lawyers and judges captured the public's attention unlike ever before by boldly deposing a military dictator and ushering in what was publicized as an era for the rule of law.[19]

Eventually some in the public resented the Lawyers' Movement,[20] while others argued that the movement was not populist but a "power grab by the members of the legal community."[21] Most damning and leading to severe damage "to the credibility of the higher judiciary" were allegations that Chief Justice Chaudhry's son was engaged in corrupt practices.[22]

While the bar and bench were joined together in the struggle to reinstate Chief Justice Chaudhry, their alliance did not survive the interventionist strategies of the Chaudhry Court. Various bar associations and leading lawyers began publicly rebuking the Court's overuse of judicial review as destabilizing to the country's democratic institutions.[23] Further, Pakistan's economic interests were harmed by "the damaging effects of the four years of unrestrained judicial activism," according to the former governor of the State Bank of Pakistan.[24]

All of this highlights the importance of Chief Justice Jillani's explanation that "legitimacy of our [the Supreme Court's] judgments would arise from our impartial application of law, [so] we should not overstep our lawful authority."[25] Therefore, the Court's adoption of a justiciability standard and institutionalization of judicial restraint could address a prudential[26] concern for the Court: public credibility. As Owen Fiss explains, the judge "is entitled to exercise power only after they have participated in a dialogue about the meaning of the public values."[27] Another theorist cited by Pakistan's Supreme Court explains that

> one of the principal aims of a system of judicial review must be to maintain a high level of public confidence in the administrative decision making process and this must also be borne in mind in assessing the level of judicial intervention which is desirable.[28]

While it is important to remember that elected branches must concentrate on appeasing "public opinion [which] is always changing," the Court does not face elections and thus should act as a "check against these political decisions."[29] One way to ensure that the Court's directives will be respected and enforced by the political branches is for the Court to maintain a sufficient level of public support. As political figures must represent the will of the electorate, it is important for the electorate to respect the work of the Supreme Court, especially when the Court has historically lacked public support. In order to address the Court's recent loss of public credibility due to the overactive policies of Chief Justice Chaudhry, the Court should institutionalize judicial restraint and adopt a justiciability standard. This strategy would show that the Court is operating under a set of rules that apply equally to all litigants.

iii. Post-Chaudhry era of restraint

While a standard has not been institutionalized, the Chief Justices who have served after Chaudhry have adopted an overall policy of judicial restraint. Chief Justice Nasirul Mulk has "carried forward the policy of judicial restraint of his predecessor, Justice Tassaduq Hussain Jillani staying away from the affairs of other institutions, taking few suo motu notices and focusing the attention on disposing cases of ordinary litigants."[30] Further, "chief justices Tassaduq Hussain

Jillani and Nasirul Mulk turned a new leaf by refusing to interfere in politics, governance and economic policymaking."[31]

Judicial restraint was examined in various judgements by the Court, including one opinion authored by Chief Justice Jillani that concluded that:

> the legitimacy of its [the Court's] does not arise from the beauty of the language or the use of populist rhetoric. Rather it radiates from . . . judicial restraint displayed in deference [to] the principle of trichotomy of powers and in an impersonal impartial application of the law.[32]

While Chief Justice Jillani recognizes the "significant growth" of judicial review around the world, he concluded that

> this expansion has taken place in the shadow of competing concerns for "vigilance" and "restraint" . . . and it is faithfulness to these dual concerns of "vigilance" and "restraint" which produces the unique supervisory jurisdiction which is the landmark of judicial review.[33]

Chief Justice Jillani wrote in a case concerning contempt of court that "the principle of showing judicial restraint . . . is by now a well-recognized principle in our judicial history, which has been time and again reiterated by the Court."[34] Demonstrating commitment to this principle, Chief Justice Jillani ordered a review to establish "parameters over the use of the Supreme Court's suo motu powers."[35] Most recently, Chief Justice Anwar Zaheer Jamali explained that petitions challenging issues that "fall within the policy realm of the executive" would not be granted relief because "this Court has always shown restraint in interfering into this domain."[36] Based on this restraint, "unless the constitutionality of the law is tested on the touchstone of constitutional provisions and struck down, it will remain law of the land and duty of the Court would be to enforce the same."[37]

Accordingly, the Court had originally dismissed initial petitions calling for the Supreme Court to disqualify the Prime Minister for corruption charges in 2016 as being frivolous.[38] Though the Court reversed this decision in 2017, there are other examples of the Court dismissing petitions based on justiciability considerations since 2013. While these cases demonstrate the Court's openness to adopting self-restraint doctrines, the Court has failed to adopt a method and binding standard for case-selection and justiciability. Solidifying the current wave of restraint and preventing a future Chief Justice from abusing the Supreme Court's judicial review powers will require the adoption of a regulated justiciability standard and process.

iv. Improving quality of judgments

Along with constitutional analysis, the Court has also quantitatively attempted to address its issues with backlog and workload management, as detailed in Chapter 5. Dealing with 18,000 petitions per year, not including 1.2 million Human Rights Cell requests,[39] is a monumental task.[40] Further, the Supreme Court's hyper-activism under the Chief Justice Chaudhry's leadership led to a wave of public interest litigation.[41] Even in defense of the Supreme Court's capability, the Registrar of the Supreme Court reported that "in the wake of heightened public expectations . . . [the Supreme Court] strived hard to meet those expectations . . . it was no easy task since it necessitated undertaking a heavy workload and longer working hours."[42]

The quality of judgments from the Supreme Court is also impacted by the quantity of cases.[43] This is especially important when one remembers that "there is none above the Supreme Court to correct its errors."[44] Therefore, any mistakes or misstatements of law at the Supreme Court cannot be appealed to any higher court and stand as written until overruled in a subsequent case.[45] Accordingly, to improve the quality of judgments from the Supreme Court it is important to limit the number of cases it accepts for hearing and review. The combination of the Court's current heavy workload and recently adopted judicial restraint policy presents an opportune moment to adopt a justiciability standard and process.

The standard proposed by this study is adaptable to the unique context of judicial power in Pakistan. Flexibility is especially important due to the historical, structural, and jurisprudential uniqueness of Pakistan that has been described throughout this study.

II. Context for judicial review

As stated in Chapters 2 and 3, in order to properly contextualize judicial review in Pakistan, one must understand the differentiating colonial legacies in the American and Indian colonies and how this impacted early use of judicial review by the courts of Pakistan, India, and the United States. Subsequently, in Chapter 4, structural differences between the three countries were examined in order to assess the judicial review powers the founders of each country wanted to grant to the judiciary. Pakistan's socio-political factors have also been compared in Chapter 4 to the United States and India in order to understand the distinct need for flexibility in legal standards based on Pakistan's unique political history. Finally, the differences in existing justiciability procedures and standards were examined in Chapter 5. Each of these points will be summarized below in order to illustrate the context for this study's prescription.

III. Repeatable restraint standard

Despite the recent overuse of judicial review, an absence of structuralized judicial restraint principles, and unique socio-political conditions in Pakistan, the Supreme Court must take the opportunity to establish a justiciability standard that can regulate the Court's use of its review powers. The Supreme Court of Pakistan should create a new standard for the exercise of its jurisdiction under Article 184(3) for both public interest and suo motu litigation. As stated by Babar Sattar, "it is essential for the Supreme Court to constitute a larger bench and clearly lay out the basis for exercise of suo motus so that they get delinked from the whims and wishes of an incumbent CJ."[46]

The following four-part standard could be introduced by the Supreme Court based on a review of its own jurisprudence.

i Does the petition present a matter of public importance?
ii Does the petition raise the enforcement of fundamental rights?
iii Is there an alternative remedy readily available at either the High Court or at an executive agency?
iv Would the exercise of judicial review disturb the trichotomy of powers by violating democratically delegated constitutional powers in the Parliament or Prime Minister's office?

It is important to keep in mind the two kinds of litigation that will be impacted most by the adoption of this standard. When it comes to suo motu litigation based on Article 184(3), the Chief Justice should apply this standard before taking notice of a case to ensure that he or she does not overuse the Court's judicial review power or run afoul of the separation of powers doctrine. When it comes to public interest litigation, the same standard would apply. However, it would be applied by the Justiciability Council through the new bifurcated petition process rather than by the Chief Justice. Both the Chief Justice and the Justiciability Council will need to rely on this standard as a primary hurdle that all parties must pass before gaining access to the Supreme Court.

A. Elements 1 & 2: matter of public importance for enforcement of a fundamental right

Without a standard, the Supreme Court is only limited by the language of 184(3), which requires a matter of public importance concerning a fundamental right. Therefore, the proposed standard accepts these two elements as the foundation of its evaluation of justiciability. The Supreme Court has recognized that

> each petitioner, in order to be able to successfully invoke this jurisdiction, is required to satisfy the Court about the two-fold requirement stipulated in Article 184(3), viz., the petition raises a question of public importance with reference to the enforcement of Fundamental Rights.[47]

However, the interpretation of what constitutes a "matter of public importance" concerning a fundamental right is rather expansive.[48] For example, in the *Memo-gate* controversy, the Supreme Court ruled that an accusation of treason against Ambassador to the United States Husain Haqqani passed the two-part requirement for Article 184(3).[49] Criticism was raised against this decision, which essentially allowed the leader of the political opposition, Nawaz Sharif, to have standing to bring a claim that was meant to embarrass and perhaps dislodge the ruling People's Party of Pakistan's administration.[50]

When Sharif himself became Prime Minister again in 2013 and was faced with allegations of corruption, the Court temporarily rejected petitions against him as non-justiciable.[51] Yet, since the Court failed to enact a narrower interpretation of Article 184(3) generally, eventually petitions against Sharif lodged by his political opponents were accepted for review by the Court. This ultimately led to the Supreme Court of Pakistan dismissing its second prime minister within five years. The Court's failure to establish jurisprudence that narrows the interpretation of these two elements in Article 184(3) can partly explain the decision of the Court to controversially grant standing to a party whose interests seemed more political than legal.

Accordingly, the Supreme Court will need to evolve and narrow its interpretation of the first two elements. The Court could alter and adapt concepts of standing and ripeness from the United States, and engage in a critical evaluation of whether litigants before the court have suffered direct, imminent or actual harm rather than suffering "in some indefinite way in common with people generally."[52]

As discussed in Chapter 5, the Supreme Courts of Pakistan and India have both rejected the restrictive interpretation of standing developed by the U.S. Supreme Court. However, this should not preclude the Court from critically evaluating whether the disputed law or executive action actually produces an imminent and tangible harm to fundamental rights.[53] Such a change would not extinguish public interest litigation or suo motu altogether, but rather would allow the Court to reserve its powers for matters that are properly within the purview of the judiciary while restraining itself from deciding non-legal matters.

While the Supreme Court of India has not adopted the more rigid standing requirements of the United States, it has examined ripeness and imminence in its decision in *S.M.D. Kiran Pasha vs Government of Andhra Pradesh*, where the Court held that it must protect a plaintiff if he or she can provide "sufficient particulars of proximate actions as would imminently lead to a violation of right."[54] Therefore, the inclusion of "imminent harm" would improve case filtering practices for the Supreme Court of Pakistan while respecting the Court's historical policy of ensuring access to justice for aggrieved parties.

Despite suggesting a narrowing of the interpretation of Article 184 (3) in order to ease the Court's workload, this study takes into account that the Supreme Court of Pakistan, like India's, has historically recognized the right to challenge governmental violations of fundamental rights even when traditional locus standi requirements could not be met. However, narrowing the interpretation of "public importance" and "fundamental rights" will improve the ability of the Supreme Court of Pakistan to avoid granting hearings to petitioners who have not suffered a legal violation of their fundamental rights, but rather are attempting to use the Court for political ends. A critical evaluation in conjunction with the narrow interpretation of these two elements will allow non-governmental organizations or other civic groups representing the interests of poor or disenfranchised communities to continue to bring claims before the court. Further, the Court could continue to exercise its suo motu powers, albeit in more limited circumstances.

B. Element 3: alternative remedies

The third element addresses the potential for an alternative remedy from either the High Courts or an administrative agency. This element is indirectly embedded in the Supreme Court process, as formal complaints must describe whether the plaintiff sought relief from a High Court before approaching the Supreme Court.[55] However, the Supreme Court has often set aside the duty of litigants to seek remedy from the High Courts.[56]

While the High Courts of Pakistan have varying levels of effectiveness, they are often superseded by the Supreme Court's broad interpretation of its powers under Article 184(3). The High Courts are often ignored in order to accelerate the remedy for parties. However, this discourages the High Courts from improving their functionality and often allows the Chief Justice to ignore the need for institutional reforms in the High Courts. Further, when the Supreme Court becomes the first forum for a dispute, the parties' right to appeal can sometimes be denied as there is no higher court before which one could appeal the Supreme Court's decision. Therefore, the addition of a third element in the test for Article 184(3) serves three purposes:

- i protects parties' right to appeal by sending them to a lower court before coming to the Supreme Court,
- ii allows the Supreme Court to redirect petitions to the lower court for adjudication, and
- iii encourages Chief Justices to make institutional improvements to the administration of the High Courts.

The second part of the third element mentions executive agencies, which are utilized in the Human Rights Cell of Pakistan's Supreme Court. As the Cell is able to dispose of over 100,000 complaints per year by working cooperatively with executive agencies,[57] the Supreme Court should consider transferring more petitions for resolution by the Cell before granting hearings to petitioners under Article 184(3).

C. Element 4: trichotomy of powers

The fourth element is perhaps the most substantive addition to the Court's consideration of justiciability. While the Supreme Court has discussed the trichotomy of powers and the role of the court vis-à-vis political branches in various judgments, this question has not been systematically addressed whenever the Court exerts its powers under Article 184(3). Therefore, adding this to the four-part test for justiciability requires the Court to consider the ramifications of its actions in a three-branch system. The language of the standard is flexible to allow the Court to develop its interpretation over time, but the Court will need to use this element to begin seriously considering when its exercise of judicial review violates the separation of powers laid down by the Constitution.

This standard could eventually play a role similar to *Baker v. Carr*, where the U.S. Supreme Court defined non-justiciable issues based on several factors such as:

- i "a textually demonstrable constitutional commitment of the issue to a coordinate political branch"
- ii "the impossibility a Court's undertaking independence resolution without expressing lack of respect due to coordinate branches of government"
- iii "a lack of judicially discoverable and manageable standards for resolving it"
- iv "the impossibility of deciding without an initial policy determination of a kind clearly for nonjudicial discretion"
- v "the potentiality of embarrassment from multifarious pronouncements by various departments" and
- vi "an unusual need for unquestioning adherence to a political decision already made."[58]

If the Supreme Court of Pakistan were to consider these types of factors as part of its trichotomy analysis, the Court could reserve its right to exercise judicial review for proper cases while deferring to the political branches for policy decisions or the execution of duties vested in those branches by the Constitution.

This standard would coincide with the suggestions of Tayyab Mehmud, in his seminal article *Praetorianism and Common Law in Post-Colonial Settings: Judicial Responses to Constitutional Breakdowns in Pakistan.*[59] Mehmud argues that the Supreme Court should adopt the political question doctrine in order to avoid exercising judicial review to legitimize extra-constitutional regimes like military dictatorships. He states that "judicial oversight of extra-constitutional regimes will be facilitated if courts develop consistent yardsticks of judicial review when constitutional orders are in place."[60] While *this* study does not propose the wholesale adoption of the political question doctrine as it exists in U.S. jurisprudence, the fourth element of the justiciability standard requires the Court to critically examine several factors to ensure that it is operating within its constitutionally designated bounds and is paying proper deference to decisions made by the elected branches where it is due.

While this standard should be implemented by the Supreme Court Chief Justice in their consideration of exercise suo motu, there must be a separate system installed to evaluate the thousands of other claims that arrive in the Registrar's office each year. The creation of a Justiciability Council will ensure the long-term success of the justiciability standard as a means of addressing the critiques of the Court's abuse of its judicial review powers and to address the logistical concerns of an often overburdened apex court.

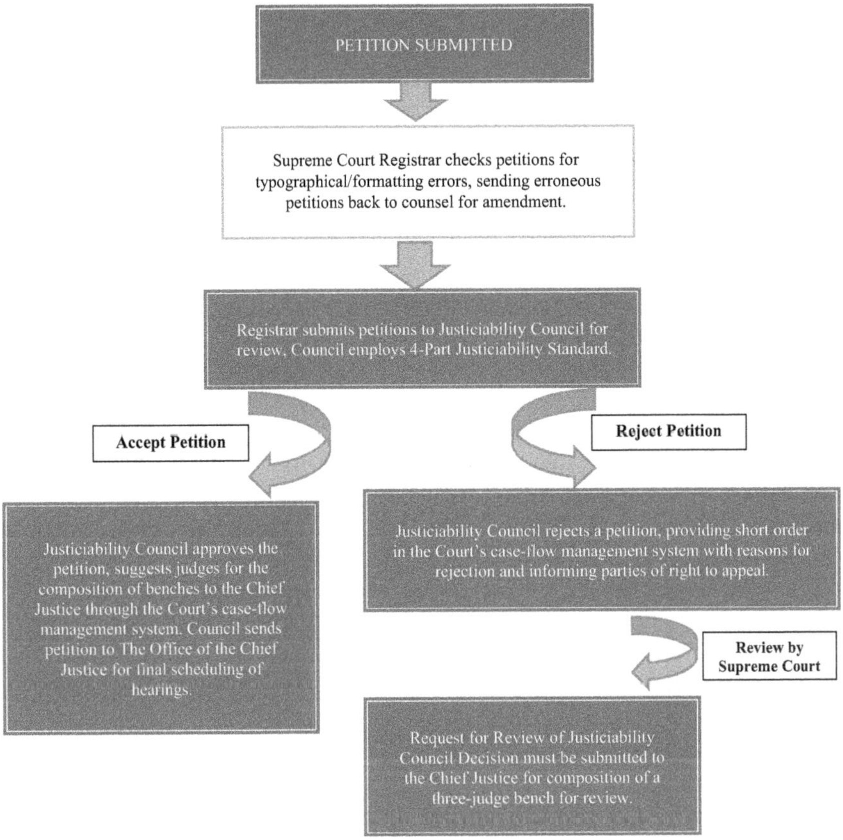

Figure 7.1 Proposed process

IV. Creation: constitutional amendment, law, or Supreme Court Rules change

The Justiciability Council could be established through three methods: Parliament could amend the Constitution to create the Council, Parliament could pass a statute creating the Council, or the Supreme Court could alter its own Rules. The first two options would mean that the elected branches would write legislation creating the Council, allowing the democratic process to shape the judicial review exercised by the Court. This would adhere to what Justice Alvin Robert Cornelius recognized as a "universal rule that the will of the people is sovereign."[61] However, as with the *Munir Hussain Bhatti* case, the Supreme Court of Pakistan errs towards invalidating statutes or constitutional amendments that allow Parliament to exert some degree of control over the Court's use of judicial review.[62] It is likely that if the legislative method were adopted, the establishment of Justiciability Council could be invalidated by the Supreme Court.

The more viable option is for the Supreme Court itself to amend the Supreme Court Rules of 1980. The Rules have been changed several times, and in 2014 Chief Justice Nasirul Mulk established a two-judge committee to revisit the Rules of the Court in order to address the problem of case backlog.[63] In a similar manner, the Supreme Court, under the leadership of the Chief Justice, could call for a commission to investigate changing the Rules to establish the Justiciability Council. Once the commission explores the Council's creation, they would likely need the approval of the Chief Justice to alter the Rules, who would need to file a notification in the federal government notification system.[64]

There is a risk and opportunity with this strategy: the risk is that according to this plan, the creation of the Council would hinge completely on the Chief Justice calling for this sort of change. The opportunity is that for the first time in the Court's history, it could set up its own institution for restraint, rather than having one imposed upon it through a military dictate or parliamentary constitutional amendment. If the judiciary were to take this step itself, the often-repeated claim that any control exerted by Parliament over the Court's exercise of judicial review endangers judicial independence could be invalidated.

The plan to establish the Council through the Supreme Court is a compromise and it lacks the involvement and approval of the political branches that embody the democratic will of the people. However, the in-house method of amending the Supreme Court Rules avoids the minefield of the historically contentious relationship between Parliament and Prime Minister on one side and the Court on the other when it comes to controlling the Court's power.[65]

Further, even if the Court created the Council through its rules, salaries could not be paid to those Council members without approval from either Parliament or the Prime Minister.[66] Through the creation of the federal budget each year, the President and Prime minister can with the approval of Parliament determine the salaries and benefits of all government employees, which would include the Council members.[67] Alternatively, Parliament could pass a bill to allow the Council members to be paid. A similar bill has been debated in 2016 in the National Assembly to pay for the salaries of the Election Commission of Pakistan members.[68] Therefore, a salary and benefits bill will need to be passed by Parliament, or the Prime Minister will need to set aside funds in the annual budget for Council salaries even if the Supreme Court creates the Justiciability Council itself through a change in the Supreme Court Rules.[69] This would allow elected branches to exercise the power of the purse in the creation of the Council, a power that the Supreme Court constitutionally lacks.

V. Composition and appointment of the Justiciability Council

The composition of Pakistan's Justiciability Council is a departure from the examples of the United States and India, as both countries require their currently serving judges to hold admissibility meetings regularly.

However, in the United States during the 1970s a blue ribbon study was commissioned by Chief Justice Warren E. Burger to "examine the Supreme Court's burgeoning case load."[70] This study recommended the creation of a National Court of Appeals, which would "screen all petitions for certiorari and appeals which now would be filed in the Supreme Court, and to refer only the most 'review-worthy' to that Court for disposition."[71] The suggestion was dismissed by retired Chief Justice Earl Warren[72] and there was a "massive outpouring of learned criticism of the national court, much of it from present justices and judges,"[73] while members of the study group attempted to defend the recommendation.[74] Justice Arthur Goldberg concluded in an opinion column published in the *New Republic* that there is only one Supreme Court and this creation of a National Court of Appeals may be unconstitutional as it stripped the Supreme Court of the right to determine which cases it would hear.[75]

Many of the concerns about such a proposal can be allayed by the composition of Pakistan's Justiciability Council being six *retired* judges:

- i one retired Chief Justice of the Supreme Court,
- ii one retired justice of the Supreme Court, and
- iii four retired Supreme Court justices, each with experience of serving on a High Courts so that all four High Courts (Punjab, Sindh, Balochistan, and Peshawar) are represented.

The inclusion of retired justices addresses one of the major critiques raised against the National Court of Appeals in the United States: that this institution would be seen by Supreme Court justices as usurping their power and acting in a supervisory role over the court. By restricting membership to former justices of the High and Supreme Courts, the Justiciability Council of Pakistan will be composed of members that are familiar with the jurisprudential trends and personalities of the Court. This will allow the relationship between the Council and the Supreme Court of Pakistan to be cooperative rather than adversarial. If properly established, the Council would be seen by the justices of the Supreme Court as supporters of the Court's overall mission to deliver quality judgments to the proper litigants.

The creation of a separate Justiciability Council in Pakistan is based on the same problem as was addressed by the American study group that recommended the National Court of Appeals: to help the Court manage its heavy workload. Without a separate Council, the Supreme Court of Pakistan would be overwhelmed by the multi-step justiciability standard this study presents. Designating one day each week for admissibility or justiciability conferences to analyze this standard would limit the amount of time the Court can spend hearing cases or drafting judgments. Therefore, shifting some of the work of disposing improper petitions to the Council will facilitate the Supreme Court's work.

Further, the appointment of retired justices to the Justiciability Council is in line with a newly developing practice in Pakistan to appoint retired judges to quasi-judicial roles. For example, a commission appointed in 2016 to conduct an inquiry into corruption claims against Prime Minister Sharif was headed by a former justice of the Supreme Court.[76] The formula for the composition of the Justiciability Council can also be found in the Election Commission of Pakistan, which has five seats filled by one retired justice from the Supreme Court[77] and a retired judge from each of the four High Courts.[78] The inclusion of a justice from each of the High Courts in the Justiciability Council is especially important as a means to ensure that Element 3 (alternative remedies available at a High Court) is properly analyzed. In order to understand whether alternative remedies are readily available at the High Courts, the Council members must possess knowledge about each of the High Courts. As former members of the High Court and the Supreme Court, the four Council members will have intimate knowledge about the effectiveness of their respective High Court and whether litigants will be able to receive justice at that level.

However, unlike the Election Commission,[79] which is appointed directly by the President with the advice of the Prime Minister, the appointment of Justiciability Council members must be executed according to Article 175A of the Constitution. Because of the judicial nature of their activity, the Councilmembers should undergo the same scrutiny that justices for the Supreme Court must face. The final change to the judicial appointment process came with the passage of the Nineteenth Amendment and the crafting of Article 175A. As it stands, according to Article 175A, the Chief Justice will nominate candidates to the Judicial Commission for discussion and consideration. If the Commission approves an appointment, it is sent to Parliament for review. If the Parliamentary Committee approves the nomination, it is forwarded to the President for formal confirmation. However, if the Committee rejects the nominee it must provide written reasons to the Judicial Commission for their rejection. This process should be used in order to select the proper set of judges for the Justiciability Council.

VI. Rule of Three and short order

The U.S. Supreme Court has adopted the Rule of Four, which allows the Court to grant writs of certiorari to a case if four of the nine justices believe the petition presents a justiciable question.[80] However, with six members on the Justiciability Council, a Rule of Three could be introduced in Pakistan whereby any petition that is deemed justiciable by at least half of the Council will be submitted to the Office of the Chief Justice for scheduling. This decision would not be binding on the Supreme Court, as the judges subsequently assigned to the case could dismiss a case as non-justiciable after initial oral hearings are held.

However, if the petition is deemed non-justiciable by four or more members of the Council according to the standard proposed above, the petition would be dismissed without the scheduling of a hearing before the Supreme Court. The Rule of Three would do away with a majority rule in order to facilitate the goal of the Council, which should be a meaningful and critical discussion regarding the justiciability of claims.

If a petition were to be rejected, the Council would need to distribute a short order to the parties through the Registrar. In order to facilitate the work of the

Court and Council and the sharing of information between the two, the Council should use the same digital case-flow management system used by the Supreme Court.[81] Using this system, the Council could publish its short order for any justice, their staff, and the concerning litigants to review.

While the short order would not carry the same legal weight or provide extensive reasoning like a Supreme Court judgment, it would provide a brief explanation of the reasons why the petition was rejected. This short order will serve two very important purposes. First, the Council explaining its reasons for rejection could help educate litigants about which claims the Council will submit to the Court. Eventually, this could have the effect of creating a self-filtering system among Supreme Court advocates once they know the types of claims the Justiciability Council will refuse to send to the Chief Justice for scheduling. Secondly, the reasons given in the short order would allow the three-judge justiciability appeal bench, which will be described below, to conduct a procedural review of the Council's decision without having to review all submissions made by both parties.

The inclusion of retired justices may be critiqued for not going far enough to restrain the Supreme Court from overusing its judicial review powers. Retired justices may share ideas with those currently serving on the Court concerning the proper extent of the Court's power. This is especially true when one considers that the appointments to the Council will continue to originate from the office of the Chief Justice as designated by Article 175A of the Constitution. There is a possibility that the Council could be packed by the Chief Justice and Judicial Commission with activist members who approve every petition for review, leaving the Justiciability Council meaningless as a filter for the Supreme Court.

However, as described above, appointment under Article 175A does not merely include the Chief Justice, but a council of members and a parliamentary oversight committee. It is unlikely that unqualified candidates with close personal relationships or a similar judicial perspective to the Chief Justice could be appointed. Rather, through the rigorous multi-step nomination, confirmation and appointment process of Article 175A, the Council's members will need to possess the requisite level of skill and expertise to be appointed and then properly execute their functions.

The method of the Council's establishment and its composition will be key to establish whether it can actually perform its function or be relegated to a rubber-stamp institution, granting hearings for all petitions based on the pretense that they are protecting judicial independence by allowing all litigants to come before the Supreme Court. However, if the Council's function is properly framed by the Chief Justice and through the language of the Supreme Court Rules as being a substantive forum for the critical evaluation of justiciability, the Council could truly serve judicial independence. By being critical in the analysis of justiciability, the Council would be assisting the Supreme Court in allocating its time and resources to proper cases that require the Court's attention and power. Not only would this serve the independence of the Supreme Court but it would also help the Court maintain its public credibility and legitimacy by restraining the Court in some instances, while allowing it the flexibility to take action in exigent circumstances.

VII. Review by three-judge Supreme Court bench

Another way this process confronts the Supreme Court's historical turf-protection is to grant petitioners the right to appeal a rejection by the Justiciability Council. The appeal would need to be examined by three Supreme Court judges (i.e. two-judge bench), who would conduct a procedural review of the Council's decisions. As discussed above, by requiring the Council to provide reasons for finding a petition non-justiciable, the justiciability procedure facilitates a procedural review by the two-judge bench.

The review conducted by the appeals bench should be similar to judicial review of administrative agency action. According to this type of review, the appeals bench will weigh the Council's judgment based on "the thoroughness of evidence in its consideration, the validity of its reasoning, its consistency with earlier and later pronouncements and all those factors which give it power to persuade, if lacking power to control."[82] During these reviews, the appeals bench will be provided with the short order from the Justiciability Council as well as the original petitions submitted by the parties in order to evaluate the following:

i whether the Council acted beyond its designated authority[83] or right to discretion,[84]
ii whether the Council's rejection was arbitrary,[85] and
iii whether the Council's rejection failed to respect procedural requirements.[86]

In the United States, the Administrative Procedure Act[87] lays out many issues that are designated as non-reviewable, which, if employed by the Supreme Court of Pakistan's appeals bench, could limit the scope of review without overburdening the Court.[88] In any event, the two-judge review should normally defer to the Council's ruling and limit its review to procedural issues relating to the Council's decision.

The right to appeal will raise an immediate complaint about the proposed justiciability procedure: namely, that every party whose petition is rejected by the Council will appeal. This would essentially require a three-judge bench to be composed for every rejected petition, which would not serve the purpose of this procedure to ease the workload of the Supreme Court while institutionalizing a justiciability standard. However, the likelihood of appeal will likely depend on how often the appeal bench overturns the decision of the Justiciability Council. If the appeals bench consistently overturns the Council's rejection of petitions, the need for the Council would become questionable as Council members would continue to feel pressured to grant oral hearings to all petitioners.

If, however, the Council correctly applies the justiciability test and the appeals bench upholds most of the Council's determinations, litigants' desire to appeal the justiciability decision will be greatly diminished. One way to accomplish a cooperative relationship between the appeals bench and the Justiciability Council is having the Council composed of senior retired members of the 'judicial family.' Based on the composition of the Council and the proper execution of its duties, eventually, parties will seldom expend the time and resources needed to appeal a dismissal, knowing the appeal will most likely be dismissed as well.

Granting the right to appeal reserves the right of the Supreme Court to deliver the final word on the Court's exercise of judicial review, ensuring that the Justiciability Council does not threaten judicial independence as understood by the Court in its prior jurisprudence. Further, it guarantees that the parties can appeal the decision to a higher authority, which is one of the problems with the apex court's expansive use of judicial review as it often limits the parties' right to appeal when the forum of first instance in a case is the highest court of the land.

VIII. Application

The proposed four-part justiciability standard and Justiciability Council could provide a method for the Supreme Court of Pakistan to retain its role as constitutional guardian while systematically restraining its use of judicial review. Further, this could serve to solidify the current judicial trend of judicial restraint proposed by each Chief Justice that has succeeded Chief Justice Chaudhry in 2013.

The proposed standard and case-selection process has been designed in a manner suited to the uniquely tumultuous political climate of Pakistan and takes into account the Supreme Court's insistence on easing access to justice for disadvantaged groups in the society. Though there might be reluctance among judges in Pakistan to immediately implement such a change, this study has described the immediate need for adopting a standard and identified methods and merits of establishing a Justiciability Council. To show the applicability and effectiveness of the standard, this section will outline how the Justiciability Council may interpret the justiciability of petitions seeking the disqualification of a future Prime Minister for allegations of corruption.

Petitions to the Supreme Court requesting the dismissal of the Prime Minister based on corruption allegations have become par for the course since the *Gilani* case, as demonstrated by Nawaz Sharif's subsequent dismissal by the Court. As described in Chapter 6, five years after the Court unilaterally dismissed Prime Minister Gilani, the Court reaffirmed its decision by disqualifying Prime Minister Sharif for possessing unreported and uncollected assets from his foreign corporation. Going forward, the winner of the 2018 elections will likely face similar petitions that could be effectively resolved by the Court if the justices follow the proposed justiciability procedures and standard from this study.

Without a standard, it would be reasonable to expect a more activist justice like Chaudhry in the future to pursue the disqualification proceedings much further than the restraint-oriented Chief Justices who succeeded Chaudhry. While these Chief Justices have provisionally emphasized restraint in order to prohibit the Court from abusing its judicial review authority, a justiciability standard and procedure could accomplish a similar result but in a way that could bind the hands of a future overly activist Chief Justice.

In relation to future corruption claims against the Prime Minster of 2018, according to the proposed standard and procedure, parties would need to submit their petitions to the Justiciability Council via the Registrar. The Justiciability Council could apply the four-part justiciability standard by beginning with the first two elements: whether the issue presents a matter of public importance for the enforcement of fundamental rights. Following much of the Supreme Court's jurisprudence, it is likely that the Justiciability Council would rule that the people of Pakistan are impacted by corruption that may have cost the Exchequer 50–70 billion dollars per year,[89] and that their fundamental rights to "access to justice and independence of the judiciary" were impacted by the Prime Minister's corruption.[90]

In the evaluation of the third element, the Court must determine if there is an effective alternative remedy available. This was examined by the Supreme Court in the 2016 pleas for disqualifying Prime Minister Sharif for comments he made in a Parliamentary speech, and the Registrar determined that one of the reasons that PTI's petition was not justiciable was because the petitioners had not exhausted lower court remedies, like the High Court.[91]

Other than seeking remedy at a High Court, another alternative could be the kind of commission suggested by Nawaz Sharif to investigate the accusations against his family for corruption in 2016. However, based on the statement of Chief Justice Anwar Zaheer Jamali,[92] it is likely that the Council would evaluate whether the Commission was in fact 'toothless' and thereby not an effective alternative remedy. Nevertheless, if the Commission were to be given some substantive powers and deemed effective by the Justiciability Council, the Council could dismiss the petition for failing the third element of the test.

Finally, the Court would need to consider the fourth element and determine what impact its decision to disqualify the Prime Minister would have on the trichotomy of powers. The ability of the petition to pass the Justiciability Council's analysis would depend on the remedy requested by the petitioners. If petitioner sought to have the Supreme Court unilaterally disqualify and remove the Prime Minister as it did for Prime Minister Gilani[93]and later for Nawaz Sharif,[94] the Council would likely determine that the petition failed to satisfy the fourth element as it would demonstrate a disregard for the constitutionally mandated delegation of duties and separation of power. The actual disqualification of the Prime Minister is a right vested in the Speaker of the House and the Election Commission.[95] The only way to respect the trichotomy of powers is to reject petitions requesting a remedy involving the Court's circumvention of Parliament and the Election Commission in disqualifying the Prime Minster.

However, the determination by the Council could be different if the petitioner called for a different kind of remedy. The petition could pass the Council's fourth element review so long as the petitioner narrowly requests the court to interpret either Article 248[96] or Article 63[97] in relation to allegations against Prime Minister Sharif without calling for the Court to override the Election Commission or Speaker of the National Assembly.

Such a remedy would respect the trichotomy of powers, as the Court could take action within its proper purview of assessing legal claims while the Parliament and Election Commission handles the political job of disqualification. Further, jurists have raised specific legal questions relating to executive immunity under Article 248, which only explicitly prohibits criminal prosecutions of the President and Governor, but not the Prime Minister. Additionally, there is the issue of the scope of the Prime Minister's immunity in relation to other articles in the Constitution, like Article 25, which guarantees the equality of all citizens before the law,[98] or Article 10A, which protects the right to fair trial.[99]

While these issues may have political consequences, they are founded in a legal inquiry concerning the interpretation of the law, which Chief Justice John Marshall famously wrote was "emphatically the province and duty of the judicial department."[100] Therefore, the type of relief requested by the parties would control the Justiciability Council's decision. The Council would be obliged to reject petitions that hinged on the unilateral disqualification of the Prime Minister by the Supreme Court. However, the Council would likely accept that the fourth element of the justiciability standard was satisfied by petitions requesting the Court to interpret executive immunity or demand prosecution of the Prime Minister to be initiated by the Attorney General.[101] Either of these requested remedies would fall in line with the U.S. Supreme Court's decision in President Nixon's case, which revolved around the legal question of immunity while leaving the impeachment to the legislative branch.

Lastly, in relation to the fourth element, the Council would need to assess the political climate to understand whether a decision by the Court to disqualify the Prime Minister could lead to a military coup, suspension of the Constitution, and ultimate deprivation of judicial independence and the trichotomy of powers. Though the likelihood of a coup is currently low, it could change since some political parties have recently called for a military takeover and the installation of a non-elected technocratic government.[102] If the Council assesses the likelihood of a coup as high, it may reject any petitions relating to the disqualification or prosecution of the Prime Minister based on element four of the test, because such an action could invite the extra-legal dismissal of the whole elected government, as has happened in the past. The imposition of a coup following the disqualification of future Prime Minister of 2018 would deprive every branch of government of its rights to rule as elected representatives or properly appointed judges. This would need to be taken into account by the Court in assessing the justiciability of a petition seeking the Prime Minister's disqualification. Unlike the Supreme Courts of India and the United States, the Supreme Court of Pakistan must consider the drastic impact of its decisions in such an unstable political environment.

IX. Conclusion

The future of the Pakistani Supreme Court's judicial review power rests on whether the Court can adopt a policy of repeatable restraint that leaves room for proper judicial responses to politically unique situations like military takeovers. Implementing a system for repeatable restraint will require the adoption of a new justiciability standard and the establishment of a Justiciability Council composed of retired justices from the Supreme Court. This proposed standard and Council would allow public interest litigation and suo motu to continue, providing the Court with flexibility in times of constitutional crisis. However, this new system would foster a critical analysis of the justiciability of petitions during periods of relative political stability and democratic rule.

The Council would assist the Supreme Court practically by disposing of non-justiciable petitions and theoretically by applying and interpreting the proposed justiciability standard. In relation to requests that the Supreme Court unilaterally dismiss the future Prime Minister of 2018 as it did with Prime Minster Gilani, the Court could avoid repeating its past excesses by limiting its query to legal questions of immunity. Further, this proposed method of repeatable restraint would allow the Court to avoid micromanaging judicial appointments and allow some input from elected representatives in the process.

Notes

1 Alexander M. Bickel, *The Least Dangerous Branch: The Supreme Court at the Bar of Politics* (2nd ed., 1986).

2 Anita Joshua, *Coup Fears Return to Pakistan*, The Hindu, June 23, 2012. http://m.thehindu.com/opinion/op-ed/coup-fears-return-to-pakistan/article3559757.ece (last accessed on Oct. 14, 2016). Citing blog by Yasser Latif Hamdani, famous attorney and civil rights activist.

3 Wischa Ngarmgoonanant, *Dictatorial Tendencies: Chaudhry and Pakistan's Supreme Court*, Yale Rev. Int'l Stud. (Jan. 2014). Available at http://yris.yira.org/essays/1236#_edn29 (last accessed on Oct. 14, 2016). ("If Chaudhry continues to expand his authority, Pakistan may be headed toward a dictatorship of the judicial branch.")

4 Interview with Zeeshan Hashmi, Former Clerk for the Supreme Court of Pakistan, in Lahore (Mar. 5, 2015). (Zeeshan Hashmi, former clerk for Chief Justice Iftikhar Chaudhry, Supreme Court of Pakistan, 2009).

5 Interview with retired Chief Justice Tassaduq Jillani, in Lahore (Mar. 9, 2015). (Hon. Justice Jillani served on the Supreme Court between 2004–2014, and was Chief Justice immediately after Chief Justice Chaudhry from 2013–2014.)

6 Babar Sattar, *Judicial Restraint or Complacency?* Dawn, July 14, 2014. Available at www.dawn.com/news/1118993 (last accessed on July 25, 2016).

7 Sindh High Court Bar Association v. Federation of Pakistan (2009) — PLD (SC) 879 (Pak.) Available at https://pakistanconstitutionlaw.com/p-l-d-2009-sc-879-2/

8 *Muhammad Azhar Siddique v. Federation of Pakistan* (2012) Const. Petition No.40 of 2012 & CMA No.2494/2 (SC) (Pak.), at Para 13.

9 Interview with Babar Sattar, High Court Advocate, in Islamabad (Mar. 18, 2015). (Babar Sattar is one of the most prolific and well-known legal scholars in Pakistan. He was threatened with contempt of court by the Supreme Court for writing an op-ed criticizing judicial trends under the Chaudhry Court especially as it relates to the Court's populist use of suo motu powers. See Babar Sattar, *Hubris as Justice*, Dawn, July 30, 2013. Available at www.dawn.com/news/1032941 (last accessed on Oct. 14, 2016). See Saad Rasool, *I am Babar Sattar*, Pakistan Today, Aug. 4, 2013. Available at www.pakistantoday.com.pk/2013/08/04/comment/columns/i-am-babar-sattar/ (last accessed on Oct. 14, 2016).

10 Id.

11 Interview with CJ Jillani, *supra* note 5.

12 Hasnaat Malik, *2014: From Judicial Activism to Judicial Restraint*, Express Tribune, Dec. 31, 2014. Available at http://tribune.com.pk/story/814921/2014-from-judicial-activism-to-judicial-restraint/ (last accessed on July 24, 2016.)

13 Hasnaat Malik, *Chief Justice Bows Out This Week*, Express Tribune, June 30, 2014. Available at http://tribune.com.pk/story/728986/chief-justice-jilani-bows-out-this-week/ (last accessed on Oct. 14, 2016).
14 Sattar, *supra* note 6.
15 Justice (r) Khalil-ur-Rehman Ramday, Interview on Mar. 12, 2015. (Justice Ramday gave a general description of the internal process without discussing specifics, but did cite one example relating to a project in Muree wherein the Chief Justice was moved to take suo motu notice after a justice recommended the case through a note to the Chief Justice.)
16 Tayyab Mahmud, *Praetorianism and Common Law In Post-Colonial Settings: Judicial Responses to Constitutional Breakdowns in Pakistan*, 1993 Utah L. Rev. 1225 at 1239. Citing Governor-General's Case, 1955 P.L.D. (F.C.) (Pak.) at 511 (Cornelius, J., dissenting), at 515–16.
17 Anwar Syed, *Judiciary and Public Opinion*, Dawn, Jan. 31, 2010. Available at www.dawn.com/news/843451/judiciary-and-public-opinion (last accessed on Oct. 14, 2016).
18 For example, *Medhi v. Pakistan International Airlines Corp* (1998) 793 PLD (SC) (Pak.)
19 See Moeen S. Cheema & Ijaz Shafi Gilani, *The Politics and Jurisprudence of the Chaudhry Court 2005–2013* (2015). Justice Khalil-Ul-Ramday Foreword.
20 Sattar, *supra* note 6. ("average Joe mocking the lawyers' movement and its wages.")
21 Ngarmgoonanant, *supra* note 3. Citing Haris Gazdar, *One Step Forward, Marching to the Brink*, 44 Econ. & Pol. WKLY. 9 (2009).
22 Faisal Siddique, *Judicial Accountability*, Dawn, Aug. 1, 2016. Available at www.dawn.com/news/1274492/judicial-accountability (last accessed on Oct. 14, 2016).
23 Qaiser Zulfiqar, *PM Contempt: Asma Jahangir Terms August 8 as a 'black day in judicial history'*, Express Tribune, Aug 8. 2012. Available at http://tribune.com.pk/story/419356/pm-contempt-asma-jahangir-terms-august-8-as-black-day-in-judicial-history/ (last accessed on July 29, 2016). *Most of suo motu Notices of Former CJP Iftikhar Chadhry Were Beyond Law: President SCBA (Supreme Court Bar Association)*, The Nation, Nov. 11, 2015. Available at http://nation.com.pk/national/11-Nov-2015/most-of-suo-motu-notices-of-former-cjp-iftikhar-chaudhry-were-beyond-law-president-scba (last accessed on July 31, 2016) ("[Barrister Ali Zafar stated that] most of the suo motu notices taken during the term of former CJP Iftikhar Chaudhry were beyond law. They should be reviewed.")
24 Malik, *supra* note 12. ("The risk profile of Pakistan, which was already quite high, has been elevated with the addition of Litigation Risk.")
25 Interview with CJ Jillani, *supra* note 5. Citing judgment in *Dossani Travels v. Federation of Pakistan*, Civil Appeal No. 800 of 2013. (SC) (Pak.)
26 Bickel, *supra* note 1, at 27.
27 Owen M. Fiss, *The Forms of Justice*, 93 Harv. L. Rev. 1, 13 (1979).
28 *Dossani Travels v. Federation of Pakistan*, Civil Appeal No. 800 of 2013. (SC) (Pak.) Citing Mike Radford, "Mitigating the Democratic Deficit? Judicial Review and Ministerial Accountability," in Peter Leyland and Terry Woods, eds., *Administrative Law Facing the Future* (1997), at 57.
29 Ngarmgoonanant, *supra* note 3. Citing Haris Gazdar, *One Step Forward, Marching to the Brink*, 44 Econ. & Pol. WKLY. 9.
30 Hasnaat Malik, *Supreme Court's Year of Transition*, Express Tribune, Dec. 31, 2015. Available at http://tribune.com.pk/story/1019061/supreme-courts-year-of-transition/ (last accessed on July 24, 2016.)
31 Malik, *supra* note 12.
32 *Dossani Travels, supra* note 28.
33 Id at Para 27. Citing *Michael Fordham, Judicial Review Handbook* (2nd ed., 1997), at 148–77

34 Criminal Original Petition No.92 of 2013 (Contempt proceedings against Imran Khan Chairman, Pakistan Tehreek-i-Insaf). (SC) (Pak.), at Para 9.
35 *SC Suggests Review of Suo Motu Powers*, Express Tribune, Apr. 4, 2014. Available at http://tribune.com.pk/story/691250/sc-suggests-review-of-suo-motu-powers/ (last accessed on Oct. 14, 2016).
36 Aamir Zahoor-ul-Haq v. Federation of Pakistan (2016) Civil Review Petition No. 561 (SC)(Pak.) at Para 13.
37 Id at Para 21.
38 Hasnaat Malik, *Top Court Rejects PTI Plea to Disqualify PM Nawaz Over Panamagate*, Express Tribune, Aug. 30, 2016. Available at http://tribune.com.pk/story/1172878/top-court-rejects-pti-plea-disqualify-pm-nawaz-panamagate/ (last accessed on Oct. 15, 2016).
39 While a small number of these petitions are forwarded to the Chief Justice for review by the Supreme Court, most of the Human Rights petitions are settled without the involvement of the justices on the Supreme Court.
40 Pakistan Supreme Court Annual Report, 2014–2015 at 113. Available at www.supremecourt.gov.pk/links/sc-a-rpt-2014-15/index.html (last accessed Oct. 17, 2016).
41 Maryam Khan, *Genesis and Evolution of Public Interest Litigation in the Supreme Court of Pakistan: Toward a Dynamic Theory of Judicialization*, 28 Temple Int'l & Comp. L. J., 285 (2015).
42 Supreme Court Registrar Annual Report, 2010–2011, Available at www.supremecourt.gov.pk/Annual_Rpt/Registrar%20Report.pdf (last accessed Oct. 17, 2016).
43 See Vernon Valentine Palmer & Mohamed Y. Mattar, *Mixed Legal Systems, East and West* (2016), at 89 (When examining the Cypriot Supreme Court, author states "We must not underestimate, however, the impact of the quantity- and quality- of the case load. An important factor has to do with numbers.")
44 Markandey Katju (retired Chief Justice of India), *The Philosophy of Judicial Restraint,* Express Tribune, July 22, 2011. Available at http://tribune.com.pk/story/406897/the-philosophy-of-judicial-restraint/ (last accessed on Oct. 15, 2016).
45 See Pakistan Supreme Court Rules (1980), Order XXVI, Rule 1 ("Subject to the law and the practice of the Court, the Court may review its judgment or order in a Civil proceeding on grounds similar to those mentioned in Order XLVII, rule I of the Code and in a criminal proceeding on the ground of an error apparent on the face of the record.")
46 Sattar, *supra* note 6.
47 *Muhammad Azhar Siddique*, *supra* note 8, at Para 13.
48 Al-Jehad Trust (1996) PLD (SC) 324 (Pak.), at 429 ("Thus, the approach, while interpreting a constitutional provision should be dynamic, progressive, and oriented with the desire to meet the situation, which has arisen, effectively. The interpretation cannot be a narrow and pedantic. But the Court's efforts should be to construe the same broadly, so that it may be able to meet the requirements of ever changing society.")
49 *Watan Party and Others v. Federation of Pakistan and Others* (2012) PLD (SC) 292 (Pak.), at Para 9A (majority opinion) Available at www.supremecourt.gov.pk/web/user_files/File/Const.P. 77-78-79%20[Memogate]DetailedOrder.pdf (last accessed Oct. 16, 2016). (The Court recognized that the fundamental rights impacted included Article 9: Security of Person, Article 14: Dignity of Man, and Article 19A: Right to Information in matters of public importance.)
50 Marvi Sirmad, *Memogate: Public Interest or Political Interest,* Daily Times, Dec. 19, 2011. Available at https://marvisirmed.com/2011/12/20/memogate-public-interest-or-political-interest/ (last accessed on Aug. 2, 2016).
51 *Supreme Court Rejects Petitions in PM Disqualification Case*, Express Tribune, Dec. 9, 2014. Available at http://tribune.com.pk/story/804091/sc-rejects-petitions-in-pm-disqualification-case/ (last accessed on July 30, 2016).
52 Frothingham v. Mellon, 262 U.S. 447 (1923) at 488. ("the party who invokes the [judicial review] power must be able to show not only that the statute is invalid but that he has sustained or is immediately in danger of sustaining some direct injury as the result

of its enforcement, and not merely that he suffers in some indefinite way in common with people generally.")

53 Imminent harm inquiry is used in both standing and ripeness evaluations by the United States Supreme Court. See generally for ripeness, *Abbott Laboratories v. Gardner*, 387 U.S. 136 (1967). See also for standing, *Lujan v. Defenders of Wildlife*, 504 U.S. 555 (1992).

54 *S.M.D. Kiran Pasha v. Government of Andhra Pradesh* (1989) SCR, Supl. (2) 105 1990 SCC (1) 328 (India), at Para 21.

55 For example: Supreme Court Rules of Pakistan, *supra* note 45, at Order XXV, Rule 6 ("An application for the enforcement of any other fundamental right shall be filed in the Registry . . . It shall also state whether the applicant has moved the High Court concerned for the same relief and, if so, with what result.")

56 Feisal Naqvi, *Memogate Redux*, Express Tribune, Jan. 9, 2012. Available at http://tribune.com.pk/story/318897/memogate-redux/ (last accessed on Aug. 3, 2016.) ("For example, Article 199 says that a writ petition will only be maintainable if 'no other adequate remedy' is available. This requirement has never been interpreted literally but has been broadly interpreted over the past few decades so that the superior judiciary can intervene essentially whenever it feels like it.") (last accessed on Aug. 8, 2016).

57 Supreme Court of Pakistan, Annual Report 2010–2011, Available at www.supremecourt.gov.pk/Annual_Rpt/Human%20Rights%20Cell.pdf, at 129 (last accessed on Aug. 8, 2016).

58 Baker v. Carr, 369 U.S. 186 (1962).

59 Mahmud, *supra* note 16.

60 Id at 1304.

61 Governor-General's Case (1955) P.L.D. (F.C.) 511 (Pak.) (Cornelius, J., dissenting), at 515–16.

62 See generally Munir Hussain Bhatti v. Federation of Pakistan (2011) — PLD (SC) 407 (Pak.) Available at www.supremecourt.gov.pk/web/user_files/file/cps.10-18of2011.pdf

63 *SC Forms Committee to Revisit Court Rules of 1980*, Express Tribune, Sep. 25, 2014. Available at http://tribune.com.pk/story/767144/sc-forms-committee-to-revisit-court-rules-of-1980/ (last access on July 28, 2016).

64 For an example of a Supreme Court Circular to the Government, See Notification No. F. 59/80- SCA from Aug. 8, 2014.

65 See Sindh High Court Bar Association v. Federation of Pakistan (2009) PLD (SC) 879 (Pak.) Nadeem Ahmed v. Federation of Pakistan (2010) PLD (SC) 1165 (Pak.) Munir Hussain Bhatti, *supra* note 62.

66 The remuneration of justices on the Supreme Court and High Court is enumerated Pakistan Const., art. 205, Read in Conjunction with Schedule 5 of the Constitution.

67 See Gyana Ranjan Panda, *Information Kit on the Federal Budget of Pakistan, Center for Budget and Governance Accountability* (2011). Available at www.cbgaindia.org/wp-content/uploads/2016/03/Information-Kit-on-The-Federal-Budget-of-Pakistan.pdf (last accessed Oct. 17, 2016.) at 5 and 9. ("Typically, the Ministry of Finance or a division within it – coordinates and manages the formulation of the budget, requesting information from individual departments and proposing the trade-offs necessary to fit competing government priorities into the budget's expenditure totals . . . (p. 9) The second stage of the budget cycle occurs when the executive's budget is discussed in the legislature and consequently enacted into law [finance bill]. This stage begins when the executive formally proposes the budget to the legislature. The legislature then discusses the budget, which can include public hearings and votes by legislative committees. The process ends when the budget is adopted by the legislature, either intact or with amendments."

68 Amir Wasim, *NA Body to Take Up ECP Members' Salary, Allowances Bill*, Dawn, July 11, 2016. Available at www.dawn.com/news/1270079 (last accessed on July 29, 20016).

69 This would be unlike the Election Commission mentioned above, which was created by constitutional amendment. See Pakistan Const., art. 218 ("It shall be the duty of the Election Commission to organize and conduct the election and to make such arrangements as are necessary to ensure that the election is conducted honestly, justly, fairly and in accordance with law, and that corrupt practices are guarded against.")

70 *The National Court of Appeals: Composition, Constitutionality, and Desirability*, 41 Fordham L. Rev. 863 (1973) at 863.

71 Id, at 863–4. Citing Federal Judicial Center, *Report of the Study Group on the Caseload of the Supreme Court* v-vi, and AlS-A17(1972) Report Excerpts at 59 A.BAJ. 139 (1973).

72 Id at 871. ("Retired Chief Justice Earl Warrant has reportedly written a memo to all his former clerks, emphatically stating his opposition to the proposed national court on constitutional grounds.")

73 Id at 885.

74 William J. Brennan, *The National Court of Appeals: Another Dissent*, 40 U. Chi. L. R. 473 (1973). Citing Alexander Bickel, *The Overworked Court: A Reply to Arthur]. Goldberg*, The New Republic, Feb. 17, 1973, Address by Chief Justice Warren Burger to the Fiftieth Annual Meeting of the American Law Institute, May 16, 1973, reported in 41 U.S.L.W. 2627; Paul A. Freund, *Why We Need the National Court of Appeals*, 59 A.B.A.J. 247 (1973); Arthur Goldberg, One Supreme Court, The New Republic, Feb. 10, 1973, at 14–16; Eugene Gressman, *The National Court of Appeals: A Dissent*, 59 A.B.A.J. 253 (1973); Nathan Lewin, *Helping the Court with Its Work*, The New Republic, Mar. 3, 1973, at 15–19; Address by Earl Warren to the Association of the Bar of the City of New York, May 1, 1973.

75 *The National Court of Appeals, supra* note 70, at 871. Citing Alan M. Dershowitz, *No More a Court of Last Resort*, N.Y. Times, Jan. 7, 1973, and Arthur Goldberg, *One Supreme Court*, The New Republic, Feb. 10, 1973, at 14.

76 Amir Wasim, *Terms of Reference Finalised for Panama Inquiry Commission*, Dawn, Apr. 17, 2016. Available at www.dawn.com/news/1252569/tors-finalised-for-panama-inquiry-commission (last accessed on July 28, 2016.). ("Apart from finalising the ToRs, the government also decided to include banking and investigative experts in the commission, which will be headed by a retired judge – as announced by Prime Minister Nawaz Sharif in his address to the nation on Apr. 5.")

77 Pakistan Const., art. 213.

78 Pakistan Const., art. 218 (2).

79 The Election Commissioner and members of the Commission are appointed by the President according to Pakistan Const., arts 213 and 218.

80 James F. Fagan, Jr., *When Does Four of a Kind Beat a Full House? The Rise, Fall and Replacement of the Rule of Four*, 25 New Eng. L. Rev. 1101, 1105–6 (1991) ("Whether to grant a petition for writ of certiorari is determined by a rule of four, that is, the vote of at least four Justices to grant such writ.")

81 See generally Justice Mehta Kalash Nath Kohli, *Case Flow Management*, Supreme Court of Pakistan Report. Available at http://supremecourt.gov.pk/ijc/Articles/20/2.pdf (last accessed on Oct 15, 2016).

82 *Skidmore v. Swift & Co.*, 323 U.S. 134, 140 (1944).

83 Barbara Shapiro & Robert Jacobvitz, Administrative Law, 13 N. M. L. Rev. 235. ("Agency authority originates in an enabling statute in which the legislature makes an express delegation of power to the agency. If the agency acts inside the statutory limits, or vires, its action is valid; if it acts outside of those limits, or ultra vires, its action is void.")

84 Charles H. Koch Jr., *Judicial Review of Administrative Discretion*, 54 George Washington L. Rev. 469 at 470. (describes five types of discretion, two of which are not amenable to judicial review: when the agency is acting under unbridled powers granted to it by Congress or when the agency is making a "numinous decision" that is by its nature beyond the purview of judicial review.)

85 Id, at 493. ("The three reviewable types of discretion are generally covered by either the arbitrariness standard or the abuse of discretion standard.")

86 Id at 494. ("*Courts also have plenary power in reviewing procedures.* Some care should be taken here also because review of procedures is an easy way to take over substantive issues. A court is tempted to impose more formal procedures as a subterfuge to get at the substantive decision. Moreover, while more procedures will certainly improve the exercise of discretion in some instances, mere resort to formalizing procedures can do substantial harm. *It is essential that reviewing courts not impose more procedures on a program requiring the exercise of discretion merely because it cannot think of anything better to do.* Additional procedures can as easily harm these programs as help them. In lieu of doubtful procedural remedies for defective exercises of these three types of discretion, the court should usually confine itself to remedies aimed at any substantive defect. Often constructing a remedy is difficult, and courts are left with returning the decision to the agency and instructing it to try again.") (emphasis added).

87 Administrative Procedure Act (APA), Pub. L. 79–404, 60 Stat. 237.

88 Richard J. Pierce Jr., *What Do the Studies of Judicial Review of Actions Mean?*, 63 Wash. Coll. L. Admin. L. Rev. 77 (2010). Koch Jr., *supra* note 84.

89 Najma Minhas, *The Panama Papers and Pakistan: Beyond Nawaz Sharif*, The Diplomat, Apr. 11, 2016. Available at http://thediplomat.com/2016/04/the-panama-papers-and-pakistan-beyond-nawaz-sharif/ (last accessed on July 30, 2016.)

90 Muhammad Azhar Siddique, *supra* note 8, at Para 9.

91 Malik, *supra* note 38. ("The registrar office held that the plea prima facie appeared to be frivolous and the petitioner did not approach any High Court for the redress of grievance in the instant matter.")

92 Raza Khan, *CJP Declines to Form 'toothless commission' on Panama Leaks*, Dawn, May 13, 2016. Available at www.dawn.com/news/1258127 (last accessed on July 30, 2016).

93 Muhammad Azhar Siddique, *supra* note 8.

94 *Imran Ahmad Khan v. Miam Muhammad Nawaz Sharif*, Const. Petition No. 29 of 2016 (SC) (Pak.)

95 Pakistan Const., art. 63.

96 Pakistan Const., art. 248 "Protection to President, Governor, Minister, etc."

97 Id, at art. 63 "Disqualifications for membership of Majlis-e-Shoora (Parliament)"

98 Id, at art. 25 (1). ("All citizens are equal before the law and entitled to equal protection of law.")

99 Id, at art. 10A. ("Right to fair trial. – For the determination of his civil rights and obligations or in any criminal charge against him a person shall be entitled to a fair trial and due process.")

100 Marbury v. Madison, 1 Cranch 137 (1803).

101 This was the initial request from the Supreme Court regarding Prime Minister Gilani: to order the prosecution of President Zardari, which most would agree was within the purview of the Court. However, the Court overstepped its bounds after Gilani refused to execute the order, leading to his eventual illegitimate dismissal by the Supreme Court.

102 Muhammad Daim Faxil, *Pakistan at Risk for a Coup?*, The Diplomat, July 26, 2016. Available at http://thediplomat.com/2016/07/is-pakistan-at-risk-for-a-coup/ (last accessed on July 30, 2016).

References

Chapter 1 references

Books

Chandrachud, Abhinav. *An Independent, Colonial Judiciary: A History of the Bombay High Court During the British Raj, 1862–1947*. (Oxford University Press, 2015).

Cheema, Moeen, & Gilani, Ijaz Shafi. *The Politics and Jurisprudence of the Chaudhry Court 2005–2013*. (Oxford University Press, 2015).

Crosskey, William W. *Politics and the Constitution in the History of the United States*. (University of Chicago Press, 1953).

Haley, John O., & Takenaka, Toshiko. *Legal Innovations in Asia: Judicial Lawmaking and the Influence of Comparative Law*. (Edward Elgar Pub, 2014).

Hirschl, Ran. *Towards Juristocracy: The Origins and Consequences of the New Constitutionalism*. (Harvard University Press, 2007).

Holland, Kenneth M. *Judicial Activism in Comparative Perspective*. (Palgrave Macmillan, 1991).

Khan, Hamid. *Constitutional and Political History of Pakistan*. (2nd ed., Oxford Press Pakistan, 2009).

New York State Bar Association, *Yearbook* (1915).

Perry Jr, H.W. *Deciding to Decide: Agenda Setting in the United States Supreme Court*. (Harvard University Press, 1994).

Roosevelt, Kermit. *The Myth of Judicial Activism: Making Sense of Supreme Court Decisions*. (Yale University Press, 2008).

Schlesinger, Jr. Arthur M. *A Life in the 20th Century: Innocent Beginnings 1917–1950*. (Houghton Mifflin Co., 2000).

Schwartz, Herman. *Right Wing Justice*. (Nation Books, 2004).

Shesol, Jeff. *Supreme Power, Franklin Roosevelt vs. the Supreme Court*. (W.W. Norton Company, 2011).

Tushnet, Mark & Khosla, Madhav. *Unstable Constitutionalism*. (Cambridge University Press, 2015).

Academic articles

Brilmayer, Lea. *The Jurisprudence of Article III: Perspectives on the "Case or Controversy" Requirement*, 93 Harv. L. Rev. 297 (1979).

Canon, Bradley C. *Defining the Dimensions of Judicial Activism*, 66 JUDICATURE 236 (1982–83).

Cappelletti, Mauro. *Judicial Review in Comparative Perspective*, 58 Cal. L. Rev. 1017 (1970).

Chase, Harold. *Federal Judges: The Appointing Process*, 51 MINN. L. REV. 185 (1966–1967).

Edwin C. Surrency, *The Courts in the American Colonies*, 111 AMER. J. LEG. HIST. 253 (1967).

Faqir, Khan, Islam, Fakhrul & Rizvi, Shahid Hassan. *The Lawyers Movement for Judicial Independence in Pakistan: A Study of the Musharraf Regime*, 2 Asian J. Soc. Sci. & Human. 345 (2013).

Green, Craig. *An Intellectual History of Judicial Activism*, 58 Emory L. J. 1195 (2009).

Hirschl, Ran. *The New Constitution and Judicialization of Pure Politics Worldwide*, 75 FORD. L. REV. 721 (2000).

Khan, Maryam S. *Genesis and Evolution of Public Interest Litigation in the Supreme Court of Pakistan, Toward A Dynamic Theory of Judicializatio*n, 28 Temp. J. Intl. & Comp. L. 284 (2015).

Mahmud, Tayyab. *Praetorianism and Common Law in Post-Colonial Settings: Judicial Responses to Constitutional Breakdowns in Pakistan*, 1993 Utah L. Rev. 1225 (1993).

Plucknett, Theodore F.T. *Bonham's Case and Judicial Review*, 40 Harv. L. Rev. 30 (1926).

Ross, Frank B., & Lindquist, Stefani. *The Decisional Significance of the Chief Justice*, 154 U. Pa. L. Rev. 1665 (2006).

Sharafi, Mitra. *A New History of Colonial Lawyering: Likhovski and Legal Identities in the British Empire*, 32 L. & Soc. Inquiry 1059 (2007).

Thayer, James B. *The Origin and Scope of the American Doctrine of Constitutional Law*, 7 Harv. L. Rev. 3 (1893).

Young, Earnest A. *Judicial Activism and Conservative Politics*, 73 U. Colo. L. Rev. 1139 (2002).

Periodicals

Faisal Siddiqi, *Judicial Accountability*, Dawn, Aug. 1, 2016. Available at www.dawn.com/news/1274492/judicial-accountability (last accessed on August 1, 2016).

Jamali, Jamaluddin. *'PPP lawyers, Asma Jahangir rant against SC verdict'*, Pakistan Today, Apr. 27, 2012. Available at www.pakistantoday.com.pk/2012/04/27/news/national/ppp-lawyers-asma-jahangir-rant-against-sc-verdict/?printType=article (last accessed on June 20, 2016).

Malik, Hasnaat. *2014: From Judicial Activism to Judicial Restraint*, Express Tribune, Dec. 31, 2014. Available at http://tribune.com.pk/story/814921/2014-from-judicial-activism-to-judicial-restraint/ (last accessed on July 24, 2016).

Panamagate Decision: Musharraf Congratulates Nation on SC's Verdict, Geo News, July 28, 2017. Available at www.geo.tv/latest/151432-panama-verdict-musharraf-congratulates-nation-on-scs-decision (last accessed on October 14, 2017).

Petition Against Judge's Appointment Dismissed, Express Tribune, Aug. 2, 2016. Available at http://tribune.com.pk/story/1153901/petition-judges-appointment-dismissed/ (last accessed on Aug. 13, 2016).

Sattar, Babar. *Judicial Restraint or Complacency?* Dawn, July 14, 2014. Available at www.dawn.com/news/1118993. (last accessed on July 25, 2016).

Schlesinger, Jr., Arthur M. *The Supreme Court: 1947*, Fortune, Jan. 1947.

Zulfiqar, Qaiser. *PM Contempt: Asma Jahangir Terms August 8 as Black Day in Judicial History*, Express Tribune, Aug. 10, 2012. Available at http://tribune.com.pk/story/419356/pm-contempt-asma-jahangir-terms-august-8-as-black-day-in-judicial-history/ (last accessed on Aug. 11, 2016).

Cases

UK

Dr. Bonham v. College of Physicians, (1610) 77 Eng. Rep. 638, 8 Co. Rep. 107.

United States

Nixon v. United States, 418 U.S. 683 (1974).

India

In re Special Reference No. 1 of 1998, 1998 7 SCC 739 (India).
Indira Nehru Gandhi vs. Shri Raj Narain, 1975 (Supp) SCC1, 2 SCR 347 (India).
Supreme Court Advocates-on-Record Ass'n v. Union of India, 1993 4 SCC 441 (India).

Pakistan

Imran Ahmed Khan v. Mian Muhammad Nawaz Sharif, C.M.A. No. 4978/2017 in Constitutional Petition No. 29/2016 and C.M.A. No. 2939/2017 in Constitutional Petition No. 29/2016. (SC) (Pak.) (July 28, 2017.) Available at www.supremecourt.gov.pk/web/user_files/File/Const.P._29_2016_28072016.pdf
Muhammad Azhar Siddiqui and others v. Federation of Pakistan and others, (2012) – PLD (SC) 774 (Pak.)
Nadeem Ahmed v. Federation of Pakistan, (2010) – PLD (SC) 1165 (Pak.) Available at www.supremecourt.gov.pk/web/user_files/file/18th_amendment_order.pdf
Sindh High Court Bar Association v. Federation of Pakistan, (2009) – PLD (SC) 879 (Pak.) Available at https://pakistanconstitutionlaw.com/p-l-d-2009-sc-879-2/

Miscellaneous

Barrett, John Q. *Arthur M. Schlesinger, Jr. – in Action, in Archives, in History*. Available at http://thejacksonlist.com/wp-content/uploads/2014/02/20071015-Jackson-List-re-Arthur-Schlesinger.pdf (last accessed on Oct. 31, 2016).
Interview with retired Chief Justice Tassaduq Hussain Jillani, Supreme Court of Pakistan, in Lahore (March 9, 2015).
Jetly, Rajshree. *Pakistan's Supreme Court and the National Reconciliation Ordinance: What now for Pakistan?*' Inst. S. Asian. Stud. Brief No. 147 (December 2009). Available at www.files.ethz.ch/isn/110966/148.pdf
Mate, Manoj S. *The Variable Power of Courts: The Expansion of the Power of the Supreme Court of India in Fundamental Rights and Governance Decisions* (University of California, 2010). Available at http://escholarship.org/uc/item/3f1640wm (last accessed on Oct. 31, 2016).

Moin, Umama, *Parliament and the Supreme: The Indian Experience*(Aligarh Muslim University, 2011). Available at http://shodhganga.inflibnet.ac.in/handle/10603/11379 (last accessed on Oct. 31, 2016).

Sale, Anna. *Obama vs. SCOTUS: Learning from FDR's Court Comeback*, New York Public Radio (Mar. 28, 2012). Available at www.wnyc.org/story/194795-last-incumbent-courtwatcher/.

Shapiro, Ilya. *Obama's Abysmal Record Before the Supreme Court*, Cato Institute, (Feb. 11, 2016.). Available at www.cato.org/blog/obamas-abysmal-record-supreme-court (last accessed on Oct. 22, 2016).

Chapter 2 references

Books

Amar, Akhil Reed. *America's Unwritten Constitution: The Precedents and Principles We Live By*. (Reprint ed., Basic Books, 2015).

Amar, Akhil Reed. *America's Constitution: A Biography*. (1st ed., Random House, 2010).

Aumann, Francis R. *The Changing American Legal System*. (Ohio State University Press, 1940).

Baylyl, C.A. *Rulers Townsmen and Bazaars: North Indian Society in the Age of British Expansion 1770–1870*. (Cambridge University Press, 1988).

Canny, Nicholas. *The Oxford History of the British Empire: Volume I: The Origins of Empire: British Overseas Enterprise to the Close of the Seventeenth Century: British Overseas Enterprise to the Close of the Seventeenth Century*. (Oxford University Press, 1998).

Chandrachud, Abhinav. *An Independent, Colonial Judiciary: A History of the Bombay High Court during the British Raj, 1862–1947*. (Oxford University Press, 2015).

Dharker, C. D. *Lord Macaulay's Legislative Minutes*. (Oxford University Press, 1946).

Durfee, Thomas. *Gleanings from the Judicial History of Rhode Island*. (S.S. Rider, 1883).

French, Laurence. *Native American Justice*. (Rowman & Littlefield, 2003).

Friedrich, Carl J. *The Impact of American Constitutionalism Abroad*. (Boston University Press, 1967).

Hamid, Abdul. *A Chronicle of British Indian Legal History*. (RBSA Publishers, 1991).

Hilkey, Charles Joseph. *Legal Development in Colonial Massachusetts, 1630–1686* (Hard-Press Publishing, 2013).

Kolff, D.H.A., *The Indian and the British Law Machines: Some Remarks on Law and Society in British India, in European Expansion and Law*. (Berg, 1992).

Macafee, Thomas. *Inherent Rights, The Written Constitution, and Popular Sovereignty: The Founder's Understanding*. (Greenwood Press, 2000).

McEwan, Cheryl. *Postcolonialism and Development*. (Routledge, 2008).

Olson, James. *Historical Dictionary of the British Empire*. (Greenwood Press, 1996).

Okafo, Nonso. *Reconstructing Law and Justice in a Postcolony*. (Ashgate Publishing, Ltd., 2012).

Reinsch, Paul S. *The English Common Law in the Early American Colonies*. (University of Wisconsin, 1899).

Richards, John F. *The New Cambridge History of India. The Mughal Empire*. (Cambridge University Press, 1995).

Rudolph, Lloyd I., & Rudolph, Susanne Hoeber. *The Modernity of Tradition: Political Development in India*. (University of Chicago Press, 1984).

Setalvad, M. C. *The Common Law in India.* (Stevens & Sons, Ltd., 1960).
Siddique, Dr. Osama. *Pakistan's Experience with Formal Law: An Alien Justice.* (Cambridge University Press, 2013).
Strickland, Rennard, *Fire and the Spirits: Cherokee Law from Clan to Court.* (University of Oklahoma Press, 1975).
Vine Jr, Deloria, & Lytle, Clifford M. *American Indians, American Justice.* (University of Texas Press, 2010).
Warren, Charles, *A History of the American Bar.* (Cosimo Classics, 1913).

Book chapters

Bhattacharya, Neeladri. "Remaking Custom: The Discourse and Practice of Colonial Codification" in *Tradition, Dissent and Ideology: Essays in Honour of Romila Thapar.* (R. Champaklaksmi and S. Gopal eds., Oxford University Press, 1996).
Brutus, "Anti- Federalist #11" in *The Anti Federalist Papers and the Constitutional Convention Debates* (Ralph Ketcham, ed., Signet Classic, 2003).
Brutus, "Anti-Federalist #15" in *The Anti Federalist Papers and the Constitutional Convention Debates* (Ralph Ketcham, ed., Signet Classic, 2003).
Hamilton, Alexander. "Federalist #78," in *The Federalist Papers*, (Clinton Rossiter, ed., New American Library, 1961).
Letter from Thomas Jefferson to Edmund Pendleton (Aug. 26, 1776), in *The Papers of Thomas Jefferson.* (Julian P. Boyd ed., Princeton University Press, 1950).
Sir Bartle Frere, Minutes to the Parliamentary Debates of the Act, reprinted in Cecil Meme Putnam Cross, *The Development of Self-Government in India, 1858–1914.* (University of Chicago Press, 1922).
Washbrook, D.A., Law, "State and Agrarian Society in Colonial India," in *Power Profit and Politics: Essays in Imperialism, Nationalism and Changes in the Twentieth Century India Vol 15, Pt. 3* (C. Baker, G. Johnson, and A. Seal, eds., Cambridge University Press, 2009). (originally published as a collection of essays in a special issue of Modern Asian Studies, July 1981).

Academic articles

Datla, Kavita Saraswathi., *The Origins of Indirect Rule in India: Hyderabad and the British Imperial Order*, 33 L. & Hist. Rev. 321 (2015).
Daniels, Ronald J. et al., *The Legacy of Empire: The Common Law Inheritance and Commitments to Legality in Former British Colonies*, 59 Am. J. Comp. L. 111 (2011).
Holland, Randy J. *Anglo-American Templars: Common Law Crusaders*, 8 Del. L. Rev. 137 (2006).
Krishnan, Jayath K. *Professor Kingsfield Goes to Delhi: American Academics, the Ford Foundation, and the Development of Legal Education in India*, 46 Am. J. Legal Hist. 447 (2004).
Lofgren, Charles A. *The Original Understanding of Original Intent?* 5 Constit. Comment. 77 (1988).
MacAffee, Thomas. *Inalienable Rights, Legal Enforceability and American Constitutions: The Fourteenth Amendment and the Concept of Unenumerated Rights*, 36 Wake Forest L. Rev. 758 (2001).
Saunooke, Robert O. *Tribal Justice the Case for Strengthening Inherent Sovereignty*, 47 Judges' J. 15 (2008).

Sharafi, Mitra. *A New History of Colonial Lawyering: Likhovski and Legal Identities in the British Empire*, 32 L. & Soc. Inquiry 1059 (2007).
Stoebuck, William B. *Reception of English Common Law in the American Colonies*, 10 Wm. & Mary L. Rev. 393 (1968).
Surrency, Edwin C. *The Courts in the American Colonies*, 111 Amer. J. Leg. Hist. 253 (1967).
Wood, Gordon S. *The Origins of Judicial Review Revisited, or How the Marshall Court Made More Out of Less*, 56 Wash. & Lee L. Rev. 787 (1999).

Historical documents

A Collection of Treaties and Engagements with the Native Princes and States of Asia Concluded on Behalf of the East India Company by the British Governments in India, Viz. by the Government of Bengal Etc. Also Copies of Sunnuds Or Grants of Certain Privileges and Imunities to the East India Company by the Mogul and Other Native, United East India Company. (E. Cox and Son Printers to the Hon. United East-India Company, 1812). Available at https://archive.org/details/bub_gb_J_1RAAAAcAAJ (last accessed on Nov. 1, 2016).

Cases

Van Ness v. Pacard, 27 U.S. (2 Pet.) 137 (1829).

Miscellaneous

BBC, *Mughal Empire (1500s, 1600s)*. Available at www.bbc.co.uk/religion/religions/islam/history/mughalempire_1.shtml (last accessed on Oct. 17, 2016).
The Admission of Overseas Students to the Inner Temple in the 19th Century. Inner Temple. Available at www.innertemple.org.uk/history/historical-articles/35-admission-of-overseas?showall=&start=2 (last accessed on Oct. 17, 2016).
Joan-Pau Rubies, *Texts, Images, and the Perception of 'Savages' in Earlier Modern Europe: What We Can Learn from White and Harriot*, British Museum Organization, Available at www.britishmuseum.org/pdf/4-Rubies-Text%20Images%20and%20the%20Perception%20of%20Savages.pdf (last accessed on Oct. 17, 2016).
Mohammad Ali Jinnah Factsheet, Lincoln's Inn. Available at www.lincolnsinn.org.uk/images/word/Library/jinnah.pdf (last accessed on Oct. 17, 2016).
Mitra Sharafi, *South Asians at Inns, South Asian Legal History Resources*. Wisconsin School of Law. Available at http://hosted.law.wisc.edu/wordpress/sharafi/south-asian-law-students-at-the-inns-of-court/ (last accessed on Oct. 17, 2016).

Chapter 3 references

Books

Beck, James M. *The Constitution of the United States*. (James Truslow Adams ed., Doubleday, Doran & Company, Inc., 1941).
Blackstone, Sir William, Thomas Lee, John Eykyn Hovenden, and Archer Ryland, *Commentaries on the Laws of England: In Four Books; with an Analysis of the Work* (S. Sweet, 1829).

Bowen, Catherine Drinker. *The Lion and the Throne: The Life and Times of Sir Edward Coke (1552–1634)* (Hamilton, 1957).
Bradley, Anthony Wilfred, Ewing, Keith D. & Knight, Christopher. *Constitutional and Administrative Law*. (Pearson Books, 2014).
Bryce, Viscount James. *The American Commonwealth*. (Cosimo, Inc., 2007).
Crosskey, William W. *Politics and the Constitution in the History of the United States*. (University of Chicago Press, 1980).
Dicey, A.V. *The Law of the Constitution*. (Oxford University Press, 2013).
Goldsworthy, Jeffrey. *Parliamentary Sovereignty: Contemporary Debates*. (Cambridge University Press, 2010).
Haimes, Charles Grove. *The American Doctrine of Judicial Supremacy*. (The MacMillan Company, 1914).
Judicial Review and the Constitution (Chris Forsyth, ed., Hart Publishing, 2000).
Lalasaheb, Dr. More Atul. *An Appraisal of the Judicial System in India: A Critical Study on Judicial Independence Vis-à-vis Judicial Accountability*. (Laxmi Book Publication, 2015).
Lord, Coke, *Institutes of The Laws of England: The Fourth Part* (W. Clark and Sons, 1817).
Quincy, Jr. J. *Reports of Cases Argued and Adjudged in the Superior Court of Judicature of the Province of Massachusetts Bay Between 1761 and 1772* (1865; reissue, Russell & Russell, 1969).
New York State Bar Association, *Yearbook* (1915).
Parliamentary Sovereignty: Contemporary Debates. (Cambridge University Press, 2010).
Pylee, M.V. *The Federal Court of India*. (P.C. Manaklal and Sons Pvt. Ltd., 1966).
Ramraj, Victor V., and Thiruvengadam, Arun K. *Emergency Powers in Asia: Exploring the Limits of Legality*. (Cambridge University Press, 2010).
Singh, Virendra. *Indian Polity with Indian Constitution & Parliamentary Affairs*. (Neelkanth Prakashan, 2016).
The Genesis of the United States: A Series of Historical Manuscripts (Alexander Brown ed., Houghton, Mifflin, and Company, 1890).
Varnum, James M. *The Case Trevett v. Weeden: On Information and Complaint, for Refusing Paeper Bills in Payment for Butcher's Meat, in Market, at Par with Specie*. (Providence, 1787).
Wade, William, and Forsyth, C.F. *Administrative Law*. (Oxford University Press, 2009).
Willis, Hugh Evander. *Constitutional Law of the United States*. (The Principia Press, 1936).

Cases

UK

Ashbury Railway Carriage and Iron Company v. Riche, (1875) 14 Eng. Rep. 42, 7 L.R.C.P. (H.L.) 653.
Calvin's Case, (1608) 77 Eng. Rep. 377, 7 Co. Rep. ia, I3a (C.P.)
Case of Proclamations, (1610) 77 Eng. Rep. 1352, 12 Co. Rep. 74, EWHC KB J22.
Case of Ship-Money, (1637) 3 St. Tr. 825, reprinted in 52 L.W. Rev. 546 (1936).
City of London v. Wood, (1702) 88 Eng. Rep. 1592, 12 Mod. 669.
Colman v. Eastern Counties Railway Company, (1847) 48 Eng. Rep. 488, 10 Beav. 1.
Day v. Savadge, (1615) 80 Eng. Rep. 235 (K.B.)
Dr. Bonham's Case, (1610) 77 Eng. Rep. 638, 8 Co. Rep. 107a.

East Anglican Railway Company v. Eastern Counties Railway Company, (1868) 11 C.B. 775, 21 L.J.C.P. 23.
Lord Sheffield v. Ratcliffe, (1615) 80 Eng. Rep. 475, Hob. 334a (K.B.)
R. v. Love, (1653) 5 St. Tr. 43.
Thomas v. Sorrell, (1673) 124 Eng. Rep. 1098 (KB), EWHC J85, Vaugh 330.

United States

Bayard v. Singleton, 1 N.C. (Mart.) 48 (1787). (North Carolina)
Bowman v. Middleton, 1 S.C. (Bay) 252 (1792). (South Carolina)
Calder v. Bull, 3 U.S. (3 Dall.) 386, 1 L.Ed. 648 (1798).
Giddings v. Browne (1657), Printed in *2 Hutchinson Papers* 1 (Prince Soc., 1865).

(Massachusetts Bay)

Ham v. M'Claws, 1 S.C. (Bay) 38 (1789). (South Carolina)
Jones v. Commonwealth, 5 Va. (1 Call.) 208 (1799). (Virginia)
Williams Lindsay v. East Bay Street Com'rs, 2 S.C.L. (Bay) 38 (1796). (South Carolina)
Paxton's Case of the Writ of Assistance (1761), reported in J. Quincy, Jr., *Reports of Cases Argued and Adjudged in the Superior Court of Judicature of the Province of Massachusetts Bay Between 1761 and 1772* (1865; reissue, Russell & Russell, 1969). (Massachusetts)
Robin v. Hardaway (1772), 1 Jefferson 109, 114, 1 Va. Reports Ann. 58. (Virginia)
Rutgers v. Waddington (N.Y. City Mayor's Ct. 1784), Reprinted in Julius Goebel, Jr., *The Practice of Alexander Hamilton: Documents and Commentary Volume I*, 393–419 (Columbia University Press, 1964).
Vanhorne's Lessee v. Dorrance, 28 F. Cas. 1012, 2 Dallas (2 U.S.) 304 (1795).

India

Queen v. Ameer Khan, 6 B.L.K. 482. (India). (1871).
Reference By Governor General, (1955) – PLD (FC) 435. (India).
Secretary of State v J Moment, ILR 40 Cal 391 (1913), (1913) 15 BOMLR 27. (India).
State of Madras vs V.G. Row Union of India & State, (1952) SCR 597. (India)
The Empress vs Burah and Book Singh, 26 March, 1877 ILR 3 Cal 64 (1878). Available at http://indiankanoon.org/doc/600234/ (last accessed on Oct. 17, 2016)
Usif Patel v. The Crown, (1955) – PLD (FC) 387. (India)

Pakistan

Federation of Pakistan v. Maulvi Tamizuddin, (1955) – PLD (FC) 240 (Pak.)

Academic articles

Allan, T.R.S. Constitutional Dialogue and the Justification of Judicial Review, 23 Oxford J. L. Stud. 563 (2003)
Forsyth, Christopher. *Of Fig Leaves and Fairy Tales: The Ultra Vires Doctrine, the Sovereignty of Parliament and Judicial Review*, 55 Cambridge L.J. 122 (1996)

Gledhill, Alan. *Unconstitutional Legislation*, 9 Indian Y.B. Intl. Affairs 40 (1952).

Hamburger, Phillip A. *Revolution and Judicial Review: Chief Justice Holt's Opinion in City of London v. Wood*, 97 Colum. L. Rev. 2091 (1994).

Holland, Randy J. *Anglo-American Templars: Common Law Crusaders*, 8 Del. L. Rev. 137, (2006).

Malcolm, Joyce Lee. *Whatever the Judges Say It Is? The Founders and Judicial Review*, 26 J.L. & Pol. 1 (2010).

Montpensier, Roy Stone de. *The British Doctrine of Parliamentary Sovereignty: A Critical Inquiry*, 26 La. L. Rev. 753 (1966).

Plucknett, Theodore F. T. *Bonham's Case and Judicial Review*, 40 Harv. L. Rev. 30 (1926).

Ringhand, Lori. *Fig Leaves, Fairy Tales, and Constitutional Foundations: Debating Judicial Review in Britain*, 43 Colum. J. Transnat'l L. 865 (2005).

Sathe, S.P. *Judicial Activism: The Indian Experience*, 6 Wash. U. J.L. & Pol'y 29 (2001).

Sathe, S.P. *Judicial Review in India: Policy and Limits*, 35 Ohio St. J. 4 (1974).

Treanor, William Michael. *The Case of the Prisoners and the Origins of Judicial Review*, 143 U. Pa. L. Rev. 491 (1994).

Walters, Mark D. *The Common Law Constitution in Canada: Return of Lex Non Scripta as Fundamental Law*, 51 U. Toronto L.J. 91 (2001).

Yoo, John C., & Prakash, Saikrishna B. *The Origins of Judicial Review*, 70 U. Chi. L. Rev. 887 (2003).

Historical documents

Government of India Act, 1935, [26 Geo. 5. C. 2.]. (UK). Available at www.legislation.gov.uk/ukpga/1935/2/pdfs/ukpga_19350002_en.pdf (last accessed Jan. 2, 2017).

Letter from Thomas Jefferson to William Nicholas, Sept. 7, 1803. Constitution Society. Available at www.constitution.org/tj/ltr/1803/ltr_18030907_nicholas.html (last accessed on Jan. 5, 2017.

Mitter, Brojendra Lal. *Advocate General of India at the Inaugural Address of the Federal Court of India*, Federal Court Reports, (1939).

New York State Bar Association, Document No. 941, *Duty of Courts to Refuse to Execute Statutes in Contravention of the Fundamental Law* (1915).

Report of the Joint Committee on Indian Constitutional Reform (H. M. Stationary Office, 1934).

Statute of Proclamations, Proclamations by the Crown Act, 31. Hen. 8 (1539) (UK).

Miscellaneous

Bandaranayake, Shirani A. *The Developments in the Role of the Doctrine of Ultra Vires in Central-Local Relations*, 8 Sri Lanka J. S.S. 25. (1985). Available at http://dl.nsf.ac.lk/bitstream/handle/1/5075/JSS8_25.pdf?sequence=1 (last accessed on Oct. 17, 2016).

Bateman, David. *Judicial Review in Kingdom and Dominions: The Historical Foundations of Judicial Review in the U.K., Canada, and New Zealand* (University of Pennsylvania). Available at www.polisci.upenn.edu/ppec/PPEC%20People/bateman/LSA%20Paper%20Final1.pdf (last accessed on Oct. 17, 2016).

Cooper, Ashley, & Cooper, Stephen. *The Forty-Shilling Freeholder*, Chivalry and War, Available at www.chivalryandwar.co.uk/Resource/THE%20FORTY%20SHILLING%20FREEHOLDER.pdf (last accessed on Oct. 17, 2016).

Karim, Justice (r) Fazal. *Paper on Judicial Review of Administrative Actions*, Supreme Court of Pakistan. Available at www.supremecourt.gov.pk/ijc/articles/16/2.pdf (last accessed on Oct. 17, 2016).

Legal History of New York, New York Courts, Available at www.nycourts.gov/history/legal-history-new-york/legal-history-eras-02/history-new-york-legal-eras-rutgers-waddington.html (last accessed on Oct. 17, 2016).

Moin, Umama. Parliament and the Supreme: The Indian Experience (2011) (Aligarh Muslim University). Available at http://shodhganga.inflibnet.ac.in/handle/10603/11379 (last accessed on Oct. 31, 2016).

Shabbir, Syeda Saima. *Judicial Activism Shaping the Future of Pakistan*, International Islamic University Islamabad, Jan. 30, 2013. Available at http://papers.ssrn.com/sol3/papers.cfm?abstract_id=2209067. (last accessed on Nov. 1, 2016).

United Kingdom Parliament. Birth of English Parliament: The Knights of the Shire. Available at www.parliament.uk/about/living-heritage/evolutionofparliament/originsofparliament/birthofparliament/overview/knights/ (last accessed on Mar. 1, 2017).

Chapter 4 references

Books

Ackerman, Bruce. *The Failure of the Founding Fathers: Jefferson, Marshall and the Rise of Presidential Democracy*. (Harvard University Press, 2007).

Chaudhri, Nazir Hussain. *Chief Justice Muhammad Munir: His Life, Writings, and Judgements*. (Research Society of Pakistan, 1973).

Dahl, Robert Alan. *How Democratic Is the American Constitution?* (Yale University Press, 2003).

Eighteenth Amendment Revisited. (Maqsudul Ali Khan, Muhammad Hanif, and Muhammad Nawaz Khan, eds., Islamabad Policy Research Institute, 2004).

Freeman, Michael (ed.) *Lloyd's Introduction to Jurisprudence* (8th ed., Sweet and Maxwell, 2014).

Gerber, Scott Douglas. *A Distinct Judicial Power: The Origins of an Independent Judiciary, 1606–1787*. (Oxford University Press, 2011).

Grossberg, Michael, & Tomlines, Christopher. *The Cambridge History of Law in America*. (Cambridge University Press, 2008).

Gupta, Manik Lal. *Constitutional Development of India*. (Atlantic Publishers and Distributers, 1989).

Haqqani, Husain. *Between Mosque and Military*. (Carnegie Endowment, 2005).

Jefferson, Thomas. *Jefferson's Manual of Parliamentary Practice (1801)*, reprinted in *Constitution, Jefferson's Manual, and Rules of the House of Representatives of the United States One Hundred Third Congress* s 283 (William Holmes Brown ed., 1993).

Kelsen, Hans. *Pure Theory of Law*. (Max Knight trans., 2014). (University of California Press, 1967).

Khan, Hamid, and Rana, Muhammad Waqar. *Comparative Constitutional Law*. (2nd ed., Oxford University Press, 2014).

Newberg, Paula. *Judging the State: Courts and Constitutional Politics in Pakistan*. (Cambridge University Press, 2002).

Omar, Imtiaz. *Emergency Powers and the Courts in India and Pakistan*. (Marinus Nilhoff Publishers, 2002).

Rakove, Jack. *Original Meanings: Politics and Ideas in the Making of the Constitution*. (Knopf Doubleday Publishing, 1997).

Sethy, Rabindra Kumar. *Political Crisis and President's Rule in an Indian State*. (APH Publishing Corporation, 2003).

Siddiqa, Ayesha. *Military Inc*. (Pluto Press, 2007).

Wood, Gordon. *The Creation of the American Republic: 1776–1787*. (The University of North Carolina Press, 2011).

Wynbrandt, James. *A Brief History of Pakistan*. (Facts on File Inc, 2009).

Academic articles

Adeney, Katharine. *A Step Towards Inclusive Federalism in Pakistan? The Politics of the 18th Amendment*, 42 Publius 539 (2013).

Beato, Andrew M. *Newly Independent and Separating States' Succession to Treaties: Considerations on the Hybrid Dependency of the Republics of the Former Soviet Union*, 9 Am. U. J. Int'l L. & Pol'y 525 (1994).

Berger, Raoul. *Standing to Sue in Public Actions: Is It a Constitutional Requirement?* 78 Yale L.J. 816 (1969).

Clanton, Bradley S. *Standing and the English Prerogative Writs: The Original Understanding*, 63 Brook. L. Rev. 1001(1997).

Clark, Bradford R. *The Supremacy Clause As A Constraint on Federal Power*, 71 Geo. Wash. L. Rev. 91 (2003)

Constable, Pamela. *Pakistan's Predicament*, 12 J. Democracy 1 (2001).

Elazar, Daniel J. *Contrasting Unitary and Federal Systems*, 18 Int. Polit. Sci. Rev. 237 (1997).

Fallon, Jr., Richard H. *Marbury and the Constitutional Mind: A Bicentennial Essay on the Wages of Doctrinal Tension*, 91 Cal. L. Rev. 1 (2003).

Federalism in the Constitutional Traditions of Canada and the United States, 1990 Duke L.J. 1229 (1990).

Graber, Mark A. *Establishing Judicial Review: Marbury and the Judicial Act of 1789*, 38 Tulsa L. Rev. 609 (2003)

Holland, Randy J. *State Constitutions: Purpose and Function*, 69 Temp. L. Rev. 989 (1996)

Hopton, T.C. *Grundnorm and Constitution: The Legitimacy of Politics*, 24 McGill L. J. 72 (1978).

Jaffee, Louis L. *Standing to Secure Judicial Review: Public Actions*, 74 Harv. L. Rev. 1265 (1961).

Kelsen, Hans, & Ehrenzweig, Albert A. "Professor Stone and the Pure Theory of Law." 17 Stan. L. Rev. 1128 (1965).

Khan, Maryan S. *Genesis and Evolution of Public Interest Litigation in the Supreme Court of Pakistan: Toward a Dynamic Theory of Judicialization*, 28 Temple J. Intl. & Comp. L. 284. (2015).

Leonard, James, & Brant, Joanne C. *The Half-Open Door: Article III, The Injury-In-Fact Rule, and the Framers' Plan for Federal Courts of Limited Jurisdiction*, 54 Rutgers L. Rev. 1 (2001).

Mahmud, Tayyab. *Praetorianism and Common Law in Post-Colonial Settings: Judicial Responses to Constitutional Breakdowns in Pakistan*, 1993 Utah L. Rev. 1225 (1993).

Massey, Calvin R., *The Locus of Sovereignty: Judicial Review, Legislative Supremacy, and Federalism in the Constitutional Traditions of Canada and the United States*, 39 Duke L. J. 1229 (1990).

Mendelson, Wallace. *The Judiciary Act of 1789: The Formal Origin of Federal Judicial Review*, 76 Judicature 133 (1992).
Reitz, John C. *Political Economy and Separation of Powers*, 15 Transnat'l L. & Contemp. Probs. 579 (2006).
Rose, Leo E., & Evans D. Hugh. *Pakistan's Enduring Experiment*, 8 J. Democracy 1 (1997).
Schlueter, David A. *Judicial Federalism and Supreme Court Review of State Court Decisions: A Sensible Balance Emerges*, 59 Notre Dame L. Rev. 1079 (1984).
Sunstein, Cass R. *What's Standing After Lujan? Of Citizen Suits, "Injuries," and Article III*, 91 Mich L. Rev. 163 (1992).
Tyler, David W. *Clarifying Departmentalism: How the Framers' Vision of Judicial and Presidential Review Makes the Case for Deductive Judicial Supremacy*, 50 Wm. & Mary L. Rev. 2215 (2009).
Weill, Rivka. *Reconciling Parliamentary Sovereignty and Judicial Review: On the Theoretical and Historical Origins of the Israeli Legislative Override Power*, 39 Hastings Const. L.Q. 457 (2012).
William Delker, Neals-Erik. *The House Three-Fifths Tax Rule: Majority Rule, the Framers 'Intent, and the Judiciary's Role*, 100 Dick. L. Rev. 341 (1996).

Book chapters

Hamilton, Alexander. *The Federalist No. 73*. (Alexander Hamilton). (Clinton Rossiter ed., New American Library, 1961).
Madison, James. *The Federalist No. 48*. The Federalist Papers (Clinton Rossiter ed., New American Library, 1961).
Publius, The Federalist, No. 52. The Federalist Papers. (Clinton Rossiter ed., New American Library, 1961).

Cases

United States

Coleman v. Miller, 307 U.S. 460 (1939).
Cooper v. Telfair, 4 U.S. (4 Dall.) 14 (1800).
Dredd Scott v. Sandford, 60 US 393 (1857).
Legal Tender Cases, 79 U.S. 457 (1870).
Marbury v. Madison, 5 U.S. 137 (1803).
Stuart v. Laird, 1 Cranch 299 (1803).

Pakistan

Miss Asma Jilani vs. The Government of the Punjab and Another, (1972) – PLD (SC) 139 (Pak.) Available at www.scribd.com/document/136858296/Asma-Jalani-v-Government-of-the-Punjab
Benazir Bhutto vs. Federation of Pakistan and others, (1988) – PLD (SC) 416 (Pak.) Available at http://nasirlawsite.com/historic/pld416.htm
The State vs. Dosso & Others, (1958) – PLD (SC) 533 (Pak.)

Historical documents

An Act to Establish the Judicial Courts of the United States, ch. 20, 1 Stat. 73 (1789).

Miscellaneous

Moin, Umama. *Parliament and the Supreme: The Indian Experience.* (Aligarh Muslim University, 2011). Available at http://shodhganga.inflibnet.ac.in/handle/10603/11379 (last accessed on Oct. 31, 2016).

Nehra, Krishan S., and Shroff, Kersi B. *Suspension and Reinstatement of the Chief Justice of Pakistan: From Judicial Crisis to Restoring Judicial Independence?* Library of Congress, (Aug. 2007). Available at www.loc.gov/law/help/pakistan-justice.php. (last accessed on Oct. 31, 2016).

Nawaz, Shah. *Judicial Activism and the Problem of Governance in India* (Aligarh Muslim University, 2011). Available at http://shodhganga.inflibnet.ac.in/handle/10603/40573 (last accessed on Oct. 31, 2016).

Synthesis of Parliamentary Sovereignty and Judicial Supremacy: Some Comparison, Byjus, Available at http://byjus.com/free-ias-prep/synthesis-of-parliamentary-sovereignty-and-judicial-supremacy-some-comparison (last accessed on Oct. 31, 2016).

Chapter 5 references

Books

Bickel, Alexander M. *The Least Dangerous Branch: The Supreme Court at the Bar of Politics*. (2nd ed., Yale University Press, 1986).

Bose, Bibhuti Bhushan ed. *Supreme Court of India: Practice & Procedure a Handbook of Information.* (3rd rev. ed., Supreme Court of India, 2010).

Chang, Wen Chen, Thio, Li-Ann, Tan, Kevin Y. L. & Yeh, Jiun-Rong. *Constitutionalism in Asia: Cases and Materials* (Hart Publishing, 2014).

Chemerinsky, Erwin. *Constitutional Law: Principles and Policies*. (4th ed., Aspen Publishers, 2011).

Constitutional Law of South Africa. (2nd rev., Stuart Woolman ed., 2008).

Gressman, E. et al. *Supreme Court Practice*. (9th ed., Bureau of National Affairs, 2007).

Hall, Kermit L., Ely, James W. & Grossman, Joel B. *The Oxford Companion to the Supreme Court of the United States*. (Oxford University Press, 2005).

Mehta, Pratap Bhanu. *The Oxford Handbook of the Indian Constitution*. (Oxford University Press, 2016).

Menski, Werner, Alam, R. and Raza, *Public Interest in Litigation in Pakistan*. (Pakistan Law House and Platinum, 2000).

Moeen, Cheema, and Ijaz Shafi Gilani, *The Politics and Jurisprudence of the Chaudhry Court 2005–2013*. (Oxford University Press, 2015).

Perry Jr, H. W. *Deciding to Decide: Agenda Setting in the United States Supreme Court*. (Harvard University Press. 1994).

Razzaque, Jona. *Public Interest Environmental Litigation in India, Pakistan, and Bangladesh*. (Kluwer Law International, 2004).

Rehnquist, William H. *The Supreme Court*. (Knopf Doubleday Publishing, 2002).

Seervai, H. M. *Constitutional Law of India, Volume III*. (2nd ed., Universal Law Publishing Co. Pvt. Ltd., 2011).

Periodicals

Iqbal, Nasir. *SC Urged to Regulate Use of suo motu Powers*, Dawn, Apr. 20, 2014. Available at www.dawn.com/news/1100999 (last accessed on May 23, 2016).

Nirupama, Subramanian. *In Clash of Institutions, Pakistan's Supreme Court Sets the Pace*, The Hindu, Apr. 4, 2012. Available at www.thehindu.com/opinion/op-ed/in-clash-of-institutions-pakistans-supreme-court-sets-the-pace/article2858006.ece (last accessed on Oct. 17, 2017).

Sabir Shah, *History of Voluntary Court Initiatives in Pakistan, India, US*. The News, Aug. 25, 2015. Available at www.thenews.com.pk/print/58421-history-of-voluntary-court-initiatives-in-pakistan-india-us (last accessed on May 23, 2016).

Academic articles

Alton, Stephen R. *From Marbury v. Madison to Bush v. Gore: 200 Years of Judicial Review in the United States*, 8 Tex. Wesleyan L. Rev. 7 (2001).

Barkow, Rachel E. *More Supreme Than Court? The Fall of the Political Question Doctrine and the Rise of Judicial Supremacy*, 102 Colum. L. Rev. 237 (2002).

Brilmayer, Lea. *The Jurisprudence of Article III: Perspectives on the "Case or Controversy" Requirement*, 93 Harv. L. Rev. 297 (1979).

Deva, Surya. *Public Interest Litigation in India: A Critical Review*, 28 Civ. Just. Q. 19 (2009).

Fagan, Jr., James F. *When Does Four of a Kind Beat a Full House? The Rise, Fall and Replacement of the Rule of Four*, 25 New Eng. L. Rev. 1101 (1991).

Khan, Maryam S. *Genesis and Evolution of Public Interest Litigation in the Supreme Court of Pakistan, Toward a Dynamic Theory of Judicialization*, 28 Temp. J. Intl & Comp. L. 284 (2015).

McKee, Gwendolyn. *Standing on a Spectrum: Third Party Standing in the United States, Canada, and Australia*, 16 Barry L. Rev. 115 (2011).

Metha, Pratap Bhanu. *The Rise of Judicial Sovereignty*, 18 J. Democracy 70 (2007).

Nichol, Gene R. Jr., *Ripeness and the Constitution*, 54 U. Chi. L. Rev. 153 (1987).

Nichol, Jr, Gene. *Abusing Standing: A comment on Allen v. Wright*, 133 U. Pa. L. Rev. 635 (1985).

Redish, Martin H. *Judicial Review and the 'Political Question'*, 79 Nw. U. L. Rev. 1031 (1984).

Robinson, Nick. *A Quantitative Analysis of the Indian Supreme Court's Workload*, 10 J. Empirical Legal Stud. 570 (2013).

Simard, Linda Sandstrom. *Standing Alone: Do We Still Need the Political Question Doctrine?* 100 Dick. L. Rev. 303 (1996).

Skinner, Gwynne. *Misunderstood, Misconstrued, and Now Clearly Dead: The "Political Question Doctrine" as a Justiciability Doctrine*, 29 J.L. & Pol. 427, (2014).

Tushnet, Mark. *The New Law of Standing: A Plea for Abandonment*, 62 Cornell L. Rev. 663 (1977).

Wechsler, Herbert. *Toward Neutral Principles of Constitutional Law*, 73 Harv. L. Rev. 1 (1959).

Cases

United States

Abbott Labs. v. Gardner, 387 U.S. 136 (1967)

Baker v. Carr, 369 U.S. 186 (1962).

Bush v. Gore, 531 U.S. 98 (2000).
Califano v. Sanders, 430 U.S. 99 (1977).
DeFunis v. Odegaard, 416 U.S. 312 (1974).
Flast v. Cohen, 392 U.S. 83 (1968).
Frothingham v. Mellon, 262 U.S. 447 (1923).
Hein v. Freedom From Religion Foundation, Inc., 551 U.S. 587 (2007).
North Carolina v. Rice, 404 U.S. 244 (1971).
Lujan v. Defenders of Wildlife, 504 U.S. 555 (1992).
Roe v. Wade, 410 U.S. 113. (1973).
S. Pac. Terminal Co. v. Interstate Commerce Comm'n, 219 U.S. 498 (1911)

India

Asif Hamid v. State of Jammu and Kashmir, (1989) S.C.R. (3) 19 (SC). (India).
A. K. Roy, Etc vs Union of India & Anr, (1982) S.C.R. (2) 272 (India).
Dr. D. C. Wadhwa & Ors vs State of Bihar & Ors, (1987) S.C.R. (1) 798 (1986). (India).
Fertilizer Corporation Kamgar Union (Regd.) Sindri v. Union of India, (1981) S.C.R. (2) 52.

(India)

Gurudevdatta Vksss Maryadit & Ors vs State of Maharashtra & Ors, A.I.R. 2001 SC 1980 (India).
I. C. Golaknath & Ors vs State of Punjab & Anrs., (1967) SCR (2) 762 (India).
Ram Jawaya Kapur v. State of Punjab, A.I.R. 1955 SC 549. (India).
S.P. Gupta vs President of India & Ors., (1982) S.C.R. (2) 365 (India).

Pakistan

Asma Jilani v. Government of Punjab, (1972) – PLD (SC) 139 (Pak.)
Benazir Bhutto v. Federation of Pakistan, (1998) – PLD (SC) 416 (Pak.)
Darshan Masih v State, (1990) – PLD (SC) 513 (Pak.)
Dossani Travels v. Federation of Pakistan, Civil Appeal Nos 800-L, 801-L & 802-L OF 2013 & Civil Petition Nos 1148/2013 & 1348/2013. (SC) (Pak.)
Hakim Muhammad Anwar Babri v. Pakistan (1973) – PLD (Lah.) 817 (Pak.)
Medhi v. Pakistan International Airlines Corp, (1998) – PLD (SC) 793 (Pak.) Available in Chang, Wen Chen, Thio, Li-Ann, Tan, Kevin, Y.L. & Yeh, Jiun-Rong. *Constitutionalism in Asia: Cases and Materials* (Hart Publishing, 2014).
Muhammad Nawaz Sharif v. Federation of Pakistan (1993) – PLD (SC) 433 (Pak.) Available at https://pakistanconstitutionlaw.com/p-l-d-1993-sc-473/
Province of East Pakistan v. Mehdi Ali Khan, (1959) – PLD (SC) 387 (Pak.). Available at www.uniset.ca/islamicland/PLD1959SCPak387.html.
Rolling Mills v. Province of West Pakistan, (1968) – SCMR (SC) 318 (Pak.)
Watan Party and Others v. Federation of Pakistan and Others, (2012) – PLD (SC) 292 (Pak.) Available at www.supremecourt.gov.pk/web/user_files/File/Const.P. 77-78-79%20 [Memogate]DetailedOrder.pdf.

Miscellaneous

Aqduz, Izzat Jahan, & Ahmed, Saleem (eds.), Pakistan Supreme Court Annual Report, May 2014- May 2015. Available at www.supremecourt.gov.pk/links/sc-a-rpt-2014-15/index.html (last accessed on Oct. 17, 2016).

Customs Act, No. IV of 1969, The Gazette of Pakistan Extraordinary, Dec. 31, 1969.

Director-General of the Civil Rights Cell, Supreme Court of Pakistan, Press Briefing, Feb. 20, 2014. Available at www.supremecourt.gov.pk/web/user_files/File/pb_dg_hrcell_dt_20.02.2014.pdf (last accessed on Oct. 17, 2016).

Hon. Mr. K. G. *Balakrishnan, Chief Justice of India, Address at the Trinity College of Dublin.* (Oct. 14, 2009). Available at www.sci.nic.in/speeches/speeches_2009/judicial_activism_tcd_dublin_14-10-09.pdf (last accessed on Apr. 6, 2017).

Mate, Manoj S. *The Variable Power of Courts: The Expansion of the Power of the Supreme Court of India in Fundamental Rights and Governance Decisions*. (University of California, 2010). Available at http://escholarship.org/uc/item/3f1640wm (last accessed on Oct. 31, 2016).

Pakistan Code of Criminal Procedure

Pakistan Supreme Court Annual Report, April 2010-December 2011. Available at www.supremecourt.gov.pk/Annual_Rpt/Human%20Rights%20Cell.pdf (last accessed on Oct. 17, 2016).

Pakistan Supreme Court Rules, 1980. Available at www.supremecourt.gov.pk/web/user_files/File/The_Pakistan_Supreme_Court_Rules.pdf (last accessed on Jan. 2, 2017).

Rehnquist, William H. *The 2003 Year-End Report on the Federal Judiciary* (Jan 2004). Available at www.supremecourt.gov/publicinfo/year-end/2003year-endreport.aspx (last accessed on Oct. 17, 2016).

Singh, Rekha Kumari R. *An Analytical and Critical Study on Judicial Activism vis-à-vis Judicial Overreach with Respect to Legislative Function of the Indian Parliament* (Veer Narmad South Gujarat University, 2015). Available at http://shodhganga.inflibnet.ac.in/handle/10603/32340. (last accessed on Oct. 31, 2016).

Supreme Court (Number of Judges) Amendment Act 2008, Act 11 of 2009, Gazette of India Extraordinary Part II, Sec. I., Feb. 6, 2009. Available at www.egazette.kerala.gov.in/pdf/2010/18/part_01/supreme_court.pdf (last accessed on Dec. 28, 2016).

Taft, William Howard, *Three Needed Steps of Progress*, 8 A.B.A.J. 34 (Address to the Chicago Bar Association) (Jan. 1922).

Chapter 6 references

Books

Ackerman, Bruce. *The Failure of the Founding Fathers: Jefferson, Marshall, and the Rise of Presidential Democracy*. (Harvard University Press, 2005).

Baumgartner, Jody C., & Kada, Naoko. *Checking Executive Power: Presidential Impeachment in Comparative Perspective*. (Greenwood Publishing, 2003).

Berger, Raoul. *Impeachment: The Constitutional Problems*. (Harvard University Press, 1974).

Cheema, Moeen, & Gilani, Ijaz Shafi. *The Politics and Jurisprudence of the Chaudhry Court 2005–2013*. (Oxford University Press, 2015).

Constable, Pamela. *Playing with Fire: Pakistan at War with Itself*. (Random House Publishing, 2011).

Gerhardt, Michael J. *The Federal Impeachment Process: A Constitutional and Historical Analysis*. (Duke University Press, 2000).

Jacobsohn, Gary J. *Constitutional Identity*. (Harvard University Press, 2010).

Jayapalan, N. *Constitutional History of India*. (Atlantic Publishers and Distributers, 1998).

Kochanek Stanley A. & Hardgrave, Robert L. *India: Government and Politics in a Developing Nation.* (7th ed., Thomson Wadsworth, 2007).
Labovitz, John R. *Presidential Impeachment.* (Yale University Press, 1978).
Leibowitz, Arnold H. *An Historical-Legal Analysis of the Impeachments of Presidents Andrew Johnson, Richard Nixon, and William Clinton: Why the Process Went Wrong.* (Edwin Mellen, 2011).
Records of the Federal Convention, Volume II. (Max Farrand, ed., Yale University Press, 1911).
Stone, Geoffrey R. *Constitutional Law.* (Walters Kluwer, 2001).
Story, Joseph, & Cooley, Thomas M. *Commentaries on the Constitution of the United States: With a Preliminary Review of the Constitutional History of the Colonies and States Before the Adoption . . . Notes and Additions by Thomas M. Cooley.* (Lawbook Exchange Limited, 2008).
Tushnet, Mark, & Khosla, Madhav. *Unstable Constitutionalism: Law and Politics in South Asia.* (Cambridge University Press, 2015).
Van Meter, Larry A. *United States V. Nixon: The Question of Executive Privilege.* (Chelsea House Publications, 2007).

Book chapters

Hamilton, Alexander. "Federalist #65," *The Federalist Papers.* (Clinton Rossiter, ed., New American Library, 1996).
Rao, P.P. "The Supreme Court Versus The Constitution: A Challenge to Federalism." *The Constitution, Parliament, and the Judiciary*, Pran Chopra. (Sage Publications, 2016).

Cases

United States

Powell v. McCormack, 938 F. 2d 239 (D.C. Cir. 1969).
Richard M. Nixon v. United States, 418 U.S. 683 (1974).
United States v. Mitchell, 377 F.Supp. 1326 (D.C. 1974).
Walter Nixon v. United States, 506 U.S. 224 (1993).

Pakistan

Baz Mohammad Kaker v. Federation of Pakistan, Constitution Petition No.77 of 2012 & CMA No.3057/2012. (SC) (Pak.) Available at https://pakistanconstitutionlaw.com/constitution-petition-no-77-of-2012-detail-order/
Contempt Proceedings against Syed Yousaf Raza Gillani, Suo Motu Case No. 04 of 2010, Criminal Original petition No. 06 of 2012. (SC) (Pak.) Available at www.supremecourt.gov.pk/web/user_files/File/Crl.O.P. 6of2012.pdf
Dr. Mobashir Hassan v. Federation of Pakistan (2010) – PLD (SC) 256 (Pak.)
Imran Ahmad Khan v. Miam Muhammad Nawaz Sharif, Const. Petition No. 29 of 2016 (SC) (Pak.)
Imran Ahmed Khan v. Mian Muhammad Nawaz Sharif, C.M.A. No. 4978/2017 in Constitutional Petition No. 29/2016 and C.M.A. No. 2939/2017 in Constitutional Petition

No. 29/2016. (SC) (Pak.) (July 28, 2017.) Available at www.supremecourt.gov.pk/web/user_files/File/Const.P._29_2016_28072016.pdf

Muhammad Azhar Siddique v. Federation of Pakistan, Const. Petition No. 40 of 2012 & CMA No.2494/12 etc. (SC) (Pak.) (Detailed Order) Available at www.supremecourt.gov.pk/web/user_files/File/Const.P. 40of2012-DetailJudgment-dt-3.7.2012.pdf

Muhammad Azhar Siddique v. Federation of Pakistan, Suo Motu Case No. 04 of 2010& CMA No.2494/12 etc. (SC) (Pak.) (Short Order) Available at www.supremecourt.gov.pk/web/user_files/File/Const.P. 40of2012-ShortOrder[19.06.2012].pdf

India

I. C. Golaknath v. State of Punjab, (1967) S.C.R. (2) 762 (India)

Indira Nehru Gandhi vs. Shri Raj Narain, (1976) S.C.R. (2) 347 (1976) (India).

Sub-Committee On Judicial Accountability vs Union Of India And Ors, Etc., (1991) S.C.R. Supl. (2) 1. (1992) (India).

The State of Uttar Pradesh v. Raj Narain, (1975) S.C.R. (3) 333 (India).

Uttar Pradesh v. Raj Narain, (1975) S.C.R. (3) 333 (India).

Periodicals

A Judicial Coup, Express Tribune, June 12, 2012. Available at http://tribune.com.pk/story/396001/a-judicial-coup/ (Accessed on June 20, 2016).

Ahmed, Khaled. *Restraint must follow Activism*, Friday Times, Feb. 3, 2012. Available at www.thefridaytimes.com/beta2/tft/article.php?issue=20120203&page=2 (last accessed on July 9, 2016).

Andhyarujina, T. R. *When the Bench Buckled*. The Indian Express, July 8, 2015. Available at http://indianexpress.com/article/opinion/columns/when-the-bench-buckled/ (last accessed on July 5, 2016).

Bhatti, Haseeb. *Nawaz Sharif Files 3 Petitions Challenging Panamagate Verdict in SC*, Dawn, Aug. 15, 2017. Available at www.dawn.com/news/1351705 (last accessed on Oct. 14, 2017).

Bhushan, Prashant. *A Historic Non-Impeachment: An All-Round System Failure*, Frontline, June 4, 1993. Available at http://bharatiyas.in/cjarold/files/cover_story_ramaswami.pdf. (last accessed on July 10, 2016).

Bilal, Mohammad. *ECP to Hear PTI's Foreign Funding, Imran Khan's Alleged Contempt of Court Cases Separately*, Dawn, May 08, 2017. Available at www.dawn.com/news/1331825 (last accessed on Oct. 14, 2017).

Boone, Jon. *Pakistan's Prime Minister Yousuf Raza Gilani Disqualified by Supreme Court*, The Guardian, June 19, 2012. Available at www.theguardian.cmom/world/2012/jun/19/pakistan-prime-minister-yousuf-gilani-disqualified (last accessed on June 20, 2016).

Cheema, Hasham. *How Pakistan's Panama Papers Probe Unfolded*, Dawn, July 29, 2017. Available at www.dawn.com/news/1316531 (last accessed on Oct. 14, 2017).

Cheema, Moeen. *Back to the Future: The Pakistan Supreme Court's NRO Judgment*, Juris-Forum, Jan. 14, 2010. Available at www.jurist.org/forum/2010/01/back-to-future-pakistan-supreme-court-s.php. (last accessed on June 21, 2016).

Datar, Arvind P. The Case That Saved Indian Democracy, *The Hindu*, Apr. 24, 2013. Available at www.thehindu.com/opinion/op-ed/the-case-that-saved-indian-democracy/article4647800.ece (last accessed on July 5, 2016).

Gilani Family's Predicament Remains Unexplained, Dawn, Nov. 15, 2012. Available at www.dawn.com/2012/11/15/gilani-familys-predicament-remains-unexplained/ (last visited June 21, 2016).

Greenhouse, Linda. *Court Upholds Shortcut Used in Ousting 2 Judges*, The New York Times, Jan. 14, 1993. Available at www.nytimes.com/1993/01/14/us/court-upholds-shortcut-used-in-ousting-2-judges.html (last accessed on July 10, 2016).

Ijaz, Saroop. *The Case for Judicial Minimalism in Pakistan*, Jurist-Forum, Oct. 11, 2010. Available at http://jurist.org/forum/2010/10/the-case-for-judicial-minimalism-in-pakistan.php. (last accessed on Oct. 20, 2016).

Ineligibility Case: Imran Khan Submits Reply in Supreme Court, Dunya News, May 29, 2017. Available at http://dunyanews.tv/en/Pakistan/390506-Ineligibility-case-Imran-Khan-submits-reply-in-Su (last accessed on Oct. 14, 2017).

Jaffry, Nasir. *Speaker Backs Gilani*, The Telegraph, May 24, 2012. Available at www.telegraphindia.com/1120525/jsp/foreign/story_15530347.jsp (last accessed on June 21, 2016).

Jamali, Jamaluddin. *PPP lawyers, Asma Jahangir Rant Against SC Verdict*, Pakistan Today, Apr. 27, 2012. Available at www.pakistantoday.com.pk/2012/04/27/news/national/ppp-lawyers-asma-jahangir-rant-against-sc-verdict/?printType=article. (last accessed June 20, 2016).

Kilpatrick, Carroll, *Nixon Resigns*, Washington Post, Aug. 9, 1974, at A01.

Lyons, Richard, & Chapman, William. *Judiciary Committee Approves Article to Impeach President Nixon, 27 to 11, 6 Republicans Join Democrats to Pass Obstruction Charge*, Washington Post, July 28, 1974 at A01.

Malaviya, Satya Prakash. *Removal of Judges*, The Hindu, June 11, 2002. Available at www.thehindu.com/thehindu/op/2002/06/11/stories/2002061100010200.htm. (last accessed July 8, 2016).

Nauman, Qasim, & Allbritton, Chris. *Pakistan PM Charged with Contempt in Case That Could Drag on*, Reuters, Feb. 13, 2012. Available at www.reuters.com/article/us-pakistan-politics-idUSTRE81C0D820120213 (last accessed on June 22, 2016).

Nawaz's Disqualification: What Legal Experts Say, Geo News, July 29, 2017. Available at www.geo.tv/latest/151531-legal-heavyweights-weigh-in-on-scs-decision-on-panama-case (last accessed on Oct. 14, 2017).

PM Says 'few thousand' Chanting 'Go Nawaz Go' Can't Make Him Leave, Pakistan today, Sep. 17, 2014. Available at www.pakistantoday.com.pk/2014/09/17/pm-says-few-thousand-chanting-go-nawaz-go-cant-make-him-leave/ (last accessed on Oct. 14, 2017).

Prakash, Satya. *The Court Verdict That Prompted Indira Gandhi to Declare Emergency*, Hindustan Times, June 26, 2015. Available at www.hindustantimes.com/india/the-court-verdict-that-prompted-indira-gandhi-to-declare-emergency/story-uaDsy0j3B0vSdiPn-2md9WO.html (last accessed on June 20, 2016).

Rosenbaum, David E. *Rodino Unit Issues Report Describing Case Against Nixon*, New York Times, Aug. 23, 1974.

Supreme Court Dismisses Sharif Family's Review Petitions in Panama Case, The News, Sep. 15, 2017. Available at www.thenews.com.pk/latest/230142-Supreme-Court-concludes-hearing-in-Panama-case-review-petitions (last accessed on Oct. 14, 2017).

Swiss Close Case Against Zardari; $60 mln Unfrozen, Reuters, Aug. 26, 2008, Available at www.reuters.com/article/us-swiss-pakistan-zardari-idUSLQ17107020080826 (last accessed on June 20, 2016).

Timeline: Gilani vs. Supreme Court: PM Disqualified. India Today, June 19, 2012. Available at http://indiatoday.intoday.in/story/timeline-gilani-vs-supreme-court-pm-disqualified/1/201390.html. (last accessed on July 4, 2016).

Waraich, Omar. *Pakistan's Supreme Court vs. Everybody, but Most of All the Prime Minister*, Time, Feb. 13, 2012. Available at http://content.time.com/time/world/article/0,8599,2106725,00.html (last accessed on June 21, 2016).

Academic articles

Gerard, Jules B. *Review of "Impeachment: The Constitutional Problems,"* 1974 Wash. U. L. Q. 179 (1974). Available at: http://openscholarship.wustl.edu/law_lawreview/vol1974/iss1/14 (last accessed on April 6, 2017).

Gerhardt, Michael J. *Rediscovering Nonjusticiability: Judicial Review of Impeachments After Nixon*, 44 Duke L.J. 231 (1994).

Narayan, Jenna. *'Defect-Shun': Understanding Schedule X to the Constitution of India*, 3 India L. J. 1. Available at http://indialawjournal.com/volume3/issue_1/article_by_jenna.html (last accessed on July 7, 2016).

Robinson, Nick. *Expanding Judiciaries: India and the Rise of the Good Governance Court*, 8 wash. u. global stud. l. rev. 1 (2009).

Verkuil, Paul R. *Separation of Powers, the Rule of Law and the Idea of Independence*, 30 Wm. & Mary L. Rev. 301 (1989).

Miscellaneous

Doyle, Charles. Cong. Research Serv., RL95–1135, *Federal Grand Jury*. (2010).

India Const. art 71, amended by The Thirty-Ninth Amendment Act, 1975.

Jetly, Rajshree. *Pakistan's Judicial Renaissance: A New Phase?* 166 Institute of South Asia Studies Brief 1 (2012). Available at www.files.ethz.ch/isn/143505/ISAS_Insights_166_-_email_-_Pakistan_Judicial_Renaissance_-_A_New_Phase_01062012162914.pdf (last accessed on Apr. 6, 2017).

Jetly, Rajshree. *Pakistan's Supreme Court and the National Reconciliation Ordinance: What Now for Pakistan?* Institute for South Asia Studies Brief 147 (Dec. 22, 2009). Available at www.files.ethz.ch/isn/110966/148.pdf (last accessed on April 6, 2017).

Pakistani Judicial System Groans Under Corruption, Volume of Cases, Public Radio International, Feb. 3, 2012. Available at www.pri.org/stories/2012-02-03/pakistani-judicial-system-groans-under-corruption-volume-cases (last accessed on June 22, 2016).

Priyadarshi, Divyanshu. *Case Study: Smt. Indira Nehru Gandhi vs. Shri Raj Narain and Anr. on 7 November, 1975*, Symbiosis Law School, Sep. 13, 2012. Available at http://ssrn.com/abstract=2146120 (last accessed on Nov. 6, 2016).

The International Consortium of Investigative Journalists, The Panama Papers, Available at https://panamapapers.icij.org (last accessed on Oct. 14, 2017).

Yaniv, Roznai, *Unconstitutional Constitutional Amendments: A Study of the Nature and Limits of Constitutional Amendment Powers* (London School of Economics, Feb. 2014). Available at http://etheses.lse.ac.uk/915/1/Roznai_Unconstitutional-constitutional-amendments.pdf (last accessed on July 11, 2016).

Chapter 7 references

Books

Administrative Law Facing the Future. (Leyland, Peter & Woods Terry, eds.). (Blackstone Press, 1997).

Cheema, Moeen S., & Gilani, Ijaz Shafi. *The Politics and Jurisprudence of the Chaudhry Court 2005–2013*. (Oxford University Press, 2015).

Fordham. Michael. *Judicial Review Handbook*. (2nd ed., Hart Publishing, 1997).

Grote, Rainer, & Röder, Tilmann. *Constitutionalism in Islamic Countries: Between Upheaval and Continuity*. (Oxford University Press, 2012).

Menski, Werner, Alam, R. & Raza, M. *Public interest in litigation in Pakistan*. (Platinum and Pakistan Law House, 2000).

Palmer, Vernon Valentine, & Mattar, Mohamed Y. *Mixed Legal Systems, East and West*. (Routledge, 2016).

Pylee, M. V. *The Federal Court of India*. (Manaktalas, 1966).

Wynbrandt, James. *A Brief History of Pakistan*. (Facts on File Publishing, 2009).

Periodicals

Anwar Syed, *Judiciary and Public Opinion*, Dawn, Jan. 31, 2010. Available at www.dawn.com/news/843451/judiciary-and-public-opinion (last accessed on Oct. 14, 2016).

Baloch, Shezad. *PM's Disqualification Case: Supreme Court Refers Petition to Chief Justice*, Express Tribune, Nov. 10, 2014. Available at http://tribune.com.pk/story/788661/pms-disqualification-case-supreme-court-refers-petition-to-chief-justice/ (last accessed on July 30, 2016).

Bickel, Alexander. *The Overworked Court: A Reply to Arthur]. Goldberg*, The New Republic, Feb. 17, 1973.

Dershowitz, Alan M. *No More a Court of Last Resort*, New York Times, Jan. 7, 1973.

Faxil, Muhammad Daim. *Pakistan at Risk for a Coup?*, The Diplomat, July 26, 2016. Available at http://thediplomat.com/2016/07/is-pakistan-at-risk-for-a-coup/. (last accessed on July 30, 2016).

Goldberg, Arthur. *One Supreme Court*, The New Republic, Feb. 10, 1973.

Hasnaat, Malik. *Top Court Rejects PTI Plea to Disqualify PM Nawaz Over Panamagate*, Express Tribune, Aug. 30, 2016. Available at http://tribune.com.pk/story/1172878/top-court-rejects-pti-plea-disqualify-pm-nawaz-panamagate/ (last accessed on Oct. 15, 2016).

Iqbal, Nasir. *SCBA Suggests Changes in Judicial Appointment Procedure*, Express Tribune, Jan. 19, 2016. Available at www.dawn.com/news/1233916/scba-suggests-changes-in-judicial-appointment-procedure (last accessed on July 31, 2016).

Joshua, Anita. *Coup Fears Return to Pakistan*, The Hindu, June 23, 2012. http://m.thehindu.com/opinion/op-ed/coup-fears-return-to-pakistan/article3559757.ece (last accessed on Oct. 14, 2016).

Katju, Markandey. *The Philosophy of Judicial Restraint*, Express Tribune, July 22, 2011. Available at http://tribune.com.pk/story/406897/the-philosophy-of-judicial-restraint/ (last accessed on Oct. 15, 2016).

Khan, Raza. *CJP Declines to Form 'toothless commission' on Panama Leaks*, Dawn, May 13, 2016. Available at www.dawn.com/news/1258127 (last accessed on July 30, 2016).

Lewin, Nathan. *Helping the Court with Its Work*, The New Republic, Mar. 3, 1973.

Malik, Hasnaat. *2014: From Judicial Activism to Judicial Restraint*, Express Tribune, Dec. 31, 2014. Available at http://tribune.com.pk/story/814921/2014-from-judicial-activism-to-judicial-restraint/ (last accessed on July 24, 2016).

Malik, Hasnaat. *Chief Justice Bows Out This Week*, Express Tribune, June 30, 2014. Available at http://tribune.com.pk/story/728986/chief-justice-jilani-bows-out-this-week/ (last accessed on Oct. 14, 2016).

Malik, Hasnaat. *CJ Constitutes Seven-Member Bench to Hear PM's Disqualification Case*, Express Tribune, Nov. 26, 2014. Available at http://tribune.com.pk/story/797590/pms-disqualification-case-cj-constitutes-7-member-bench-to-hear-the-case/ (last accessed on July 30, 2016).

Malik, Hasnaat. *SC Office Returns Imran's 'frivolous' Plea Against PM*, Express Tribune. Aug. 31, 2016. Available http://tribune.com.pk/story/1173204/sc-office-returns-imrans-frivolous-plea-pm/ (last accessed on Oct. 15, 2016).

Malik, Hasnaat. *Supreme Court's Year of Transition*, Express Tribune, Dec. 31, 2015. Available at http://tribune.com.pk/story/1019061/supreme-courts-year-of-transition/ (last accessed on July 24, 2016.)

Minhas, Najma. *The Panama Papers and Pakistan: Beyond Nawaz Sharif*, The Diplomat, Apr. 11, 2016. Available at http://thediplomat.com/2016/04/the-panama-papers-and-pakistan-beyond-nawaz-sharif/. (last accessed on July 30, 2016).

Most of suo motu notices of former CJP Iftikhar Chadhry were beyond law: President SCBA (Supreme Court Bar Association), The Nation, Nov. 11, 2015. Available at http://nation.com.pk/national/11-Nov-2015/most-of-suo-motu-notices-of-former-cjp-iftikhar-chaudhry-were-beyond-law-president-scba (last accessed on July 31, 2016).

Naqvi, Feisal. *Memogate Redux*, Express Tribune, Jan. 9, 2012. Available at http://tribune.com.pk/story/318897/memogate-redux/ (last accessed on August 3, 2016.)

Plea in SC: PTI Finally Decides to Seek PM's Disqualification, Express Tribune, July 29, 2016. Available at http://tribune.com.pk/story/1151524/plea-sc-pti-finally-decides-seek-pms-disqualification/ (last accessed on July 30, 2016.)

Rasool, Saad. *I am Babar Sattar*, Pakistan Today, Aug. 4, 2013. Available at www.pakistantoday.com.pk/2013/08/04/comment/columns/i-am-babar-sattar/ (last accessed on Oct. 14, 2016).

Sattar, Babar. *Hubris as Justice*, Dawn, July 30, 2013. Available at www.dawn.com/news/1032941 (last accessed on Oct. 14, 2016).

Sattar, Babar. *Judicial Restraint or Complacency?* Dawn, July 14, 2014. Available at www.dawn.com/news/1118993. (last accessed on July 25, 2016).

Siddique, Faisal. *Judicial Accountability*, Dawn, Aug. 1, 2016. Available at www.dawn.com/news/1274492/judicial-accountability (last accessed on Oct. 14, 2016).

SC Forms Committee to Revisit Court Rules of 1980, Express Tribune, Sep. 25, 2014. Available at http://tribune.com.pk/story/767144/sc-forms-committee-to-revisit-court-rules-of-1980/ (last accessed on July 28, 2016).

SC Suggests Review of Suo Motu Powers, Express Tribune, Apr. 4, 2014. Available at http://tribune.com.pk/story/691250/sc-suggests-review-of-suo-motu-powers/ (last accessed on Oct. 14, 2016).

Sirmad, Marvi. *Memogate: Public Interest or Political Interest*, Daily Times, Dec. 19, 2011. Available at https://marvisirmed.com/2011/12/20/memogate-public-interest-or-political-interest/ (last accessed on Aug. 2, 2016).

Supreme Court Rejects Petitions in PM Disqualification Case, Express Tribune, Dec. 9, 2014. Available at http://tribune.com.pk/story/804091/sc-rejects-petitions-in-pm-disqualification-case/ (last accessed on July 30, 2016).

Walsh, Declan. *Political Instability Rises as Pakistani Court Ousts Premier*, New York Times, June 19, 2012. Available at www.nytimes.com/2012/06/20/world/asia/political-instability-rises-as-pakistani-court-dismisses-prime-minister.html? r=0 (last accessed on July 30, 2016).

Wasim, Amir. *NA Body to Take Up ECP Members' Salary, Allowances Bill*, Dawn, July 11, 2016. Available at www.dawn.com/news/1270079 (last accessed on July 29, 2016).

Wasim, Amir. *Terms of Reference Finalised for Panama Inquiry Commission*, Dawn, Apr. 17, 2016. Available at www.dawn.com/news/1252569/tors-finalised-for-panama-inquiry-commission (last accessed on July 28, 2016).

Weinbaum, Dr. Marvin, and Naveed, Nasir. *Fallout in Pakistan from the Panama Papers*, Middle East Institute. May 17, 2016. Available at www.mei.edu/content/article/fallout-pakistan-panama-papers. (last accessed on July 30, 2016).

Zulfiqar, Qaiser. *PM Contempt: Asma Jahangir Terms August 8 as a 'black day in judicial history'*, Express Tribune, Aug 8. 2012. Available at http://tribune.com.pk/story/419356/pm-contempt-asma-jahangir-terms-august-8-as-black-day-in-judicial-history/ (last accessed on July 29, 2016).

Cases

United States

Baker v. Carr, 369 U.S. 186 (1962).

Frothingham v. Mellon, 262 U.S. 447 (1923).

Skidmore v. Swift & Co., 323 U.S. 134 (1944).

Pakistan

Aamir Zahoor-ul-Haq v. Federation of Pakistan, (2016) Civil Review Petition No. 561 (SC) (Pak.). Available at www.supremecourt.gov.pk/web/user_files/File/C.R.P._561_2015.pdf

Dossani Travels v. Federation of Pakistan, Civil Appeal No. 800 of 2013. (SC) – (Pak.) Available at www.supremecourt.gov.pk/web/user_files/File/C.A.800Lof2013etc.pdf

Governor-General's Case, (1955) – PLD (F.C.) 511 (Pak.)

Imran Khan v. Federation of Pakistan, Criminal Original Petition No.92 of 2013 (Contempt proceedings against Imran Khan Chairman, Pakistan Tehreek-i-Insaf). (SC) (Pak.) Available at www.supremecourt.gov.pk/web/user_files/File/Crl.O.P. 92of2013-dt-9-10-2013.pdf

Medhi v. Pakistan International Airlines Corp, (1998) – PLD (SC) 793 (Pak.)

Muhammad Azhar Siddique v. Federation of Pakistan, (2012) Const. Petition No.40 of 2012 & CMA No.2494/2 (SC) (Pak.) Available at (Detailed Order) Available at www.supremecourt.gov.pk/web/user_files/File/Const.P. 40of2012-DetailJudgment-dt-3.7.2012.pdf

Munir Hussain Bhatti v. Federation of Pakistan, (2011) – PLD (SC) 407 (Pak.) Available at www.supremecourt.gov.pk/web/user_files/file/cps.10-18of2011.pdf

Nadeem Ahmed v. Federation of Pakistan, (2010) – PLD (SC) 1165 (Pak.) Available at www.supremecourt.gov.pk/web/user_files/file/18th_amendment_order.pdf

Sindh High Court Bar Association v. Federation of Pakistan, (2009) – PLD (SC) 879 (Pak.) Available at https://pakistanconstitutionlaw.com/p-l-d-2009-sc-879-2/

Tikka Iqbal Muhammad Khan v General Pervez Musharraf, (2008) – PLD (SC) 6 (Pak.) (short order). Available at https://pakistanconstitutionlaw.com/order-of-the-supreme-court-in-constitutional-petition-nos-87-and-88-of-2007-against-the-proclamation-of-emergency-and-provisional-constitution-order-no-1-of-2007-dated-23rd-of-november-2007/

Watan Party and Others v. Federation of Pakistan and Others, (2012) – PLD (SC) 292 (Pak.) (Detailed Order) Available at www.supremecourt.gov.pk/web/user_files/File/Const.P. 77-78-79%20[Memogate]DetailedOrder.pdf

India

S.M.D. Kiran Pasha vs Government of Andhra Pradesh, (1989) S.C.R. (2) 105 (1990) (India).

Academic articles

Brennan, William J. *The National Court of Appeals: Another Dissent*, 40 U. Chi. L. R. 473 (1973).

Fiss, Owen M. *The Forms of Justice*, 93 Harv. L. Rev. 1 (1979).

Freund, Paul A. *Why We Need the National Court of Appeals*, 59 A.B.A.J. 247 (1973).

Gazdar, Haris. *One Step Forward, Marching to the Brink*, 44 ECON. & POL. WKLY. 9. (2009).

Gledhill, Alan. *Unconstitutional Legislation*, 9 Indian Y.B. Intl. Affairs 40. (1952).

Gressman, Eugene. *The National Court of Appeals: A Dissent*, 59 A.B.A.J. 253 (1973).

Khan, Maryam. *Genesis and Evolution of Public Interest Litigation in the Supreme Court of Pakistan: Toward a Dynamic Theory of Judicialization*, 28 Temple Int'l & Comp. L. J. 285 (2016).

Koch Jr., Charles H. *Judicial Review of Administrative Discretion*, 54 Geo. Wash. L. Rev. 469 (1986).

Mahmud, Tayyab. *Praetorianism and Common Law in Post-Colonial Settings: Judicial Responses to Constitutional Breakdowns in Pakistan*, 1993 Utah L. Rev. 1225 (1993).

Ngarmgoonanant, Wischa. *Dictatorial Tendencies: Chaudhry and Pakistan's Supreme Court*, Yale Rev. Int'l Stud. (Jan. 2014). Available at http://yris.yira.org/essays/1236#_edn29 (last accessed on Oct. 14, 2016).

Pierce Jr., Richard J. *What Do the Studies of Judicial Review of Actions Mean?*, 63 Wash. C. L. admin. l. rev. 77 (2010).

Robinson, Nick. *A Quantitative Analysis of the Indian Supreme Court's Workload*, 10 j. Empirical legal stud. 570 (2013).

Shapiro, Barbara, & Jacobvitz, Robert. Administrative Law, 13 N. M. L. Rev. 235. (1983).

Walters, Mark D. *The Common Law Constitution in Canada: Return of Lex Non Scripta as Fundamental Law*, 51 U. Toronto L.J. 91 (2001).

Walters, Mark D. *The National Court of Appeals: Composition, Constitutionality, and Desirability*, 41 fordham l. rev. 863 (1973).

Miscellaneous

Address by Chief Justice Warren Burger to the Fiftieth Annual Meeting of the American Law Institute, May 16, 1973, reported in 41 U.S.L.W. 2627.

Administrative Procedure Act (APA), Pub. L. 79–404, 60 Stat. 237. (1946).

Aqdus, Izzat Jahan, & Ahmed, Saleem, eds. Pakistan Supreme Court Annual Report: May 2014–May 2015. Available at www.supremecourt.gov.pk/links/sc-a-rpt-2014-15/index.html (last accessed Oct. 17, 2016).

Federal Judicial Center, *Report of the Study Group on the Caseload of the Supreme Court* and AIS-A17(1972) Report Excerpts at 59 A.B.A.J. 139 (1973).

Gyana Ranjan Panda, *Information Kit on the Federal Budget of Pakistan*, Center for Budget and Governance Accountability (2011). Available at www.cbgaindia.org/wp-content/uploads/2016/03/Information-Kit-on-The-Federal-Budget-of-Pakistan.pdf. (last accessed Oct. 17, 2016).

Interview with Zeeshan Hashmi, former Clerk of the Supreme Court of Pakistan, in Lahore (March 5, 2015).

Interview with retired Chief Justice Tassaduq Jillani, Supreme Court of Pakistan, in Lahore (March 9, 2015).

Interview with retired Justice Khalil-ur-Rehman Ramday, Supreme Court of Pakistan, in Lahore (Mar. 12, 2015).

Interview with Babar Sattar, High Court Advocate, in Islamabad (Mar. 18, 2015).

Kohli, Justice Mehta Kalash Nath. *Case Flow Management*, Supreme Court of Pakistan Report. Available at http://supremecourt.gov.pk/ijc/Articles/20/2.pdf (last accessed on Oct. 15, 2016).

Notification No. F. 59/80- SCA from August 8, 2014. (SC) (Pak.)

Pakistan Supreme Court Annual Report: 2010–2011. Available at www.supremecourt.gov.pk/Annual_Rpt/Human%20Rights%20Cell.pdf (last accessed on Aug. 8, 2016).

Public Interest Litigation: Scope and Problems, Human Rights Commission of Pakistan Seminar, Mar. 28, 2010. Available at http://hrcp-web.org/hrcpweb/wp-content/pdf/ff/26.pdf (last accessed on Aug. 2, 2016).

Index

For Product Safety Concerns and Information please contact our EU representative GPSR@taylorandfrancis.com
Taylor & Francis Verlag GmbH, Kaufingerstraße 24, 80331 München, Germany

www.ingramcontent.com/pod-product-compliance
Ingram Content Group UK Ltd.
Pitfield, Milton Keynes, MK11 3LW, UK
UKHW011013180926
475701UK00004B/718
* 9 7 8 0 3 6 7 5 9 1 7 7 9 *